COLLECTED WORKS OF CHARLES BAUDOUIN

Volume 5

THE MIND OF THE CHILD

THE MIND OF THE CHILD
A psychoanalytical study

CHARLES BAUDOUIN

Translated by
EDEN AND CEDAR PAUL

LONDON AND NEW YORK

First published in English in 1933
This edition first published in 2015
by Routledge
27 Church Road, Hove BN3 2FA

and by Routledge
711 Third Avenue, New York, NY 10017

Routledge is an imprint of the Taylor & Francis Group, an informa business

© 1931 Charles Baudouin

All rights reserved. No part of this book may be reprinted or reproduced or utilised in any form or by any electronic, mechanical, or other means, now known or hereafter invented, including photocopying and recording, or in any information storage or retrieval system, without permission in writing from the publishers.

Trademark notice: Product or corporate names may be trademarks or registered trademarks, and are used only for identification and explanation without intent to infringe.

British Library Cataloguing in Publication Data
A catalogue record for this book is available from the British Library

ISBN: 978-1-138-82541-3 (Set)
eISBN: 978-1-315-73901-4 (Set)
ISBN: 978-1-138-82653-3 (Volume 5)
eISBN: 978-1-315-73903-8 (Volume 5)

Publisher's Note
The publisher has gone to great lengths to ensure the quality of this reprint but points out that some imperfections in the original copies may be apparent.

Disclaimer
The publisher has made every effort to trace copyright holders and would welcome correspondence from those they have been unable to trace.

The

MIND OF THE CHILD

A PSYCHOANALYTICAL STUDY

by

CHARLES BAUDOUIN

TRANSLATED BY
EDEN AND CEDAR PAUL

LONDON
GEORGE ALLEN & UNWIN LTD
MUSEUM STREET

*The French original, entitled "L'âme enfantine et la psychanalyse,'
was published in* 1931 *by Delachaux et Niestlé of Neuchâtel and
Paris.*

FIRST PUBLISHED IN ENGLISH 1933

All rights reserved

PRINTED IN GREAT BRITAIN BY
UNWIN BROTHERS LTD., WOKING

To

MISS EMMA THOMAS

AND HER COLLABORATORS IN THE
FELLOWSHIP SCHOOL AT GLAND
IN THE HOPE THAT THIS
STUDY MAY HELP THEM
IN THEIR VALUABLE
WORK

AUTHOR'S NOTE

THE author wishes to express his thanks to those who have aided him in collecting the data used in the present work, namely:

Mesdames and Mesdemoiselles Canivé, Clay, Ith, Rechbach, Shapiro, Stump, and Vougman.

Messrs. Ith and Navon, Drs. Bischler and G. Richard.

He is also indebted to the Jean Jacques Rousseau Institute for having guided him into this field of study and for having aided him in its cultivation.

Finally he would like to make special mention of the "Zeitschrift zur psychoanalytischen Pedagogik," issued under the auspices of Drs. Federn and Meng, a periodical to which he owes much, and which may be confidently recommended to educators in search of further information concerning the topics with which this book deals.

CONTENTS

INTRODUCTION

THE CHILD'S COMPLEXES AND THEIR CLASSI-
FICATION

PAGE

17

PART ONE

COMPLEXES OF THE OBJECT

CHAPTER ONE

CAIN OR FRATERNAL RIVALRY 35

CHAPTER TWO

OEDIPUS AND FILIAL AFFECTION 50

CHAPTER THREE

DESTRUCTION 67

1. SADISTIC TRENDS 67
2. ANAL TRENDS 70
3. MASOCHISTIC TRENDS 73

CHAPTER FOUR

DISPLAY AND MYSTERY 84

1. DISCLOSURE 84

PART TWO

COMPLEXES OF THE EGO

CHAPTER FIVE

MUTILATION 107

12 THE MIND OF THE CHILD

CHAPTER SIX

PAGE

DIANA: WOULD YOU RATHER BE A GIRL OR A
BOY?   125

CHAPTER SEVEN

BIRTH   149

1. CHILDREN'S THEORIES   149
2. REBIRTH: EXPLANATION AND COMPENSATION   158

PART THREE

COMPLEXES OF ATTITUDE

CHAPTER EIGHT

WEANING   171

CHAPTER NINE

RETREAT   187

PART FOUR

RELATIONS AND REGULATIONS

CHAPTER TEN

POINTS OF INTERSECTION OF THE VARIOUS
COMPLEXES   207

CHAPTER ELEVEN

TWO TYPICAL MOTIFS   221

1. I AM SHUT OUT   221
2. THE VICTIMISED WOMAN   237

CONTENTS 13

CHAPTER TWELVE

	PAGE
THE SUPER-EGO	245
1. IDENTIFICATION	245
2. THE FATHER-IDEAL	247
3. CONSCIENCE	250
4. SELF-CHASTISEMENT	255

CONCLUSION

HINTS TO EDUCATORS	265

BIBLIOGRAPHY	271
INDEX	279

INTRODUCTION

THE CHILD'S COMPLEXES AND THEIR CLASSIFICATION

In my introduction to *Freud et la psychanalyse éducative*, an anthology of essays dealing with psychoanalysis in its relation to education, I endeavoured to give precise definitions of the concepts "psychoanalysis" and "children." Here is the classification I made at the time.

1. Fundamental mechanisms. How do the vital mechanisms of the instinctive and affective life (as brought to our knowledge by Freud) present themselves to the child mind? How does it react to such phenomena as repression, transference, sublimation, introversion, identification, and so forth?

2. Complexes. What has our personal observation of children to teach us concerning those psychological constellations, those intimately interwoven conditions, which psychoanalysts term complexes? (Oedipus complex, castration complex, etc.)

3. Typical disturbances. What light has psychoanalysis to shed upon disturbances of character, of conduct, of mental or scholastic aptitudes, upon the whole gamut of affective and neurotic disorders among the children a schoolmaster or schoolmistress have under their care?

4. Methods. What methods have psychoanalysts at their disposal in dealing with children? How are we to adapt a discipline devised for adults to the needs of children, and normal children at that?

Each of these questions, simply and succinctly drawn up at the time, embodying as it were a scheme for further inquiry, might well form the topic of a separate study. Such a detached investigation I am proposing to undertake in the course of the following pages as concerns the

THE MIND OF THE CHILD

second of the before-mentioned topics. In dealing with "complexes" we are led to the heart of the matter. We are thereby induced to ask what constitutes the fundamental structure of the child mind, and we are forced to find our way among the most obscure reactions (and those which are most steadfast) of the human soul. While elucidating the problem of complexes, we shall not be able to avoid touching upon the third question enumerated above, upon that concerning disturbances in the affective life. But I intend to deal with this matter only insofar as it impinges upon a given complex, and only if it is able to elucidate or explain the latter. The pathology of the child mind will concern us less than its anatomy. In this light, the complexes should be studied; and I am increasingly convinced that the whole basis of psychoanalysis consists in the study of these same complexes. A French disciple of Freud, Marie Bonaparte, expresses the matter very well when she writes: "Just as all human beings, be they white, yellow, or black, are furnished with a liver, a heart, lungs, and nervous and vascular systems, so does the human psyche possess an analogous functional anatomy, and this despite the many divergences resulting from race or climate. The super-structure of a Hottentot or of an Einstein may appear dissimilar, but the primal complexes and the general topography of the soul remain invariably the same."[1]

According to my way of thinking these words admirably convey the idea (whether implicit or explicit) which psychoanalysts hold in regard to complexes. But the general public is not as yet so well informed. The man-in-the-street, having accepted the initial deductions of our psychoanalysts, has not got any further than to look upon such phenomena as exceptional and more or less

[1] Prophylaxie infantile des névroses, p. 2.

THE CHILD'S COMPLEXES

abnormal. In the early days of psychoanalysis, the complex appeared as a strange association of ideas, a system entirely governed by affective logic, and capable of explaining certain neurotic disorders. On closer investigation, however, it was found that the complexes observed among neurotics existed likewise among normal individuals. We may each of us exhibit what may be termed "personal complexes"; yet these are merely ramifications of the universally present "primitive complexes" and we can easily discover the point at which they make their entry. Thus, since psychoanalysis has become the vogue, people are inclined to excuse themselves for having certain complexes as they do when they are suffering from a headache. But in so acting they are under a misapprehension; they are confusing the illness with the afflicted organ. It is as if one were to complain of having a heart or a liver on the pretext that one or the other was causing pain. Complexes in themselves are not pathological; it is only when they become modified or hypertrophied that they can be looked upon as morbid.

The more detailed study of complexes during recent years is of great importance; for, pari passu with this study, the whole science of psychoanalysis has developed and we have come to realise that what was at one time considered pathological is nothing other than a normal psychological phenomenon. Realising the truth of this, we shall meet with less resistance when we endeavour to apply psychoanalytical methods to the education of our young charges. The resistance we encounter is natural enough, for parents and guardians have a right to ask themselves whether the children are not being treated as neuropaths. To-day we are in a position to quash such a demurrer. Psychoanalysis has quite definitely become the concern of psychologists and pedagogues;

THE MIND OF THE CHILD

only in occasional instances is it the affair of a medical practitioner.[1]

Though psychoanalysis is primarily of interest in its application to the entire field of normal psychology, we have nevertheless to recognise that it has very special affinities to child psychology. In general the complexes (which constitute the particular investigations of psychoanalysts) are formed by the time a child has reached the age of six. Ernest Jones writes: "I would go so far as to maintain that no entirely new form of interest or type of mental reaction can enter the mind after the age of four or thereabouts. The same is true of character tendencies."[2] Direct observation of children has enabled us to witness the actual creation of these vast constellations which the psychoanalysis of grown-ups could only subsume under the name of "the unconscious." The farther we probe into the matter the more clearly do we perceive that the Freudian unconscious is essentially the survival of infantile conscious mentation, of those processes which are formed by the time a child reaches the age of six, and which thereafter are so completely and unaccountably forgotten that we have as it were to dig them up out of the adult unconscious. If we study our children in the light of psychoanalysis we may expect an abundant harvest, for in such cases we are applying the psychoanalytical method in a direct and concrete fashion without having to resort to induction and supposition, since we can use our senses both of touch and vision. After thirty years of labour, Freud, in 1925, came to the unexpected conclusion that the child constitutes the most admirable object for psychoanalytical research.[3]

[1] Cf. Freud, Psychanalyse et médecine.
[2] Papers on Psychoanalysis, p. 639.
[3] Cf. Freud, in his preface to A. Aichhorn's book, Verwahrloste Jugend.

THE CHILD'S COMPLEXES

This assertion ought to put an end to a second objection which the general public is apt to raise in regard to applying psychoanalytical methods to education. People would fain ignore the sexual aspect of psychoanalysis, and would dissociate it completely from all that concerns the child. Here we are up against a misconception on the part of the layman. Freud, without ascribing an exclusive role to the notion of sexuality within the realm of the unconscious, nevertheless gives the sexual life a very important position. But he attaches a special meaning to the term sex. We have to remember that when he speaks of sexual phenomena he refers in especial to "infantile sexuality." One may be entitled to complain of this expression from the terminological point of view, he may not have been quite happy in his choice of words; but we need merely remember that "sex" in the Freudian sense is not what Mr. Everyman understands by the word. What is to be understood is those elements of diffused sexuality, of affectivity, of love, which constitute in the child no more than the germ of what will become truly genital in the adult. Psychoanalysis enables us to assert categorically that the sexual instincts of children are in very truth the germs of what in later life become genuine forms of sexuality, for the methods devised by psychoanalytical practitioners enable us to follow with absolute exactitude the progressive and hidden transformation from one kind into the other. We might even say that infantile sexuality is an elliptical expression which comprehends within itself the close, curious, and unexpected relationships which Freud discovered to exist between the adult genital life and infantile affectivity. But the non-medical reader will be rendered more sympathetic to psychoanalytical ideas if we lay rather less stress on the word "sexuality" and rather more on

22 THE MIND OF THE CHILD

the word "infantile," thus leading him to perceive that psychoanalysis is not so much concerned with the sexual life as with the psychology of the child.

When we speak of analysis we imply a resolution into simple elements. In old days the psychology of associations sought for these elements in the sensations. Nowadays, for numerous reasons, we are led to find them in the instinctive responses of the individual to his environment. Such is, indeed, the attitude adopted by psychoanalysts. A study of instinctive actions constitutes the basis of psychological investigation; wishes, cravings, form the next step. In a spirit of depreciation, certain persons have been wont to say that psychoanalysis is nothing better than a rehash of the old associationist psychology. It has, indeed, been a great mistake to poke fun at the "association of ideas" beloved of the psychologist of an earlier epoch. This was a necessary stage, and we are further in error when we fail to recognize that psychoanalysts, while making use of the method, have gone far beyond its scope. What legacy still remains to us from the associationist psychology is the analytical viewpoint, is the endeavour to reduce psychological facts to their primal elements. Insofar as a psychoanalyst is an analyst, he could not very well proceed otherwise, even though in the end he were led to the conclusion that the analytical point of view is not exhaustive, that, indeed, it needs to be completed, to be rounded off by other methods. But whereas in the case of the associationist psychology we had to do with the association of ideas, that is to say (in the last analysis) with the association of images, which are the vestiges of sensations, the psychoanalyst deals with the association of active elements, such as instincts, wishes, tendencies, and the like. The association of ideas and of images is

THE CHILD'S COMPLEXES

merely utilised nowadays in order to reveal more clearly the active associations of the subject. This method has proved fertile in results, since psychoanalysts have thereby been led to identify a goodly number of concrete and stable associative systems, i.e. the various complexes. The associationist psychology reconstructed the human mind, on general and theoretical principles, by means of problematical or merely possible elements; psychoanalysis, on the other hand, gives one the impression of dealing with actual and specific elements which can be described and named.

It would be presumptuous were our psychoanalysts to declare that they had laid bare the ultimate and irreducible elements of the human mind. Even in the case of quite young children, personal observation makes us aware of the fact that psychological development is singularly far advanced already at a tender age, and that we have good warrant for speaking of "complexes." Despite the assertions of too simple-minded materialists, the child is much more than a little animal; it possesses a mind, a soul—call it what you will—though this mind or soul be still at a stage of infantile evolution. The aim of analytical investigation is to dissect psychological phenomena, to reduce them to their "instinctive" elements; and our studies along these lines have shown that many a survival from our instinctive past lingers on in our minds and characters. In 1922, when writing my *Studies in Psychoanalysis*, I realised that the next task awaiting the psychologist was to trace step by step the gradual transformation of the instincts into sentiments and thoughts. Encouraged by Freud's studies concerning the sexual instinct and its metamorphoses, by Adler's considerations of the instinct for wielding power, by Drever's book on *Instinct in Man*, by Bovet's work on *The Fighting Instinct*,

24 THE MIND OF THE CHILD

and by the endeavours on the part of certain authors to connect war neuroses with the instinct for self-preservation, I thought that the next step on the road to elucidating various knotty points in psychoanalysis would be the writing of a series of monographs on the different instincts. Eight years of observation and reflection have now led me to think that this task will not be accomplished quite as speedily as I had hoped. We cannot afford to skip any phases of the investigation, and the more detailed the study, the more frequent must be our stopping places and the more numerous our helpers.

In the early days of "scientific psychology" our students were fired with the ambition to constitute a system of psychophysics out of hand. It had become evident that there existed a considerable gap between body and mind, which must be bridged by physiology. This was the origin of the science of psychophysics. But ere long a second intermediary between physiology and psychology was disclosed, this time in the field of biology, for, connecting the functions of the body with the actions of the mind a whole universe, the world of the instincts, was found to exist. Out of this realisation a new aspect of the science was created, one which we might term "psychobiology," wherein William James from one outlook and Sigmund Freud from another give pride of place to the notion of the instincts.

Nor has the matter ended there. Not content with demonstrating the relationships between the instincts and the psyche, Freud has furnished us with a very precise method for exploring these relationships. We have thus been led to discover that between instinct and the higher phases of mentation there is yet another stage which consists of the complexes.

For the nonce, psychoanalysts do not directly relate

THE CHILD'S COMPLEXES

the higher mental processes to the instincts but to the complexes. Nevertheless certain instinctive elements are plainly manifest in the complexes, and we are forced to admit, after a more careful study of the complexes, that there exists a law which is of supreme importance and which I propose to formulate in the following terms: In every complex several instincts are represented in an extremely intimate state of combination; and, on the other hand, all the primal instincts are represented in each of the more important of the complexes.

This law which brings vividly before our eyes the fact that the complexes form a stage between instinct and the higher processes of mentation helps us to understand and to explain the divergences of interpretation which from the very outset arose among psychoanalysts when they endeavoured to establish a connecting link between higher affective phenomena and the instinctive life. Freud was by no means mistaken, nor was he guilty of exaggeration, when he detected almost universal traces of the sexual instinct; nor were other investigators led astray when, in identical phenomena they detected an extension of the instinct of self-preservation, or of the will-to-power, or of the social instinct, and so forth. These various interpretations begin to clash only when their protagonists endeavour to link in too direct a manner higher phenomena with the instinctive elements discovered therein. Actually, such higher phenomena ought to be connected up with a complex wherein numerous instincts are inextricably interwoven. It was towards some such conclusion that I was striving when I wrote my *Psychanalyse de l'art*. Later, when more sure of my own ground, I proposed that alongside the notion of the "libido" we should place that of the "potential," and

26   THE MIND OF THE CHILD

psychoanalysts have not been slow to adopt the idea. Freud, arriving at a similar conclusion by methods of his own, has given them a most lucid explanation in recent writings, such as *Das Unbehagen in der Kultur* (Civilisation and its Discontents, 1930). In my book *Mobilisation de l'énergie* (1930), I endeavoured to show the full significance of this evolution in psychoanalytical theory, and the modifications which Freud, with his customary straight-forwardness, has introduced into certain of his concepts, as for instance in his interpretation of the libido and of sadism. Freud no longer accounts for sadism as an essentially sexual manifestation, but links it up, rather, with the aggressive tendencies and with the instinct to kill. Thus we see that though Freud discerns sexual elements in phenomena where most people do not expect to find them, he is not deterred by the fact that sadism is almost universally regarded as a sexual perversion to discover in it other, non-sexual, elements. There is no contradiction here. We are merely in presence of two applications of the principle that the latent content of things differs from the manifest content.

Such being the condition of affairs, I have felt it incumbent upon me to devise a method whereby higher phenomena can be deliberately referred, not to instincts, but to complexes. This means that I shall have to postpone to a later day the resolution of each individual complex into its instinctive elements, for, in the actual state of our knowledge, we are not yet in a position to do so. The method I am proposing to adopt has this further advantage that it transcends the dissensions between the various schools of psychoanalytical theory, and brings into relief the points upon which our authors may easily come to a common understanding (since we are dealing with facts). Thus the practical analyst may continue his

THE CHILD'S COMPLEXES

labours with enhanced energy and he may expect better results, since he will be working on a solid foundation, and upon ground already tilled. Furthermore his achievements will bear richer fruit, seeing that his practice will not be encumbered with premature theoretical discussions.

I hold that our instinctive energies, before they can fecundate our sentiments and the higher mental processes, must pass through the region of the complexes as through a sieve. In this region the energies generated by each separate instinct are split up and dissociated from their elements, to be once more regrouped in the most unexpected manner. Energies derived from several instinctive sources enter into the fresh mosaics thus formed, and an identical instinct may be found repeating itself in several of the newly-formed groups. The groups or mosaics constitute what psychoanalysts term the complexes which have been discovered in the subterranean regions of the adult mind. But when we come to analyse children we find these same complexes occupying the front row of the stalls—if I may be permitted so concrete an image. We cannot, therefore, deal in any detail with child psychology without in the first instance furnishing a description of these mosaics or groupings. This is the task I have set myself in the present volume.

I cannot hope in one short book to deal with the whole list of the complexes, and shall confine myself to a study of the more obvious ones and to those upon which psychoanalytical experience can furnish the most numerous and precise data.

At the outset let me endeavour to classify these complexes. Such a classification cannot attempt more than to put some sort of order in our study. It is

28 THE MIND OF THE CHILD

anything but perfect, and can only be looked upon as provisional.

1. First of all we shall have to consider those complexes which are formed by acquisitive tendencies and by the desire to attain an exterior object. These I propose to term complexes of the object. In this group there is the Cain complex, the rivalry arising among brothers and sisters for the sole possession of the mother or of the family goods; the Oedipus complex which gives expression to the child's love for one parent and hatred of the other; the destruction complex (sadistic-anal) where the impulse to destroy an object or to injure a fellow-mortal is manifest; the spectacular complex which embodies the group of tendencies wherein the subject wishes to be seen or wishes to see, to discover, to contemplate a given object or to be appreciated and admired by this object.

2. By an almost imperceptible transition (and we shall constantly be faced by such transitions in the domain we are now exploring), the last-named complex leads to a second group of tendencies. The spectacular attitude, though of interest to the subject, nevertheless lacks something in regard to the subject: to be seen or to contemplate an object is not possession. Furthermore, a person who wishes to be admired is very near the point of self-admiration. Again, curiosity, which goads the subject to wish to see, reacts upon the subject himself, so that he asks: "What am I?" Thus one passes little by little into a state of mind wherein the subject is himself the centre of preoccupation. Here we may speak of complexes of the ego. In this class of complexes we encounter the mutilation [castration] complex which plays so vital a part and which (pari passu with the Oedipus complex) was one of the first to be distinguished by Freud. The subject compares himself with the world around him; a

THE CHILD'S COMPLEXES

child of the male sex will contrast himself with a child of the other sex (a little boy will thus imagine that the little girl he plays with has been mutilated); his mind is preoccupied with problems concerning the more and the less. Such circumstances give rise to feelings of inferiority and to the wish to be superior. This complex takes on a particular form among little girls, and I have, therefore, devoted a special chapter to what I name the Diana complex. A little girl, thinking herself to be inferior, would prefer to be a boy. But the child does not solely seek to find its own level in regard to its environment. At a very early date it wants to know what it is, whence it comes, how babies are born. This is known as the birth complex. A child has its own theories on the problem of birth: a baby comes into this world by way of the anus, and so forth—unless, indeed, its origins are to be sought in the magic sphere of fable.

3. Children's interests are never purely theoretical. The birth complex is teeming with other fantasies, such as a desire to return to the mother's womb, and the closely related desire to find a refuge. Again, by progressive stages, we thus pass on to certain affective systems which we may term complexes of attitude. In such cases we are no longer concerned with the individual's position in relation to the environment, nor with the aggressive assertion of the ego, nor with a personal chase after an object in order to possess it. We are here faced by an attitude which recurs again and again in respect of a vast number of objects, in respect of life itself, and which colours the most divergent tendencies. The weaning complex is very definitely linked up with the shock of being deprived of the maternal milk, with the desire for a definite object. But as between the words "desire" and "object," the main stress may just as well be transferred

30 THE MIND OF THE CHILD

from the latter to the former. The object, having become unattainable, is given up; the desire, the craving remains; in a word, an attitude of mind is created, and this attitude arises in regard to the most multifarious objects under the form of demands, avidity, etc. The attitude which arises in connexion with the weaning complex presupposes, in addition, a regret for the loss of babyhood, a regret which finds expression in various ways and which introduces us to the flight complex. This last-named complex is composed of attitudes of regret, of regression, and of introversion; it is for ever underlaid by the search for a refuge—which leads us back by a detour to one of the ramifications of the birth complex. Furthermore, narcissism is closely correlated to the flight complex, and at the same time has obvious connexions with the ego complex seeing that narcissism is an affective falling-back upon the self. But perhaps this falling-back upon the self is less tinged with ego love than with the desire to flee from life and the world.

4. Such are the three classes of complex I feel entitled to establish. The Oedipus complex and the mutilation complex (termed by Freud the castration complex) have become classical. Those concerning birth and weaning are not so widely accepted. I myself am responsible for coining the terms Cain complex, destruction complex, spectacular complex, Diana complex, and flight complex in order to designate certain regions more or less exactly identified by other psychoanalysts, regions which until now lacked synthesis and a perfectly clear definition. It is obvious that my classification corresponds to a difference powerfully stamped upon the very nature of things. The complex is a bundle of tendencies, and can only be explained by a study of the tendencies. But every tendency, every action (like every sentence in a language), must

THE CHILD'S COMPLEXES

contain an object, a subject, a verb, as one might say; and according to the word we choose to emphasise at the moment we have to do with complexes of the object, complexes of the ego, and complexes of attitude. Nevertheless, though the above classification may appear natural enough, it cannot pretend to be more than approximative. Even in so short an enumeration, we have found it impossible to draw any precise lines of demarcation. The complexes shoot out ramifications into one another's domains; constantly we are being hauled back from one to the other, and from one class into another. Thus the destruction complex classified above among the complexes of the object, is, when contemplated from certain angles, a complex of attitude, and we shall see later on in this study that the "anal character" which derives from the destruction complex becomes a genuine attitude towards life.

We have, therefore, to correct the too rigorous distinctions we have drawn while endeavouring to search for relationships between the complexes, and this I propose to do in Part Four. We are in a position to describe points of contact between various complexes, and in doing so we shall perceive that these encounters are not due to chance, but that it is in the nature of certain complexes to link themselves on to certain typical motifs which often enough assume a similar aspect. I shall describe in detail two examples of such a linking up of complex and motif, under the captions: "I am shut out," and "the victimised woman." In Chapter Twelve I intend to study what Freud has called the super-ego, which is a genuine complex and represents as it were the court of moral appeal. In regard to all the other complexes this super-ego plays the part of regulator or governor, so that it has constantly to keep in touch with every complex.

32   THE MIND OF THE CHILD

This court of moral appeal, which is responsible for the aspect which the "ideal" or the "conscience" will assume in each individual, is already distinctly visible in the child; it constitutes a function of parenthood, of the earliest educators of the young, and it brings us up against the very core of the problem of education.

PART ONE

COMPLEXES OF THE OBJECT

CHAPTER ONE

CAIN OR FRATERNAL RIVALRY

In a psychoanalytical study of Victor Hugo, which formed a series of lectures I gave at the university of Geneva, the poem entitled *La conscience* was the kernel of my monograph. Here we are given a magnificent picture of Cain's remorse after the murder of his brother. Fraternal rivalry constituted one of the most violent conflicts in the poet's own unconscious. He was the youngest of three boys, the eldest of whom happened to be christened Abel. From the very outset, "little Victor," who was rather a puny child, nursed the secret ambition to become the equal of his older brothers, to outstrip them, to "take their place." When such desires arise in early childhood, they usually find expression in a wish for the rival's death. Such a wish is in reality less cruel than appears on the surface, for a little child does not know what death really is, and not infrequently uses the word as a synonym for "absence."[1] All through the life and works of our great poet the numerous ramifications of this unconscious theme may be followed in all their details. Was I animated with a desire to prove that "little Victor" was a monster? Of course not. His case is exceptional because he happened to be a genius and was able to sublimate in a truly beautiful manner his infantile complex of rivalry.

But the complex itself is not exceptional by any means; it is, rather, the rule. Human nature is thus constituted and we have to bow before the fact. A youngster who

[1] Cf. Freud, The Interpretation of Dreams (La science des rêves, p. 238).

36   THE MIND OF THE CHILD

suddenly has a little brother or sister foisted upon him usually reacts at first by a violent fit of jealousy, a feeling purely animal in its nature. The feeling of jealousy continues to exist, but in a latent state, and is more or less successfully held in leash. I have observed analogous reactions in animals. When my eldest boy was born, we had a little black cat which was a singularly faithful and affectionate pet. If we went out of an evening, it would accompany us a good part of the way and await our return at the spot where it had parted from us; even if we were away several hours it would still be there. When it first saw our baby it looked at the boy with a wicked expression in its eyes, and then went for the youngster tooth and claw. We had to give it a good lesson, whereupon the little animal disappeared and never came back again. A certain amount of hostility on the part of the younger child appears to be a natural response to the same feeling which animates the elder when a new baby joins the family circle. But it is the hostility of the older child in respect of the younger which is the most salient fact, and one upon which the most interesting observations have so far been made. The frequent quarrels between sisters and brothers are in most cases the outcome of this early rivalry which bursts forth at the slightest provocation and which is the despair of so many mothers. The ostensible and seemingly inadequate motives of such fraternal bickerings are no more than superficial pretexts: the real spur is the latent and primal jealousy.

At first we may feel inclined to object to so positive an affirmation. Yet no sooner has psychoanalysis drawn our attention to its existence than we observe countless examples all around us. Nay more, we are surprised never to have noted the phenomenon before. This is a very frequent situation in regard to psychoanalytical

CAIN OR FRATERNAL RIVALRY

observations: we did not see the fact because we did not wish to see it (repression); but once we have been made aware of its existence nothing is more obvious. Nearly all of us have passed through such phases in the course of our childhood, but they have been so successfully repressed that nothing of them remains in the memory. According to the degree of a child's moral development we find repression more or less at work from earliest infancy. Happily a large number of children are able to master their hostility quite soon, and can substitute—or, more correctly, can "superimpose"—a sincere affection. Sometimes, for the start, a child may be trained to assure all and sundry that it is very fond of its little brother or sister. But such avowals are always more or less forced, and the natural hostility thus repressed will become manifest from time to time, and invariably remains obvious to the trained observer.

In spite of the difficulties of the case, students of human nature did not have to await the results of psychoanalytical observations in order to realise the fact that infantile jealousy does indeed exist. St. Augustine writes: "I have seen and studied a child rendered quite ill through jealousy. Though it could not yet speak it was pale and cast grieved and bitter glances at its fellow sucklings." The extract is quoted by Cullerre in his book on *Les enfants nerveux* (p. 47). This same author draws our attention to the fact that analogous instances may be culled almost any day from our newspapers. Some of these are records of deeds of violence such as the following summary from the New York press: A boy, twenty months old, was jealous of his baby sister born two days before. Left alone with her, the little boy struck her so forcibly that the nurse on her return found the infant dead and covered with bruises and scratches. Her small

THE MIND OF THE CHILD

brother was leaning over the victim and gazing at her in stupefaction.

Since psychoanalysts have had their attention drawn to these facts they have collected a large number of child sayings which speak eloquently as to the true state of the mind. I had a little girl of five under my care who had just been presented with a baby brother. Jokingly she was asked whether the baby might be taken away in the wheelbarrow. "Oh yes," she replied indifferently, "only you must bring back the wheelbarrow." Linette's dislike of her brother remained very active for some time, and I shall have occasion to refer to this case again later on.

A boy of two and a half years, when shown his newly-born sister, said: "Me don't want to see that." For a whole week he refused to look at her, and when she was taking suck he wanted to tear her away from the mother's breast. Incidentally, the little boy died a short while after from bronchitis.

Here is another personal observation. Nani is four years old; her sister Zizou is three. The latter is ill after a fall and has had to be put to bed. Her mother leaves the sick room, but is promptly recalled by hearing a cry of distress. The lights have not been switched on, but in the dusk the mother can see two dark holes in Zizou's face whence blood seems to flow. Nani is standing aside in a corner, looking sheepish. The mother at first believes that the elder child has put out the younger sister's eyes. Happily matters are not as bad as this, but she discovers that Nani has emptied a bottle of tincture of iodine into Zizou's eyes. General consternation; 'phone calls to doctor and oculist; injections, and so forth.—The burns were no more than superficial and the eyes of the little girl were saved. Nani, on being asked why she had done it, at first answered: "I was a little silly." Then, with an

CAIN OR FRATERNAL RIVALRY

indefinable expression of countenance, she added: "I've spoiled Zizou's beautiful eyes." The younger girl was a very lovely child, and, above all, her eyes were constantly being commented upon in the presence of Nani. Another reason for hostility, and one which has been observed in numerous instances, was that the mother was so ill after Zizou's birth that Nani was sent away from home for six months. Such an exile is well calculated to arouse in the child mind a feeling that it is forsaken because of its younger rival, that it has lost its mother's affection—and this latter idea is of supreme importance in the genesis of infantile jealousy.

This refusal to "share mother" with any one else sometimes takes very original forms. Anna was two years old when her sister was born in a sanatorium. It was in this place that Anna first saw the baby, and she contemplated it with interest. When baby and mother came home and the infant was put to the breast, Anna began to cry. To calm the child her father had to assure her that the baby was not going to eat mother. From this moment, either directly or otherwise, Anna began to ask questions about how babies were born. Each time she asked, she was told that babies grew inside the mother's tummy. Apparently this explanation was accepted for what it was worth, but it never ousted the story about the stork which in her heart of hearts Anna continued to prefer to any other. She refused to accept the truth, maintains our author,[1] because of jealousy. Anna could not bring herself to admit of so intimate a contact between her little sister and her mother. In the end, however, she was persuaded to accept the truth, and her qualms of jealousy were assuaged by the positive assurance that

[1] Imre Hermann (Budapest), "Revue Française de Psychanalyse," vol. ii, p. 386.

40 THE MIND OF THE CHILD

she, too, had enjoyed a similar contact with her mother's body and had been suckled at the maternal breast.

Feelings of jealousy provoked by the advent of a little brother or sister often give rise to more or less unfortunate modifications in the character and behaviour of the older child. In reporting the dream of a little girl, E. Westerman Holstijn-Vissering[1] furnishes us with the following data: Maja aged three. Since the birth of her brother Yajla three months ago her character has obviously undergone a change. She will start weeping for no apparent reason, and while crying thus, she imitates the voice of the baby. Such imitation recurs in her games. She dreams:

1. It is dark; Auntie came in a car; Mummy promised to take Maja for a drive in the car, but Mummy went off alone and left Maja behind.

2. A man came into the bedroom and flung all the plates out of the window. All the plates were broken.

In the first part of the dream we see plainly how Maja feels that her mother has forsaken her. In the second part we perceive a reaction against this situation, but the reaction is masked. The truth of the matter became evident in the light of the following associations: the previous evening Maja was told that the cat had fallen out of the window and had hurt itself. "It cried and wept." The child was greatly impressed by this story. Afterwards when Maja was in the garden, she heard the baby crying, and said: "Yajla is crying, he must have fallen out of the window." One is apt to believe what one wants to believe, and Maja's supposition so gratuitously finding expression in the child's mind leaves us in no doubt at all as to her feelings in regard to her little brother and the plates which are substituted for him in the dream.

[1] Ein Traum eines dreijährigen Mädchens, p. 476.

CAIN OR FRATERNAL RIVALRY 41

The interpretation concerning the plates is all the more plausible seeing that in a goodly number of cases children accomplish in actual fact the actions which Maja does only in a dream. They throw objects out of the window. Analysis of these actions goes to prove that we are here in presence of a typical and symbolical action whereby the child indirectly expresses its desire (repressed into the unconscious) to rid itself of objectionable rivals. We have a classical example of such a deed in *Dichtung und Wahrheit*. Goethe tells of the pleasure he felt one day when he threw a great number of breakable objects out of the window, and then contemplated the veritable hecatomb of broken pieces. Psychoanalysis interprets these objects as symbolising the young poet's innumerable brothers and sisters.[1] This by no means implies that Goethe, any more than Victor Hugo, was a monster.

But the child's actions are not always as patently typical as those recorded above. Some, indeed, require careful analysis in order to reveal their true significance. Barbara Low in *The Unconscious in Action* (p. 105) tells of a boy of ten who "was ceaselessly weaving patterns of a specific kind whenever he began to do any thinking—arithmetical calculation, algebraic problems, and so on. He had no idea of any meaning attached to his patterns, he merely saw them in the air before his eyes and could not drive them away. An analysis gave some clue, for the patterns showed themselves to be connected with his very earliest experiences in connexion with bitter jealous hostilities in relation to his younger brother and mother's decided preference for the latter."

Disturbances in the character of a child, due to fraternal

[1] Cf. Freud, Eine Kindheitserinnerung aus Dichtung und Wahrheit. Also, Philipp Sarasin, Goethes Mignon, eine psychoanalytische Studie, II, Goethes Jugendgeschichte, p. 349.

42   THE MIND OF THE CHILD

rivalries, sometimes result in a family tragedy, and may continue far beyond the age of childhood. The tragical development of such a situation can often be traced throughout the whole of a long life. I recall the case of two brothers. There was only two-and-a-half years' difference in their ages. The elder boy reacted to the arrival of the younger by assuming a domineering attitude and by behaving as if the baby did not exist at all. The quality of his work, his energy and success, greatly appreciated by the father, were a perpetual source of humiliation to the younger lad. The latter, feeling left out in the cold, manifested in regard to his mother an immense longing for tender affection. This longing remained unsatisfied. Later in life he became spendthrift, and his mother had constantly to be supplying him with money. In spite of all she did for him, he felt that she was unjust towards him—for what he needed was impossible to grant: reparation for the injustice he believed himself to have suffered in childhood. He took a strong dislike for his home, ran away, and spent ever more money; he enlisted at the age of eighteen, and then deserted. His unstable and dissatisfied character made it difficult for him to remain long in any situation, to make a career for himself, whereas the elder man prospered and became well established. This only served to enhance the inequality between the two brothers. It was obvious, however, that the younger preferred to remain a child for ever in need of maternal care.

Happily things do not always come to such a pass. Nevertheless it is rare not to find secret resentments, persisting into adult life, among brothers and sisters. The resentful feelings are the vestigial remains of infantile rivalries, which those concerned justify by such excuses as: "We are so unlike "; "My brother's character is totally

CAIN OR FRATERNAL RIVALRY

different from mine"; "We are very fond of one another, but there are certain things we cannot agree about." How often do we hear phrases such as these! One might be led to believe that Dame Nature had gone out of her way to create dissimilarities between those nearest of kin. When psychoanalytical methods are applied to these cases, we very soon begin to see clear and to appraise them at their just value. Usually an improvement takes place in strained relations which at bottom are due to a very different reason than that ascribed.

Troubles of the sort do not invariably localise themselves in the behaviour and temper of the sufferer; they may also find expression in undermining the health of the subject under the form of neurotic symptoms.

Alfred Adler[1] reports the case of a girl of seven whose father was inclined to spoil her, but whose mother was very strict with her and extremely indulgent toward a younger child. Feeling herself to occupy an inferior position to this little sister, she reacted by becoming extremely conceited both at school and in the home. She had no love for her sister who was her constant rival. By making a lot of fuss about some minor ailments, she produced certain morbid symptoms by means of which she was able to gratify her feelings of revenge: her father devoted himself to her, and endeavoured to compensate her for the mother's neglect by indulging all her whims and fancies. One day the mother reproached her husband for spoiling the child so outrageously. That very night the little girl had her first fit of neurotic anxiety. This was manifestly the effect of a violent revolt on the part of the child, inasmuch as the paroxysm made it necessary for the father to give even more time and

[1] Adler and Furtmüller, Heilen und Bilden, p. 110.

44 THE MIND OF THE CHILD

trouble to his little daughter, and the mother no longer ventured to enter a protest.

In *Man's Unconscious Conflict* (p. 239) Wilfrid Lay quoting from another author[1] instances a case of psychic blindness in a little girl. The morbid condition was found upon analysis "to rest upon an analogy, the basis of similarity being the following thoughts. She did not want to have any care of her younger brothers and sisters. She knew that if she were blind she could not see to do various things for them, etc. In other words, blindness is like inability, which is in turn like irresponsibility. She did not wish to be responsible for the family nor to do for them. . . ."

I owe to one of my pupils the following case of bedwetting, which is an admirable example of masked revenge. Madeleine was seventeen months old when her sister Jaqui was born. She showed no jealousy; on the contrary, she manifested great interest in the baby, assisting at its toilet, and never allowing strangers to touch it. In her childish idiom she explained that the baby "is all for me." Jaqui was a good baby, very quiet, and no one bothered about her except at feeding times and to wash and dress her. When Madeleine was eighteen months old she rarely wetted her bed, and by the age of twenty months she practically never did so. Then, quite suddenly, she began bed-wetting frequently. This coincided with a period in the baby's growth when it needed more attention, when it was laid out on the lawn, when it began to gurgle and kick its little heels in the air, when, in short, people had to be watching it and fussing around it. At three and a half years of age Madeleine was still a confirmed bed-wetter. No methods proved of any avail in curing her of the habit. She continued to occupy herself

[1] Coriat, The Meaning of Dreams, p. 173.

CAIN OR FRATERNAL RIVALRY

with the baby and to protect it. She could be left in sole charge without anxiety. But if the parents were present her attitude changed and she went out of her way to tease little Jaqui. About the same period she began to be disagreeable towards her mother, to be disobedient, and to answer her mother's protests by threatening "to tell Daddy." At three years and seven months she was constantly accusing her mother of favouritism in regard to Jaqui, and at the same time she became affected with a nervous habit, producing a peculiar noise in her throat. The bad habit grew upon her. Thereupon she was sent to stay with some friends of the family for five days. On the very first night she refused to have the waterproof sheeting placed under her, promising that she would not wet the bed. She was allowed to do as she wished and not once during the five days of her visit did she fail to keep her promise. But immediately she returned home she started bed-wetting again. On the following evening her mother removed the waterproof sheeting, and said that Madeleine was now going to be treated as a big girl. Thenceforward she wetted her bed about every fourth night. But she now began to make comparisons between her bed and that of her sister which was larger and handsomer (the younger girl having been clean in her habits for some time past). Since they were staying temporarily in a boarding-house and could not afford to risk spoiling the mattress, the parents decided they would replace the waterproof sheeting. Madeleine thereupon started wetting her bed every night.

A few weeks later, Madeleine, Jaqui, and the mother left Germany for Geneva—the father did not go with them. Before setting forth on this long journey, Madeleine's mother said that at Geneva the little girl would have a proper bed like a big person. Madeleine was pleased

THE MIND OF THE CHILD

after a fashion, but asked suspiciously: "And Jaqui, is she too going to have a big bed like me?"—"No, hers will be smaller." Then the child's delight knew no bounds, and she kept on repeating: "I'm going to have a big bed, a bigger one than Jaqui!" At Geneva she was put to sleep in the promised big bed, and from that time onward she never wetted her bed again. As for her behaviour towards her mother, that began to improve a few days after arrival, and by the end of three weeks her manners were irreproachable. Madeleine became very affectionate and obedient; she no longer grumbled that her mother made a favourite of the younger girl.

There can be no doubt that all these disturbances, and especially the last-named case, are intimately related to the Cain complex. Bed-wetting, indeed, may nearly always be interpreted as concealing the desire to be a tiny baby which occupies the attention of grown-ups night and day. From the outset Madeleine had hesitated between two methods of resolving her mental conflict: one was a regression towards babyhood; the other was to assume a superior and possessive attitude (the little sister was "all for me") by means of which she could compensate herself for the condition of inferiority to which she felt herself reduced by the advent of the baby Jaqui. The second method was certainly a better solution than the first, and in many instances such compensations are quite happy in their results, for they satisfy the child by making it sure of enjoying a tangible superiority over the other brothers or sisters.

Children invariably drift into one solution or the other. Green reports two cases which illustrate this fact. A boy of nine, whose nose is put out of joint by the birth of a baby brother, is animated with a profound feeling of resentment against his mother and a desire to domineer

CAIN OR FRATERNAL RIVALRY

over his little brother. He dreams that he kills a tigress ("and you know a tigress is much more savage when she has a cub with her") and that he captures the baby tiger which henceforward follows him and obeys him. But the wish to dominate, to wield power, is not simply gratified by means of fantasies. In the case of the boy we are now considering, he devised a scheme whereby he kept to his room, and even remained in bed entertaining himself with tales of adventure, fairy tales, and reading books which dealt with English and with classical history. The second case is that of a girl aged three who has a sister younger than herself. She cannot bear to see her mother taking care of the baby, and solves her conflict by taking the mother's place. She endeavours to imitate her mother in every way; tries in her clumsy, childish fashion to help in looking after the baby. But since her zeal is at times inopportune, she is scolded and is asked why she makes such a nuisance of herself. Her reply is: "I want to do it."[1]

We need not, therefore, make a mountain out of a molehill in such cases. No matter how violent these childish enmities may appear, they are all capable of a happy solution. Love for the parents, and the sense of moral obligation which manifests itself at an early age, are two of the factors which promote a beneficent solution (as we shall see later on). Marie Bonaparte in her speech at the fifth congress of French-speaking psychoanalysts emphasised the advantages that accrued to children who in early life had brothers and sisters to play with. The affection which ensued amply compensated for any jealousy they might have felt at the outset, and in view of their future life among adults, rubbing shoulders with

[1] Cf. Green, Psychanalysis in the Class-Room, pp. 189 and 205.

48 THE MIND OF THE CHILD

Mr. Everyman, such comradeship was of inestimable value. The way in which a child solves the natural conflict arising between itself and its brothers and sisters tends towards repetition when it subsequently comes into contact with schoolmates and, still later, in its social relationships.

Adler has noted a certain authoritative and conservative mentality among first-born children, whereas the second is often of a rebellious disposition and the youngest tends either to be lazy because it is spoilt or to be the most original of the family. Sometimes the last-born is inordinately ambitious. These differences can be easily accounted for when we know the position each child occupied during the first years of its life. We have an admirable example of the conservative mentality in an eldest child when considering the case of Charles Maurras, the protagonist of "L'Action Française." In the very first pages of his recollections of childhood's days, he makes the following confession which, be it noted, displays keen powers of self-observation: "He [Maurras' father] told me about the coming of my younger brother, singing and capering about as he spoke. . . . I had already adopted the behaviour of an only child, and looked upon my little rival with a jealous eye, for I thought, 'How many of Mother's caresses are lost to me!' My father took me by the hand saying: 'Come on, old chap, we two are men.' "[1] Henceforward the boy took up his position among the powers of order and might. Yet another example of, this time, a younger son being inspired with inordinate ambition and great originality of thought is furnished by Victor Hugo whose case was cited above.

All the repressions and transformations of infantile jealousies end in the adoption of a specific social attitude.

[1] La musique interieure, p. 2.

CAIN OR FRATERNAL RIVALRY 49

We may even esteem that such childish rivalries are possibly the foundations of our social sentiments. According to Freud, even our feelings of justice and solidarity are coloured by infantile rivalries: if a child cannot become the first, the favourite, it desires that at least every one of its contemporaries shall be on a similar footing to itself. This is the least it can expect, and is merely a matter of "being just."

Does not this imply that a society founded purely upon the "justice" and "fraternity" advocated by certain reformers would have a very precarious existence? Justice is merely a substitute for egoism, while fraternity is, above all, rivalry. Brothers are born foes. We need to go beyond justice and to have recourse to charity whether we desire this or not; and charity is love. But love does not arise upon the soil of fraternal relations; it takes birth among the filial sentiments, and these will be the subject of our next chapter.

CHAPTER TWO

OEDIPUS AND FILIAL AFFECTION

FREUD's early definition of the Oedipus complex was no more than a summary of two tendencies intimately connected one with the other, namely: love for the parent of the opposite sex and hostility towards the parent of the same sex. I have often pointed out in my books and in the course of lectures delivered at the university of Geneva and the Jean-Jacques Rousseau Institute that in order to grasp the full significance of the Oedipus complex as we interpret it to-day, we must lose sight of the complications that arise from displacement, transference, and symbolism. A boy's hostility to his father may be transferred, for instance, to his brother, his schoolmaster, his employer, etc. Furthermore, as Freud pointed out after a while, in the course of a long and detailed analysis we find, over and above the "normal" Oedipus complex, a reversed Oedipus complex; e.g., a boy will go through a period of love for his father and enmity towards his mother, whereas a girl will, for a time, feel moved by love for her mother and dislike of her father.[1] Those who are accustomed to analyse the infantile and primitive impulses of man will find nothing to be surprised at in such a reversal of the order of things, for these contradictory reactions of the affects are constantly being juxtaposed without rhyme or reason. Are we, therefore, to declare that the famous Oedipus complex, as first conceived by Freud and upon which his whole system seemed to be based, is a worthless figment? Far from it. The "normal" Oedipus complex is considerably

[1] Cf. Freud, The Ego and the Id.

OEDIPUS AND FILIAL AFFECTION 51

more often present in our subjects than the "reversed" form. Besides, in both cases we are confronted by the same fundamental truth with which we were faced when discussing the Cain complex. This truth may be formulated as follows: in a child, love is extraordinarily wholehearted and jealous. Thus we may summarise the situation under two formulas:

1. During the period when a child, be it boy or girl, loves its father, it tends to look askance at its mother and treats her as a rival; during the period when it loves its mother, the father becomes the rival.

2. Love for the mother and hostility towards the father is more frequently met with among boys; love for the father and hostility towards the mother is more often met with among girls.

The second of these formulas, which expresses Freud's earlier conception of the Oedipus complex, is to-day corrected by the first formula. The latter is a confirmation of the essential unity of love and hostility in the heart of a child, and it helps us to understand the origin and significance of the dispute which in earlier days arose between Freud and Adler, a difference of opinion which constituted the first schism in the ranks of psychoanalysts. The phenomena which Freud interpreted as a function of the love impulse, were interpreted by Adler as a function of the will-to-power. Such a translation of functions is always feasible since infantile affection from the outset is indissolubly linked with hostility or rivalry. In love between adults, the so-called "dramas of jealousy," always represent a regression to infantile emotions. But such divergences of interpretation apply with as much force to the Cain complex as to the Oedipus complex. Conflicts arising between brothers and sisters are the outcome of a desire to dominate and to be

THE MIND OF THE CHILD

superior. Nevertheless, the crucial point of fraternal rivalry is invariably the fact of having to be satisfied with a share of maternal love. Perhaps we shall do well simply to observe the strange solidarity which exists between hostility and love, and leave it at that. Precious time will be wasted in futile theoretical discussion as to the priority of one sentiment over the other. In view of the intimate connexion which undoubtedly exists between the two instincts, any discussion of the sort is fated to lead nowhere. It is upon the intimacy of this connexion that, above all, I wish to insist when introducing my readers to the idea of the complex.

Long before the days of psychoanalysis we have instances of the working of this Oedipus complex recorded in the biographies of illustrious men. We are told that Blaise Pascal, accustomed to the individual endearments of his father and his mother, could not endure to see his parents displaying affection towards one another; if they did so, he would scream and cry, and struggle in his nurse's arms. Stendhal relates of himself, in *La vie de Henri Brulard*: "My mother was a lovely woman, and I was quite in love with her . . . I longed to cover her with kisses, and my one desire was that she she should wear no clothes. She loved me passionately, and would kiss me frequently. I returned her kisses with so much ardour that she was forced to withdraw. I hated my father when he came interrupting these caresses. . . . I felt estranged from my father, and loathed having to kiss him." He lost his mother when he was only seven years of age, and states that with her death there vanished all the joy of his childhood. As far as his father was concerned, Stendhal remained inveterately hostile. He found the elder man "wrinkled

OEDIPUS AND FILIAL AFFECTION 53

and ugly," mean, and ultra-particularist ("archi-dauphinois" in this case). When the old man died, Stendhal, with ironical humour, tells us: "During the first month after receiving the news, I tried in vain to feel sorry. My reader will say I was a bad son—and he will be perfectly right!" Between such irreconcilable hostility towards the father and such passionate love for the mother, a link undoubtedly exists: the two ramifications of the Oedipus complex are goads to one another and are coincident.

In the course of psychoanalytical treatment we are perpetually encountering sentiments of the Oedipus variety among the children placed under our care. Such feelings attain their maximum round and about the fifth year of life. Paul aged four wants to marry his mother. The latter objects. "What about Daddy?" Paul laconically answers: "Oh, he'll be deaded long ago." We have already cited the case of Madeleine who was jealous of her sister Jaqui, and who, when nearly three, exhibited a marked antagonism towards her mother, with the superadded desire for the latter's death. One day she asked: "Shall I be given a big pair of shoes?" Mother answers: "I'll buy you some."—"No," replies the child, "you'll be dead, and I'll have yours." Madeleine, as I showed above, had chosen her father as friend, and often threatened her mother with such phrases as, "I'll tell Daddy." Freud records the following words spoken by a girl of four: "Mummy's dead, and my Daddy's going to marry me so's I'll be his little wife."

As the child grows older it voices its Oedipus desires less blatantly. It is apt to repress them as culpable. Nevertheless, in the creations of its fancy, it gives such thoughts free rein. They may be found expressed in

54 THE MIND OF THE CHILD

drawings, in dreams, and so forth. Anna Freud, in her *Introduction to Psychoanalysis for Teachers*, relates the story of a little girl who, in drawings, represented her mother as a horrible virago. The child was psychoanalysed, and the virago yielded place to a queen to whom a little princess was offering a flower. Another authority reports the case of a lad, nine years of age, who had the following day-dream which admirably illustrates the Oedipus complex. He fancies himself at Rome; the emperor Augustus takes a liking for the boy and gives him a situation which brings him into close contact with the great ruler; the child fights on the emperor's behalf, lends him money; but Augustus shows no gratitude; the youngster then begins to take up arms against his former patron; he elopes with the emperor's daughter, marries her, and becomes head of the empire.

The Adlerian school has records of analogous observations, though the champions of this way of thinking express themselves in a terminology peculiar to themselves. Adler, for example, tells the story of a well-developed boy, four and a half years old, who so far had manifested no marked preference either for his father or his mother. One evening, however, he told his mother that he would like to sleep in his father's bed (which was side by side with his mother's), "and Daddy can have my cot." The mother, wishing to test her little boy's actual feelings, suggested that she should sleep in the cot and the boy in her bed. The child refused point blank. If Father was not to vacate his bed, the boy would like to sleep with Mother in her bed. Adler insists that such a state of mind in a child is normal, and he refuses to recognise in it the possible source of a neurosis. He emphasises the decision, simplicity, virility, and methodical procedure of the little boy, who knows what he wants, pursues his

OEDIPUS AND FILIAL AFFECTION 55

aim, and, without flinching, has recourse to another solution when he sees that his first proposal is not to be fulfilled.

I think that to-day all psychoanalysts are agreed that the Oedipus complex is a normal phenomenon which, in itself, cannot be the cause of a neurosis; that it only becomes so in consequence of fortuitous exaggerations and modifications. In my own practice I have had to deal with mothers who showed an exaggerated intimacy and tenderness towards their sons; of boys deprived over long periods of the presence of the father who, on returning home, is made anything but welcome by the son; of lads whose mother marries a second time and whose new husband is the object of violent jealousy on the part of the stepsons; and so on.

As with all the complexes, the Oedipus complex, thanks to transference and displacement, has an infinite number of ramifications. Hostility arising from the Oedipus complex is susceptible of a multitude of displacements, and, according as these displacements are successful or not, the subject remains normal or may present troubles of all kinds. In an article which appeared in the "Revue Française de Psychanalyse" under the title of *La psychanalyse et les écoles nouvelles*, Zulliger tells how he found that both his bicycle tyres had been punctured by one of his pupils. He detected the culprit and asked the lad a variety of questions. The result of the enquiry was to disclose that the hatred which had led the youngster to puncture the tyres was actually a sentiment felt towards the boy's father, and that the teacher had merely played the part of substitute. This discovery may have soothed Zulliger's outraged feelings —but his bicycle tyres needed repair none the less!

Displacements of the sort are liable, unfortunately, to

56   THE MIND OF THE CHILD

become fixations. In my *Psychanalyse de l'art*, I drew attention to this fact when studying the different grades of stability in dream displacements. If in certain cases, the substitute object seems to be a haphazard derivative upon which the tendency is discharged and which is thereafter forgotten, it may happen that the tendency will become permanently attached to the substitute while the primary object is gradually divested of its affective value. In such a case, we have to do with transference in the proper meaning of the term.

Ernst Schneider relates how a boy during the whole of his childhood was inordinately teased and made fun of by his father. The lad's education consisted in depriving him of every amusement suitable to his tender years and making him do things which only an adult could perform. When the child came to grief in his endeavours to accomplish tasks greatly exceeding his powers, the grown-ups would laugh at him. The child accepted this treatment in a docile spirit for he suffered from a feeling of guilt arising out of the Oedipus complex. When he was old enough to go to school his whole character underwent a change. The new surroundings brought about a reaction and he avenged himself upon his masters for all the tortures he had been forced to endure without complaint at his father's hands. He became the ringleader of every prank played upon the professors. His young comrades looked upon him as a hero, and in his present popularity he found compensation for the innumerable humiliations of earlier life. The troubles which in subsequent years arose as a consequence of these childish conflicts led our young man to the psycho-analyst's consulting room.[1]

The hostility arising out of the Oedipus complex is

[1] Ernest Schneider, Zur Psychologie des Lausbuben, p. 12.

OEDIPUS AND FILIAL AFFECTION

not infrequently transferred to every form of authority. Among Pfister's patients there was a rebel youth who held the Church, the State, and society-at-large in scorn; everybody was looked upon as an enemy; his dreams were filled with the idea of persecution. Analysis revealed that the young man's attitude resulted from deep-rooted hostility towards the father. At two years of age the boy dreamed that he saw a bear and was very much frightened by the beast. The bear was obviously a substitute for the lad's father who wore a full beard and moustache, and who, in addition, took delight in scaring the child with a little bronze bear he had bought. Since early childhood and right on till the time he was analysed, the subject suffered from wry-neck, and he had a fixed stare. These symptoms, likewise, proved to be the result of dread of the father.[1]

The symbol of a bear as substitute for the father is worth a few special remarks. Transference can take place only between objects which are reciprocally symbolical; and every transference, like every symbol, depends for its existence upon associations. Now, there exist collective associations which are identical among all human beings, and which form the bases of all the collective symbols whose interpretation presents no difficulty to those who are accustomed to unravel their meaning. Readers who are familiar with psychoanalytical procedure must forgive me if I lay stress upon this point; but experience shows that the theory of symbolism is, of all those propounded by psychoanalysts, the one that the layman finds most difficult to assimilate, and likewise the one which is considered the most arbitrary. Well-meaning critics assure us that they are ready to accept

[1] Oskar Pfister, Die Behandlung schwererziehbarer und abnormer Kinder.

58 THE MIND OF THE CHILD

our theses if only we are willing to give up this wretched theory of symbolism. But, alas, this theory is the foundation of the psychoanalytical edifice; and there is so little arbitrariness in our deductions that symbolism has become an affair of actual observation, nay, almost a matter of precise statistical data. "Symbol" is, in effect, nothing more than another word for "association"—and the latter concept will find no one to contest its authenticity. It implies merely (in addition to the accepted implications of the theory of association) that analogous affective reactions are repeated in respect of associated objects. In other words, the theory of symbolisation supplements the association of ideas by the association of tendencies. Furthermore, our psychologists are not content as were those of an earlier day to construct a theoretical framework for their ideas; they have minutely described certain of these associative groups, which have thus become, as it were, concrete facts and have acquired a particularly stable configuration. This quality is precisely what our antagonists find most difficult to accept. Now, the association of a father with, let us say, the schoolmaster, with authority in general, with certain animals of the stronger sort (a bear) is precisely one of the collective associations mentioned above. A fact worthy of note is that the elements linked together by one of these primitive and collective associations have also been linked in the experience of the individual with whom we are concerned, as if to reawaken and reinforce the association. Thus the association of "bear" with "father" is certainly a collective association, but in Pfister's subject the symbol has been crystallised, so to say, around the nucleus of the little bronze bear. The same may be observed in the case of Victor Hugo in whose life we find the father symbolised

OEDIPUS AND FILIAL AFFECTION 59

by an eagle and by an emperor, etc. These, too, are collective symbols, but they were consciously chosen by the poet in consequence of very definite personal associations; his father was a general under the empire, with the imperial eagle as emblem and with Napoleon as overlord.

On the slightest provocation such collective associations appear readily enough, and the child imagination is perpetually inventing fresh myths concerning them. Barbara Low in *The Unconscious in Action* (p. 91) furnishes us with a vivid illustration of the case in point. "A boy of six questioned his mother about God: she answered with the best resource she could, truthfully from her own standpoint, which was agnostic, but with a large measure of imaginative understanding for the child's attitude, to the effect that she thought God might be—and many people thought this—something like a father, who could do and know very wonderful things, but people like herself and him and even his own father, who could do so many wonderful things also and was so beloved, could not possibly understand much about it. Later on, he would have more thoughts himself and they would talk it over again. . . . The boy, a very happy and intelligent child, departed, satisfied, it seemed, to play in the garden. About ten minutes later he came rushing in, dragging behind him his large grey elephant mounted on wheels, and asked eagerly: 'Do you think God is rather like my elephant?' This startling query was difficult to meet, but the mother answered: 'Well, yes, perhaps in this way: You know the elephant is the most powerful of all animals, is obeyed and admired by all of them, and can do many things the others can't, with his trunk and his feet, so he is above all the others, as some people believe God is above all of us.' The boy

60 THE MIND OF THE CHILD

was most pleased, and danced around gaily, saying: 'God is like my elephant: I love my elephant—he's very, very clever, you know, *much* cleverer than you, Mummy.' . . . A little later, his mother went to look for him and found him sitting on the grass, crying. Reluctantly, he finally brought out: 'I don't want God; I hate him; he can hurt me like the nasty old elephant,' and so saying he got up and with much vigour and malice knocked over the elephant and kicked it repeatedly as it lay on the ground." Here we see collective symbolism at work and suddenly revealing itself in the boy who was merely recapitulating the behaviour of primitive man: "a mingling of a desire for the omnipotent god-figure, satisfaction in identifying it with himself (. . . *his* elephant), and fear of its power, expressed in his resentment against the elephant-god, behind which stands his real father." Darwin already drew attention to the hereditary fixation of certain associations, and it is difficult to deny the fact when faced with incidents such as those recorded above. These particular associations seem to go back, very far back indeed, in human history, and, according to Freud, must have had their origin at the epoch when totemism was in vogue. It is this same epoch to which he refers when seeking the source of the Oedipus complex so deeply rooted in us all.[1] As a matter of fact, what I have written about collective associations could very well be said anent every complex; but I needed to be specially explicit when discussing the Oedipus complex.

Many anomalies of behaviour may be traced to hostility arising out of the Oedipus complex, for this complex has the faculty of transferring itself and generalising itself. In the example we cited from Pfister's notes, we saw that the subject had a tendency to regard

[1] Sigmund Freud, Totem and Tabu.

OEDIPUS AND FILIAL AFFECTION 61

"everybody" as his enemy. Often the rivalry and hostility engendered by the Oedipus complex is transferred more or less to every partner and interlocutor. A patient of my own, Jacques, obviously recapitulated in respect of what he termed "people" the attitude of mind he had assumed in younger days towards his father. Since he had been all of a tremor whenever he felt himself under paternal supervision, he had taken his revenge by keeping a watchful eye upon his father and by endeavouring to catch his father red-handed; later on, he felt himself spied upon by "people," and, in spite of his best endeavours to counteract his evil propensity, he would spy upon the actions of these same "people," endeavouring to detect a flaw in their armour, and nevertheless invariably afflicted with a feeling of inferiority in respect of them. "Social constraint" is the equivalent of the "paternal restraint" under which a child suffers in early years, and is merely a prolongation of the latter into adult life. Thus, hostility to the father may develop into hostility to the social order as a whole.

Barbara Low gives us the case of "a man who as child, boy, and later as adult, found the utmost difficulty in speaking, either in his class-room or in taking part in a school entertainment, or later in public meetings. It was found that the main impulses involved were, first a fear of some exposure culminating in disaster (or as he first put it, the public speaking was a critical test in which he felt he was bound to fail, however much his reason pointed to the contrary); secondly, a great sense of jealous rivalry which forced him always to compare himself with the most brilliant and distinguished exponent present . . .; . . . behind his 'nervous' and 'retiring' manifestations an extreme narcissism predominated, though this latter was itself only a symptom. Both the

62 THE MIND OF THE CHILD

exposure-idea with its resultant danger and the sense of rivalry were linked to primitive early wishes, the former in connexion with his own body and the body of his mother . . . , and the latter with a jealous feeling towards his father, both of which must bring punishment in their train—the punishment of being unable to make use of his own abilities. When he was able to relinquish . . . his sense of guilt on the one hand, and on the other his rivalry for a father-figure, . . . he found himself able . . . to make quite a good use of his knowledge in debating and lecturing."[1] Thus we see that the fear was no more than a transference of the feeling of inferiority and of rivalry in respect of a father who was both inflexible judge and rival.

Wilfrid Lay records the case of a man who had had a very stern, strict, and aggressive father, and indentified himself with this early form in which the father existed for him even to the extent of acting both as aggressive father in his desires and as compliant submissive environment in his acts. He would, when caught unawares, say, "Yes, Sir!" to a gruff waiter, or meekly obey a car conductor yelling to the passengers "move forward." All the time, however, his imagination was dominated by the ideal of aggressiveness, and, when not intimidated, he was overbearing in his manner.[2]

Such essays in identification may be pushed to a greater or lesser extreme, and may produce the most varied effects. Stegman tells of a boy, nine years old, whose father was alcoholic. The family lived in want. The boy did his best to help his mother and to take his father's place; he was extremely independent and did not like his mother to give him orders. Though he tried

[1] Barbara Low, The Unconscious in Action, pp. 134–135.
[2] Wilfrid Lay, The Child's Unconscious Mind, p. 113.

OEDIPUS AND FILIAL AFFECTION 63

to uphold her authority, he nevertheless endeavoured to imitate his father's despotic demeanour towards her. This may, of course, have been the result of a partial sublimation, so that the complex found vent in fairly good behaviour.[1] In general, a successful identification with the father by a son or with the mother by a daughter is the simplest and most normal method of solving the Oedipus situation, provided (it goes without saying) that each parent happens to be a good example to follow.

But identification may likewise end in the most varied disturbances, since the issues are complicated by a sense of guilt with regard to the feelings of hostility which preceded it. A child may come to imitate the illnesses and infirmities of the parent he dreams of replacing, and this imitation will take the form of nervous disorders.

The second component of this complex, love, is equally capable of provoking disturbances in the human psyche. Thus a lad who is over fond of his mother may come to depend upon her to so great an extent as to hinder the whole of his subsequent development as a member of society. Furthermore, the two components of the complex run the risk of converging, of reacting along identical lines, seeing that resistance to paternal authority, by transforming itself into antagonism towards the social order, is an inducement to the child to withdraw into itself. Countless analyses of adults have revealed the intimate link (especially among males) which exists between the Oedipus complex and the shunning of social intercourse. The situation is already perceptible in childhood, and it is easy to watch its development.

[1] M. Stegman, Identifizierung mit dem Vater, p. 561.

64 THE MIND OF THE CHILD

Pierre P. is a boy of eleven. Up to that age he had been of a gay disposition, and was not lacking in a certain boldness. Suddenly he took to grumbling and whining, refused to go to school (where previously he went with obvious pleasure, even undertaking to escort his younger sister to the class-room). He now remained at home, keeping close to his mother all day long; literally, he clung to her skirt and thus hindered her greatly in her housewifely avocations. The father occasionally took his son by the hand and forced him to go to school, so that the mother might be free. Then the child sulked in a corner of the class-room, or gave way to prolonged fits of weeping. E. Pichon who records this case, tells us that the lad had been given a shock. During a period of convalescence from some childish ailment, Pierre had been put to sleep in his parents' bedroom and had witnessed an act of sexual intercourse between them. The Oedipus complex which up to that moment had been resolving itself along normal lines, was now brusquely and ruthlessly re-awakened. The child could not tolerate such an intimacy between his father and his mother. In his turn he pressed himself close up against his mother and refused to leave her side.[1]

Oedipus love, which is unconsciously felt to be culpable, if repressed may in its turn lead to unhappy results. A little girl took to lying after having built up the whole of her life on an unconscious lie: the pretence of being completely indifferent to her father whom she actually adored. Such repressions are apt to give an unwholesome twist to the affective life, they may nip in the bud every manifestation of love, may convince the subject that he or she is in-

[1] E. Pichon, Sur les traitements psychothérapiques courts d'inspiration freudienne chez les enfants, p. 712.

OEDIPUS AND FILIAL AFFECTION 65

capable of loving, or, indeed, of experiencing any kind of feeling.[1]

Pfister gives us the instance of a girl of sixteen who, in addition to various physical symptoms (neuralgia, insomnia), was sure she was doomed to suffer because there was no love among human beings. The analyst was not slow to appreciate that the girl's words needed interpretation, and he soon found that the young woman herself suffered from her inability to love. This inhibition of the love sentiment, in its turn, was traced to an excessive attachment to her brother. The girl's condition was completely relieved by the analysis.[2]

It would seem that the Oedipus feelings, when too robust, though they may travel along devious paths, attain the same goal in the end; namely, the inhibition of love. On the one hand, the sentiment may concentrate too exclusively upon a member of the family (father or brother among girls, and mother or sister among boys), and is, therefore, hard to dislodge and set off along more beneficent avenues. Another difficulty is that the Oedipus sentiment is subject to a kind of repression which is far more generalised than in the case of any other sort of love sentiment owing to the universally present incest taboo. Thus, because of the innate strength of the Oedipus feeling itself and because of the repression to which it is subject, an Oedipus attachment runs the risk of inducing a more or less pronounced inhibition of love in general, so that we find that sometimes sexual love suffers a blight, at other times all the tenderness natural among relations is obliterated, indeed, the whole affective life seems to succumb. Analysis, if applied in early youth, may clear up the whole Oedipus situation in the most brilliant manner, and may reawaken springs

[1] Félix Boehm, Une enfant menteuse.   [2] Love in Children.

THE MIND OF THE CHILD

which had appeared to be permanently dried up. But if the Oedipus situation is never to take a hold, we must see to it that our children are given interests outside the family circle and that they are thus led to love other members of society besides those belonging to the home.

CHAPTER THREE

DESTRUCTION

1. *Sadistic Trends*

WHILE discussing the topics of fraternal rivalry and the Oedipus situation, I had occasion to draw the reader's attention to certain bellicose and cruel tendencies among children. "At that age, a child is without pity." We must now consider them apart from the questions of rivalry and hostility. In the course of our examination we shall gradually discern that these tendencies, too, constitute the nucleus of an important system.

At the outset, the leanings towards cruelty are clearly associated with the digestive process. This is an extremely primitive order of associations, and one which may easily be traced in the kingdom of the lower animals. One has to kill if one is hungry, and thus the voluptuous sensation of slaughter became interwoven with the nutritive instinct. Among children we encounter a "cannibalistic" stage or a "sadistic-buccal" stage, which finds expression in the action of biting, and wherein the cruel tendencies are linked up with excitations of the mouth. Marie Bonaparte points out that there exist two successive phases among infants during which the mouth forms the main zone of excitation: (1) the phase of sucking, pure and simple; and (2) the cannibalistic or biting phase.[1]

A colleague has sent me the notes of the following remarkable case. François, three years of age, was a highly impressionable little boy. He was taken to a

---

[1] Marie Bonaparte, Prophylaxie infantile des névroses, p. 6.

68 THE MIND OF THE CHILD

picture gallery where he saw a canvas representing some dead ducks hung up till they should become tender. Afterwards he could talk of nothing else, but refused to go to the picture gallery again. At a first guess, we should be inclined to look upon this child as over-sensitive and too full of pity. The sequel will show that, on the contrary, the sight of the corpses had aroused cruel tendencies (hence his inability to talk of anything else) which he endeavoured to repress (by refusing to go to the picture gallery). About the same time, Toulet, the dog, caught and mauled a chicken, which François' parents ate. Some days later, a little girl was run over by a car. François said: "You know, zat lil' girl was run over by a toto, and she was deaded, and zen she was eated all up." The boy's laconic generalisation is of much the same order as that of Maja, cited on p. 40, who had been told that the cat had fallen out of the window and had "cried and wept." When, after this, she heard her baby brother crying she said: "Yajla must have fallen out of the window." A superficial observer may demur to our inferring cruelty in children as the explanation of such occurrences, and he will declare that the "association of ideas" accounts for everything. As a matter of fact it explains nothing, and it is precisely this same "association of ideas" which needs elucidation. Among the multitude of analogies a child might possibly notice, those only which correspond to its tendencies are retained in its memory. As soon as we unearth these tendencies and correlate them with our other observations the whole affair is made plain.

But let me resume the case-history of little François. He was now nearly four, and told the following tale: "Once upon a time there was an eagle who screamed very loud, and called God to come. Then God came,

DESTRUCTION 69

then God gave the eagle a kiss on its beak, then the eagle eated up God." The child continued to be profoundly impressed by any destruction of property on the catastrophic scale. When he was five years old he passed the skeleton of a house gutted by fire, and begged his companion to hold him tight by the hand. At the same date he saw a man with a wooden leg. A little girl told him that "they cut his leg off." François, quite disingenuously observed: "I should have liked to eat the meat." Then: "If I killed Daddy?—A pity!—If I killed Mummy and Daddy and every one in the house I'd have lots of food." The boy's aunt intervened: "Nice little boys don't eat human flesh; it's only savages who do that." To which François rejoined: "Mm, it's awfully good."

At five years and six months, François exclaimed: "I love stories about people who are killed. When they're going to kill some one, I'll hide behind some planks and then I'll see everything." To his father he said: "If you die before me, I'll be able to eat you; I'll cook your brain, and then your eyes and your ears. . . . If you die, I'll open your skull and your tummy to see what it looks like inside. Oh, yes, I'll do that." Mr. So and So happened to die at this juncture, and François had a great desire to see the corpse. "I could gouge out his eyes and cut him in two." The child often informed his aunt that when she died he would "plough her body" and "keep her skeleton." Once, when he was lying in his father's bed, he pulled the sheet over his head, and exclaimed: "A skeleton!" Another day he happened to see a diagram of the human anatomy, and cried out, "Meat," as he contemplated the muscular tissues. The lad's father endeavoured to explain the difference between human flesh and animal meat; but

THE MIND OF THE CHILD

the boy continued to speak of "meat," despite his father's best endeavours.

2. *Anal Trends*

Once the infantile stage is passed we find as a rule that, though this childish cruelty still remains connected with the digestive process, the buccal zone loses its importance and yields place to the anal zone. Mastication is superseded by defaecation. This constitutes a totally unexpected phenomenon, and it needed psychoanalytical observation to make us realise the very strong association between these two functions. We are constantly coming up against it in the course of analysis, and it forms the kernel of what Freud has termed the "sadistic-anal" complex. In order to explain this curious association we have to take note of the fact that cruel tendencies develop in the child at the very period when the anal region is becoming a zone capable of excitation. Further, there exists an analogy between the two terms, which the abstract word "destruction" admirably describes. Sadistic tendencies are inclined to lead persons to disfigure and to destroy, while the digestive processes, in dealing with the foodstuffs which nourish the body, spoil them and disintegrate them. It would seem natural to use the term "destruction" when describing this complex. Sabina Spielrein has recourse to the same word to describe the sadistic component of the sexual instinct; and Freud has not taken exception to the term.

The word is peculiarly apt when we come to consider certain effects this complex has upon behaviour, when we see a child spoiling everything it undertakes, and, in later years upon the whole mentality which may take an ultra-critical or negative or destructive or "mephistophelian" twist.

DESTRUCTION 71

"A girl of nine years old . . . , of marked intellectual development, an omnivorous reader, very grown-up in much of her behaviour, is, nevertheless, quite incapable of doing any small piece of writing, painting, or needlework without blots, smudges, crumplings, and knots, and her material . . . is invariably . . . spoilt soon after she handles it. In consequence she hates all such occupations, dodges them whenever possible, and has already built up within herself powerful inhibitions, which have extended to activities she enjoys . . . such as dancing, swimming, games, at which she is clumsy and inefficient. . . . She lived largely in day-dreams, and the content of these revealed two absorbing trends: one, a fantasy of herself as rich, beautiful, brilliant, admired by all and sundry, often in the role of a princess or other high-born lady; the other, preoccupation with functional interests, in a highly disguised form, coupled with frequent catastrophes and perils at the hands of alarming things—large animals, ogres, and so forth."[1] In this case, the destructive tendencies seem to have been awakened by jealousy of a younger sister who was "neat and dainty and clever in all physical activities."

Such a situation is by no means rare. I remember the case of a boy, Henri, whose development was taking place along normal lines and who seemed by the time he was five years old to have overcome the infantile anal tendencies common to babyhood. A little brother was born. Immediately thereafter the elder boy exhibited certain cruel impulses. Above all, and at the same date, he began to make blots, to become highly excited by smutty stories concerning defaecation, liked to make use of dirty words, and spent an inordinate amount of time in the w.c.

[1] Barbara Low, The Unconscious in Action, pp. 138–139.

THE MIND OF THE CHILD

In cases such as these we frequently notice that the hostility engendered in regard to brothers and sisters is transferred to animals and takes the form of actual cruelty. Pfister tells of a boy who tortured female beasts only, and especially when they were suckling their young. He was thus obviously discharging his feelings of rivalry in respect of his younger brethren and of resentment against his mother for having forsaken him.[1] More subtle displacements are likewise possible. For instance, little Henri whose case I have just cited, was not slow to overcome the hostility he felt towards his younger brother, but one day he stamped furiously upon some shoots of corn which had just flushed the earth with green.

At the moment when a child feels itself abandoned by its mother it will often find relief for its outraged feelings by a regression to the sadistic-anal stage. Disappointed in its love, it will console itself with infantile satisfactions. According to the specific circumstances of the case, the cruelty component, or, rather, the digestive component, will come into action. Thus the child will appear either to transform its love into hate (follow the typical mechanism of those "tragedies of hatred" which precisely repeat this form of regression), or it will invest the digestive processes with excessive importance—and, in the latter case, it will carry the traces of such transference with it throughout life. Kurt, for instance, feeling he had been deprived of his mother's affection, started to steal foodstuffs, and seemed to be dominated by the slogan: "Fill your stomach, my lad; thus you'll fill the hole made in your heart." Later in life, this man took a great interest in inaugurating a restaurant. In each instance, the whole complex was set into strong vibration. All children who "suddenly"

[1] Oskar Pfister, Die Behandlung schwererziehbarer und abnormer Kinder, p. 62.

DESTRUCTION

become naughty or intolerable little beasts, or greedy, cruel, prone to thieving, lying, soiling themselves, are, in reality, reverting to a primitive phase of development. Nor is it difficult to demonstrate that these disturbances in character formation, and in behaviour are due to a reactivation of the sadistic-anal phase, and are the result of disappointed love, in especial a frustrated love for the parents.

3. Masochistic Trends

Once we have started our study of sadism we very soon come up against its counterpart: masochism. The desire to suffer is akin to the desire to inflict pain. As we so often find when studying the instincts, an active tendency runs almost parallel with a passive tendency, they are easily interchangeable, and see-saw one with the other.

Pfister records the case of a boy who, between the age of six and eight years, was subject to sadistic fantasies. He imagined that he martyrised a little girl and was able to kill her by pouring boiling water over her. He succeeded in repressing this fantasy, but thereupon he was seized with a desire to die; he tried to picture what it would feel like if he committed suicide; in the end these fancies took the form of an obsession.[1]

The little girl whose case I have quoted above from Barbara Low's book *The Unconscious in Action*, was given to day-dreams wherein she herself was a prey to large and terrifying animals and to ogres. Zulliger records the history of a lad of thirteen, Tino by name, who took a delight in tormenting animals. After a while, however, he liked to be cuffed and beaten by his schoolmates,

[1] Oscar Pfister, Was bietet die Psychanalyse dem Erzieher?

THE MIND OF THE CHILD

and enjoyed a voluptuous sensation when mosquitoes sucked as much blood from him as they could hold—then he would kill them. If his father raised a hand against him, the lad yelled and struggled before any blows were rained upon him.

Innumerable combinations are possible between the active tendency and the passive. One of my pupils told me of a boy, four and a half years old, who had just been sent to school. His first reaction to contact with other youngsters of his age is definitely masochistic in character. He liked playing with them, but allowed them to deprive him of his building bricks, to pull his hair, to push him this way and that. The child seemed to take pleasure in being teased, and never complained to grown-ups. Indeed, it would appear that he endeavoured by every means to avoid coming into contact with adults, and to escape their interference. A month later this same little boy began to show aggressive inclinations: he put up a fight when attacked, but in order the better to defend himself he made an ally of another lad who treated him as a slave, so that the masochistic trend continued along another avenue. Now, if he was scolded, he took to his heels, hunched his back, and smiled slyly. A sly expression of countenance, one wholly lacking in straightforwardness, often betrays a condition which signifies that the child is not clear in its own mind as to the path along which it should travel; it remains in a state of ambivalence between two opposing tendencies (sadistic-masochistic, let us assume). When a child assumes a sly expression, this usually means that it is somewhat ashamed of itself; this condition, in its turn, may be interpreted as a state of suspense betwixt anger and fear, aggression and flight.[1]

[1] Cf. A. Gerson, Die Scham.

DESTRUCTION

75

In other cases, masochism takes precedence of all other tendencies. For example, a boy was dominated by the secret desire to be maltreated by his father. Whenever he felt that he was looked down upon in the family circle, he would pick a quarrel with some one outside the home, not so much to wreak vengeance for the insult he had suffered as in the hope of being punished. He even went so far on one occasion as to have several perfectly sound teeth extracted in order "to calm" his feelings. He endeavoured to pile proof upon proof to show how superior his father was and how great was his father's hatred, so that he might always have good reason to maintain his masochistic attitude. When he grew to manhood he avoided taking up the virile role proper to a lover, and at the age of thirty-six he picked quarrels with so many persons as seriously to impair his chances of promotion. Yet all this was no more than the reproduction in adult life of the reactions he had suffered from during childhood.[1]

Digestive troubles among children, due far more frequently than we are apt to imagine to nervous or psychological causes, are intimately connected with the trends we have just been considering. Many varieties of diarrhoea, of constipation, of enteritis, may afflict the child and may even persist into adult life. Constipation, above all, is frequently the result of retaining the faeces because such retention procures the child a pleasurable sensation around the anal zone. The same kind of excitation may, of course, arise from purely somatic disorders during infancy, such, for instance, as enteric fever, haemorrhoids, thread-worms, etc., and these troubles are likely to predispose an infant to acquiring

[1] Adler and Furtmüller, Heilen und Bilden, p. 45.

76 THE MIND OF THE CHILD

an anal complex in later childhood. There is a reciprocity of action between the disorders and the complex, so that it is sometimes hard to tell which is the cause and which the effect, to decide where the neurotic symptoms begin and the somatic end. Constipation is likewise connected with the reactions of a child in respect of "being clean." This obligation, if we reflect for a moment, brings a child for the first time face to face with "duty," with a constraint imposed upon it by society. There is a certain amount of rebellion lurking behind constipation: the child consents to be clean since its elders insist, but it takes its revenge by postponing the act of evacuation as long as it pleases. From the time it assumes this attitude, we notice an intimate relationship between constipation and obstinacy.

It is less easy to understand how stammering may be closely akin to the same complex. Nevertheless, this is frequently the case. A boy of four was torn between two wishes: that of having copious stools in order to please his mother; and that of retaining the faeces because the sensation was pleasurable to himself and failure to have a good motion of the bowels annoyed his father. He managed to get the better of his desire to "retain," but replaced the anal zone by the buccal zone and unconsciously sought to retain sounds at the moment they were about to escape from his mouth, so he began to stutter. The discovery of this anal-sadistic complex in the boy led to its solution and his stammering was completely cured.[1] Schneider further assures us that stammering is very frequently met with in cases of anal-eroticism.[2]

[1] Searl, "Internationale Zeitschrift für Psychoanalyse," vol. xiii, No. 3, quoted in the "Revue Française de Psychanalyse," 1927, p. 758, in an article entitled, Un cas de bégaiement chez un enfant.

[2] Ernst Schneider, Kinderfehler, Entstehung und Behandlung, p. 167.

DESTRUCTION

The various forms of anal-sadistic tendencies are amenable to more or less successful cure. Some cures come about spontaneously, and the educator need no more than guide the child in the proper direction. Infantile interest in its excreta may find a natural displacement on to mud, earth, or other substances. Such transferences of interest may be spontaneously directed towards a more seemly object apart from any external coercion.

Barbara Low instances the case of a boy of six who showed himself excessively interested in very "dirty" and sticky substances, such as mud, wet clay, thick wet paint, plasticine, and so forth. He had been in charge of a nurse who made strenuous effort to wean him from his really excessive preoccupation, giving him bright-coloured counters and bricks, with the result that instead of accepting these substitutes, the child became very tiresome, often slightly disordered internally, and much depressed. He was then sent to school, and it happened that he had a number of tasks set him involving the use of sticky wet materials—wet sand, clay, and plasticine—in handling which he was very successful and generally won first place in his class and his teacher's high praise. In a few months a change was apparent: the constant diarrhoea and stomach trouble disappeared, the child became far more amiable and tranquil, and began to turn to fresh objects of interest. Investigation showed that the boy's over-interest in sticky, dirty materials was itself a sublimation of his more primitive and excessive interest in excrement, and for him a very big step in sublimation. The nurse's endeavour to oust this interest gave him a sense of his own guilt, and drove him, on the one hand, into a more primitive pleasure still, that of bodily gratification expressed in his internal

THE MIND OF THE CHILD

digestive troubles, and on the other, into cantankerousness, which was his way of expressing his own guilt. When he was once more allowed to continue his own form of sublimation, at his own rate, under the teacher's encouragement, he lost his guilt-sense—a gain of the highest importance—was able to enjoy his pleasure in his home relations, and by degrees turned to substitute interests.[1] Such a process of sublimation has often and often proved to be the genesis of a vocation to pursue the plastic arts.

No fixed rule of action can be laid down for teachers in this field, and it is only by an understanding of the deeper issues involved that appropriate methods of treatment can be found. The manifest symptoms give no clue to the riddle, as is shown in the following case, where there would seem to be an analogous state of affairs to that disclosed in the foregoing example, and yet in reality we have to do with a very different problem. "A boy of six and a half, . . . intelligent beyond the average, . . . spent long periods playing with wet clay and plasticine, making nothing of definite form but mainly dabbing his fingers into the shapeless mass. Other symptoms, such as exceptional clumsiness with knife and fork and scissors, fear of the dark in bed, gave rise to the suspicion that his interest in sticky materials was not a step in sublimation but rather a regression to a more childish period revealing a large fund of emotional activity still bound up with his functioning,[2] an interest which had never had its fair share of fulfilment at the

---

[1] Barbara Low, The Unconscious in Action, pp. 158–159.

[2] That is to say, the activity was absorbed by the digestive complex instead of assimilating the complex to itself. It is often very difficult to determine which of these mechanisms is at work. Cf. my books on Psychanalyse de l'art, p. 259, and Mobilisation de l'energie, p. 284.

DESTRUCTION 79

appropriate much earlier stage, since he had been brought up by an old-fashioned nurse with drastic ideas as to training in cleanly habits. The teacher . . . encouraged his proclivity for the sand and clay, with the result that he became still more infantile in behaviour. . . . By gradual degrees harder materials were introduced, so that the boy was forced . . . to devise means to use it . . . and to join with other children for new devices in fashioning it."[1]

Such progressive displacements, which transfer a child's interest from squashy and unclean substances to hard materials, are extremely interesting to follow. Jones in his *Papers on Psychoanalysis* (p. 694), quoting Ferenczi, furnishes us with a stimulating summary. These displacements may end in an interest for pebbles, then for money. Thrift, miserliness (closely akin to constipation), enthusiasm for collections of various sorts, classified lists, all these are "anal-erotic character traits." The same traits are likewise represented by other and quite different qualities, especially by those of excessive cleanliness, of a meticulous orderliness,[2] by strange compromises such as, on the one hand, an endeavour to overcome, to "over-compensate," the tendencies to befoul and to spoil, and, on the other hand, the conservation of an obstinacy intimately connected from the outset with the anal complex.[3] It is most interesting to have a child under

[1] Barbara Low, The Unconscious in Action, pp. 161–162.

[2] Two "anal phases," following upon the two "buccal phases," have been noted as characteristic of the normal development of children. During the first anal phase a child delights in the free discharge of its excreta; during the second phase it is more interested in retaining its excreta and adopts its first "ethical standard" which Ferenczi has christened the "ethics of the sphincter muscles." Cf. Marie Bonaparte, Prophylaxie infantile des névroses, p. 6.

[3] Such a reaction is, indeed, no more than a repetition of one I drew the reader's attention to when discussing an earlier infantile

80 THE MIND OF THE CHILD

observation at the time when this compromise is taking place. We have already made little Henri's acquaintance. He had become dirty and disorderly after the birth of his brother. Thereafter, he began to demand that his clothes should be immaculate; whereas he had acquired the habit of passing an inordinate amount of time in the w.c., he now spent a disproportionate amount of time over his toilet; he, who had allowed his hair to be matted and untidy, took to combing and brushing it in and out of season so that he acquired the nickname of "the maniac." If any one disturbed him during these occupations, or ventured to criticise him, he screamed and shed bitter tears. In any case it is always unwise to criticise a child's actions unduly, for it may feel so rebuffed that it will revert to its dirty and disorderly habits. It is quite natural, during this period of transition, for a child to have alternative phases of cleanliness and of dirtiness, of order and disorder, and to show extremes in one direction or the other.

This period is fecund in the acquisition of so-called manias. A child will create a ritual for dressing and undressing; it will acquire tics, spasmodic contractions of the muscles; it will perform utterly futile actions, become pedantic, take to counting the boards of the flooring (arithmomania), and so on. When such manifestations are very marked, we are entitled to assume that the soil is favourable for the development in later life of an obsessional neurosis. Analyses have repeatedly shown that neuroses of this kind are invariably connected with the activation of the destruction complex. In severe cases, the sufferer himself feels that he has an urge to

phase of development. The child consents to be clean if the elders in charge insist, but it takes its revenge by retaining its excreta and only emptying its bowels at the moment it chooses to do so.

DESTRUCTION 81

spoil his life in his own despite, to frustrate his endeavours, to destroy his work, to annihilate himself by degrees; and he imagines that his obsessions form the tools whereby he will procure his own destruction.

Quite early in a child's life we observe these "compulsions" or, better, "obsessions" (the Germans use the word Zwang to describe such actions). Richard Sterba tells us that these "obsessive acts" begin already at the age of seven.[1] At times the relationship of such actions to the destructive impulses is very obvious. Sterba gives the instance of a little girl who felt impelled every time she was carrying a fragile object to mutter the words "with the help of God." The formula was merely a safeguard against the unconscious desire to break the object in question (destruction), and this desire, in its turn, was the expression of a feeling of antagonism in respect of the parents who had asked the child to perform this service.

Wittels describes a boy, who at the age of four behaved in a way which clearly demonstrated an obsessive act in the germ. In this case, too, hostility towards the environment and obstinacy were evident. Franzl insisted on walking twenty paces behind his grandmother in spite of her request that he should "hurry up" and come alongside her. He realised that he was not behaving nicely, but he had made up his mind to be disobedient. Then he took to counting the palings which formed part of a gateway, and, since he could only count up to three, he repeated "and another and another and another." But he was actually busy counting in his own fashion and therefore could not heed what his grandmother said.[2]

[1] Richard Sterba, Eine Zwangshandlung aus der Latenzzeit, p. 322,
[2] Fritz Wittels, Verdrängung und Zwangsideen in der Kindheit, p. 253.

F

82 THE MIND OF THE CHILD

When these obsessions persist for a long time, we encounter a kind of moral pessimism in the subject, who becomes unduly serious and morose, and falls a prey to the slavery imposed by the obsession. Anal-erotic traits are likewise present. Ernest Jones writes: "It is noteworthy that paediatrists have called attention to the fact that children who suffer much from intestinal disturbances in infancy, usually grow up to be unhappy, irritable, and unduly serious."[1]

As far as cruel tendencies are concerned, the child overcomes them by making use of a see-saw method, in a word, by transforming its sadistic impulses into masochistic impulses. But this mechanism does not suffice to solve the problem; the desire to suffer needs sublimation, it needs to cease being "an art for art's sake," a pursuit of suffering for its own sake; it needs to become connected up with rational aims, such as a mastery of oneself, asceticism, and so on.[2] Sublimation along these lines is a ticklish affair, and is often a failure. Pfister records the case of a young man who, with a moral goal in view, started on a course of ascetic exercises. Finding himself unable to overcome his instincts, he took to even more drastic measures, making a veritable martyr of himself, and inflicting an especially cruel treatment upon his genital organs. In his case, masochism had reappeared in a brutal guise.[3]

Just as when uncleanliness is being transformed into meticulous cleanliness we meet with cases of "overcompensation," so in the struggle to get the better of its cruel tendencies a child is liable to go too far. This is what Freud expresses in the following words which

[1] Ernest Jones, Papers on Psychoanalysis, p. 690.   [2] Ibid.
[3] Oskar Pfister, Was bietet die Psychanalyse dem Erzieher?

DESTRUCTION 83

cannot be too strongly recommended to the consideration of all educators: "The most selfish of children may develop into highly charitable citizens, and in adult life may prove capable of the sublimest sacrifices. Most of those who in later years become apostles of mercy, philanthropists, vindicators of the rights of animals, were, in childhood, inclined to be sadistic, and were in especial prone to torment animals."[1]

[1] Sigmund Freud, Essais de psychanalyse, La guerre et ses deceptions, p. 241.

CHAPTER FOUR

DISPLAY AND MYSTERY

1. *Disclosure*

A GIRL of twelve was brought to Dr. Sterba for consultation. She had committed petty thefts, and was prone to lying and other peccadilloes. Her physical development was somewhat backward, but she had good intellectual capacities, in especial possessed a gift for acquiring languages, and had a talent for "rhetoric" in the primary meaning of the word. The latter was probably inherited from her mother who was a Hungarian provincial actress. When the child was three years old she was taken to the artists' room and saw them making ready to appear on the stage. At other times the little girl herself was allowed to tread the boards and took great delight in this sort of display. At four years of age, in public, she gave an amusing imitation of the mayor's oratorical eloquence, and every one commented upon her cleverness. The mother's time was completely occupied with her professional duties, so that she had no leisure to see to the upbringing of her child, but confided Ilona first of all to the care of an aunt, and thereafter to a childless couple who were very strict in their educational ideas. Severity, however, had no effect in curbing Ilona's exhibitionist tendencies, and she missed no opportunity wherein to display her talents and her person. When unaccompanied, she would pull up the sleeves of her dress or her skirt as far as possible as she walked along a street or sat in a bus or a tram. Any article of clothing which might make her conspicuous was collected, so that

DISPLAY AND MYSTERY 85

she took to filching her friend's ribbons, laces, artificial flowers and so forth. She powdered her nose, blued her eyelids, reddened her cheeks and her lips. She wanted to be a coquet, for that was her ideal of what a woman should be. The analyst enquired "why?" To which the girl replied: "Because those sort of women dare everything; they choose the men they want and as many as they want because they are beautiful. They talk with these men about love and marriage, and they are embraced and kissed." The idea she had conceived of love and marriage was purely spectacular. If a woman wanted to get married, all the eligible men were drawn up in a row and the woman merely had to make her choice. Having chosen, the parties shook hands and fell in love with one another; then they kissed and were married. "If they wish to have a child, they go to the doctor; once in the consulting room, they both undress and a bandage is placed over their eyes because they are naked and one must not look at what is below. Then the couple has to be tied together, and the doctor sees that all goes well." If by some unlucky chance the man and the woman look at one another while in a state of nudity, they are punished and go to hell.

To be looked at was, for Ilona, synonymous with being loved. The day she arrived for the first time at her adoptive parents' house she was told she would be loved. She thereupon took the centre of the floor and started play-acting: this was her conception of "being loved." The pleasure Ilona experiences in showing off is associated with a similar pleasure in looking: these two traits are frequently found in conjunction one with the other. She became quite excited if she met fast women while on her walks abroad, or if she saw posters on the hoardings representing people in a state of nudity. While talking to

86 THE MIND OF THE CHILD

the analyst she would reproduce with the utmost fidelity all the things she had seen and heard. Indeed, her imitative faculty was amazing. She would imitate the behaviour of amorous couples, and then add regretfully: "But what's the good of it all? Only one person ever looks at me, and I am happy when every one looks at me."[1]

Studying the case of young Ilona we discover several of the main components of what I term the spectacular complex, such as the pleasure of being seen and of looking, coquetry and the sexual tinge applied to these delights, and the beginnings of an endeavour to sublimate these tendencies by means of theatricals and public speaking. Inaccuracy, above all the falsehoods the child told, are connected with the same complex. The two opposed impulses to display oneself and to hide oneself are intimately associated, for the latter is often aroused when the subject is trying to overcome the former. In the love of making-up, and in general when we encounter a desire to masquerade, we are in presence of "compromise formations" whereby the two contradictory impulses so akin to one another find a solution. Prevarication, too, is germane to the passion for make-up which La Bruyère termed "a species of lying,"[2] and which we have every right to treat as a symptom. The fact that the inclination to make-up is contagious changes nothing in its chief characteristics.

Pfister records the case of a boy who at the age of seven "saw the devil outside the window, looking at him with glowing eyes. . . . From the age of seven till ten, he could not go to bed unless his mother followed him with her eyes as he went to the door." The case is a

---

[1] Editha Sterba, Nacktheit und Scham, p. 58.
[2] La Bruyère, Caractères, Chapter III.

DISPLAY AND MYSTERY

typical one of the confirmed inspectionist, who suffers from an uneasy conscience, and not only demands a proof of his mother's love by insisting that she shall follow him with her eyes, but who likewise wishes to be assured that no one suspects his vicious curiosity.[1]

The act of exhibiting oneself is essentially related to our most primitive instincts and sentiments. So far as Ilona was concerned it above all signified a desire "to be loved." It likewise expresses the wish to dominate and to be appreciated. Adler has devoted special study to this aspect of the matter, as indeed to certain other neurotic symptoms closely allied, such as an uneasy feeling when the subject is at a great height, in a large square (agoraphobia). Adler interprets these symptoms as a dread of coming down from one's pedestal. This explanation needs to be completed in the light of Freudian views; but even so, we have still to do with the "spectacular complex." I had to analyse a girl under my care who at the onset of puberty developed a fear of crossing streets or public squares; the act of being seen was felt to be culpable, the girl imagining that she was guilty of showing off. We have already seen that inquisitiveness is associated with the "naked body," with curiosity as to puberal development and consequent interest in the hairy and non-hairy parts of the human anatomy. The feeling of guilt associated with the act of exhibiting one's nakedness is susceptible of unconscious generalisations and transferences of the most varied and unexpected sort. For instance, a child may find it absolutely impossible to stand and answer a question in class, or to show its good points in any way. Shyness, timidity are a reaction to the spectacular complex. "The reaction is so great that an extreme reaction takes place against the primary

[1] Oskar Pfister, Love in Children, pp. 177 et seq.

88 THE MIND OF THE CHILD

tendency, leading to undesirable and troublesome character traits. For instance, the passion for nudity, which is so strong in infancy, may lead, by way of reaction, to the opposite characteristic of excessive shyness, bashfulness, shrinking, and self-consciousness, which may be of torturing severity and greatly hampering in the practical relations of life."[1]

I have already had to make use of the terms "curiosity" and "inquisitiveness." No sooner do we become aware of the existence of the spectacular complex than we come up against the tendency to be inquisitive. The pleasure derived from seeing is prolonged by the pleasure enjoyed through knowing. A child's curiosity is early trained upon the physical attributes of youngsters of the opposite sex and upon the mystery which surrounds birth. The prohibitions placed in the path towards the acquiring of such knowledge merely serve to whet the appetite, weighting it with a sense of guilt, and either hindering its attainment or constraining it to a transference upon other objects.

Isadora, who was brought to me when she was sixteen years of age, had, since early childhood, manifested extremely active spectacular tendencies. At the age of thirteen, she was given a course of eurhythmics, and this suggested to her the choice of a profession, namely expressionist dancing. During the subsequent years her taste for this career became more and more pronounced, and in the end she proved to be really gifted. The form the sublimation took was an excellent one, but it ceaselessly betrayed its true origin: Isadora likes to dance with no other clothing than very transparent draperies; she eagerly awaits the return of springtide because, the

[1] Ernest Jones, Papers on Psychoanalysis, p. 642.

DISPLAY AND MYSTERY

weather being warmer, she is able to wear dresses of flimsy materials. She is passionately fond of making-up. When writing a French essay, she expresses her thoughts without circumlocution, whereas her schoolfellows are thoroughly conventional in their compositions. But she exaggerates the unconventionality of her ideas, and she introduces the same kind of exaggeration in her talk. "I adore exaggerations," she exclaims. This tendency, which is so strong as to approximate to a veritable mythomania, represents (as does her fondness for every kind of make-up) a clever compromise between exhibitionism and a desire to conceal. She delights in acting a part and in trying to appear different from what she really is.

Concomitantly with these developments, she had from an early age been tormented with curiosity concerning forbidden knowledge, and this was obviously the outcome of the same instinct. She wanted to know all about an elder brother's love affairs, about birth, and so on. With the connivance of one of her sisters she set about discovering "the truth"; thence she proceeded to investigate other mysteries, took a keen interest in Schuré's *Grands initiés* which happened at the time to be much under discussion in the circle of friends she frequented. The affinity of these tendencies with those enumerated above is beautifully illustrated by the following instance which occurred in class when the students were given as subject for an essay "My two greatest desires." Isadora had no hesitation in declaring that her first wish was to live in the Golden Age when nymphs bathed naked in fountains and streams; but, since this main desire could not be granted, she would be content with becoming "an initiate."

"Veils" occupy an important position in the system of her mental associations. She likes *Salambô* mainly on account of the veil scene. One shade of violet is repugnant

THE MIND OF THE CHILD

to her, whereas mauve and other tints of this colour are pleasant to her eye. When she was made to concentrate her attention upon the particular hue that displeased her, we discovered that it was the one adopted by the Catholic Church to cover the statues during Lent and Holy Week: veiled statues, uneasiness of mind caused by mysteries, both these themes vibrated in the antipathy she felt for a particular colour. Her desire to be "an initiate" was likewise a reflexion of the veil motif, for it signified the gratification of knowing what others did not know; of seeing and yet concealing that which she saw—a further method of compromise.

Lying, too, is in various ways linked up with the spectacular complex,[1] and primarily in virtue of its association with the exhibiting-concealing motif. In certain instances it may be the outcome of a moral tendency which may be explained as follows: the curb placed upon the tendency to exhibit may have been too strong, and the consequent dissimulation might very well be the outcome of a kind of moral decency carried to excess. But the most important factor contributing to the genesis of falsehood in a child is indubitably the habit of lying among the parents and other adults forming the environment. In especial, the evasive or incorrect answers furnished to a child's questions concerning birth and matters sexual do incalculable harm in this field. No matter how young the child may be it is never wholly duped by such evasions.

Half-truths, if I may speak frankly, are hardly in better case than thoroughgoing lies where children are concerned. Odier tells of a boy eleven years old, who was summoned

[1] Cf. Ernst Schneider, Kinderfehler, Entstehung und Behandlung, p. 161.

DISPLAY AND MYSTERY

to his mother's presence in order that she might inform him of the advent of another child to the family circle. She further added that the baby would come out of her body. "Which way?" asked the lad. His mother replied that every time a baby was born, it came from a different part of the body, and that this time she was sure it would come from one of her arms. The boy took counsel of a friend, and discovered that his mother had told a lie. He was not long in following suit, and soon began to suffer from mythomania. [1]

I, too, had a youth of sixteen under my care who had been brought to me on account of his lying proclivities. He started by telling me his recollections. He recalled that when he was four years old he saw his little sister for the first time, but she was already a big girl.—"Do you mean that you had never seen her before?" I asked. —"She had never lived with us before, and I did not know she was my sister. She was born at S."—"And you, don't you live at S.?"—"No, I've never lived there."— "Then your mother must have gone to S. for the birth of your sister."—"Oh, no!"—These contradictions accumulated, while the lad remained unruffled. At first I thought my patient must be telling deliberate falsehoods. Nothing of the sort. He informed me that his mother was not his real mother, that he was not absolutely sure of the identity of his mother, she was probably a lady who had disappeared when he was six years old. This lady had promised to send him some toys, but her gifts had never come. He did not go by his father's name nor by that of his "real" mother. In a word, the boy had come into this world by "illegitimate" means, and no one had ever explained the circumstances to him. He assured me that all this irregularity left him completely

[1] Charles Odier, Curiosité morbide, p. 83.

92 THE MIND OF THE CHILD

indifferent, and the tone he used to convey the information seemed to confirm the truth of his words. But the indifference was merely assumed, it formed no more than a shell to his genuine feelings. The repression of his curiosity had taken place very early in life, and it needed certain comments made by his schoolfellows to bring young Thierry to the realisation that there was something strange about his bearing the surname of neither of his so-called parents. He had sought to clear up the mystery in consultation with his sister, whose curiosity was even livelier than his own, and who, unaided, had drawn her own conclusions as to the facts of the case. Here we are given a slight modification of the typical sequence of events. The question at issue is not simply nor essentially one concerning the origins of life, but of the origins of life according to the law of the land, and the civil state of the parents. Nevertheless, the curiosity has to do with birth and with the sense of guilt arising therefrom; it is further complicated by the reticence and the lies of the parents.

The history of a young woman of twenty-four is recorded by Pfister. She lost all sense of inner peace from the day she began "the ferreting business." When she was quite little she would sit in front of something and ask herself what it was really like in its inside. "What I was especially interested in was the problem what could be inside a carved ivory dog. It seemed to be impossible that there could be nothing inside, and I felt that it must be able to think." She suffered from anxiety troubles and a sense of inferiority and guilt. Later on, she held aloof from boys, and showed no interest in the idea of being married; indeed, she was directly averse to the prospect. Her sense of inferiority was so great, that she was always asking herself whether she would ever be able to find a man

DISPLAY AND MYSTERY

"of high moral views" to consent to marry her. It seems to me that what she deemed her "guilty curiosity" lay at the foundation of her disquietude.[1]

A very different symptom, but one which nevertheless is related to the same system, is recorded by Sophie Morgenstern in her book *La psychanalyse infantile et son rôle dans l'hygiène mentale.* A very intelligent child of seven and a half years old suddenly began to stammer. His own recollection was that this habit started on the day he took to imitating a school teacher who continually punctuated her lessons with the words: "Eh ben! Eh ben!" The young woman was at the time giving a nature lesson, and was explaining how flowers were planted out, and how seeds were sown and watered. Thereafter the boy would collect seeds and sow them in flower-pots. Then he took to asking his mother if babies were sown likewise. The elucidation of this problem and the advice given to the mother sufficed to liquidate the child's difficulties. But we often find that stammering is the outcome of an uneasy conscience among individuals who wish to inquire into forbidden topics.

The most typical troubles attendant upon this complex concerning curiosity as to the nature of forbidden topics are those which affect the intelligence. Jones tells us of a boy who at the age of fifteen reverted to the conduct of a child of three. Apparently the cause of this retrogression was a desire to forget the knowledge he had acquired of sexual life and thus to be able to play the innocent.[2]

Such a case is definitely pathological, but we need not have to do with extremes of the sort to be aware

[1] Oskar Pfister, Love in Children, pp. 121 et seq.
[2] Ernest Jones, Papers on Psychoanalysis, pp. 476 et seq.

94 THE MIND OF THE CHILD

that similar tabus are placed upon certain forms of inquisitiveness, and that these tabus may become generalised so as to apply to other branches of knowledge and thus to dam up the growth of the mental faculties.

Barbara Low refers to a woman rather over forty who came to be analysed. She had experienced since the age of eight an inability to deal with any kind of problem although she possessed normal powers of handling plain and straightforward issues. "At school she had been entirely unable to work out the simplest kind of arithmetical or algebraical problem, although extremely quick in dealing with plain examples of rules: similarly in drawing, making plasticine maps, cutting out or putting together garments, or in simple scientific experiments, she was entirely baffled and perpetually asking herself, without finding an answer, 'How shall I begin?' Yet she was intellectually very quick in understanding, of marked literary and artistic tastes, and quite capable in the ordinary affairs of life. . . . It became clear that she suffered from a powerful unconscious fear of using her hands, feet, eyes, her body as a whole, and arising from that her mental 'sight' in relation to anything which was obscure, to any problem; and this fear begotten of her sense of guilt was linked up with her fantasies in relation to mother and father. . . . Any mysterious tale, detective story, or riddle was at once a delight and yet a paralysing thing, and she told me she did not think that she had solved a single riddle even once in her life."[1]

Another case bearing upon the same inhibition of painful memories is that of a boy of nine and a half who took a violent antipathy for the geography lessons and his geography teacher at school. "He could not understand the meaning of a map at all." From independent

[1] Barbara Low, The Unconscious in Action, pp. 129–130.

DISPLAY AND MYSTERY

information it appeared that the teacher was very efficient, quite amiably disposed towards her pupil, and that the geography lesson was popular with the other children in the class. But the boy complained that she was "always cross." In the course of treatment "a book lent him by the analyst which dealt in a simple way with the origins of peoples, their distribution over the globe, and the relationships between various races," gave the boy much pleasure. He began "to yield up some of his more intimate thoughts, foremost of which was this: How do differences among people come about? Why are there white, yellow, red, or black men? A matter, he complained, that his geography teacher had never talked about. . . . Still further freeing by analysis led him to cast away the disguise, and to come some stages nearer his real enquiry—namely, what was the difference between man and woman, and how did it result?" It at length became plain that repression of this fundamental problem lay at the root of his detestation for the geography lesson. His emotion was the outcome of his Oedipus conflict; behind his query, lay his disappointed love in regard to the mother and his jealous anger against his father. His genuine preoccupation was: "Why should there be this hateful and bitter disappointment for me, namely, that I am not allowed to hold first place with my mother, but must needs be thrust out on account of my father. . . ." Accompanying these feelings was a sense of guilt and a longing to know what difference there could exist between man and woman.[1]

I knew a boy named Karl who reacted in a similar manner. He was fourteen when he came to me for treatment, and in his case it was not difficult to unravel the course of events. As a small child, Karl had been

[1] Barbara Low, The Unconscious in Action, pp. 112 et seq.

96 THE MIND OF THE CHILD

very much interested in geography; subsequently he became indifferent, and ultimately took a great dislike for this subject. His antipathy spread to include various branches of the natural sciences. When I first knew him, his interests had concentrated upon the abstract sciences, upon physics and mathematics, and it was to these he wished to devote his time. Karl had been brought to me because he stammered, but the defect in his speech was merely part of the generalised complex. It is easy to understand that stuttering may be linked up with the idea "I must not speak of so and so."

The cases enumerated above show that we educators are faced with a question of primary importance in relation to school life as a whole. Inborn capacities appear to play a less important part than do affective shocks acquired in early childhood in determining a pupil's preference for this branch of study or the other, and a corresponding success in one sort of work or an incapacity to achieve anything worth while in a second or third subject. Among the complexes which correspond with these infantile shocks, those arising from a repressed curiosity as to forbidden things take pride of place. We need, however, but compare the above-cited cases to see that the reaction from the curiosity complex is very different from child to child. It is not enough merely to say "such and such a trouble is due to repressed inquisitiveness." Each case must be examined on its merits—and analysis is alone able to furnish the necessary clue—; we need to realise how the complex has developed in each particular case, or what individual complex has grafted itself upon the primary complex.

The question has been well considered by Freud in his book on Leonardo da Vinci: sometimes the repression of curiosity concerning forbidden topics leads (by trans-

DISPLAY AND MYSTERY

ference) the person concerned to enter other avenues of research, and may condition the most sublime intellectual and scientific aptitudes; at other times the repression follows the process of transference step by step, and the new perspectives become, in their turn, forbidden paths of sublimation; in the latter case, mental growth is inhibited instead of being encouraged.[1] As our psycho-analytical knowledge increases, we may hope to determine with more precision the reasons for such differences. Jones is inclined to take the following point of view. Sublimation is best achieved when there exists the most favourable distance in the associations between the object of the sublimated tendency (intellectual interests) and the object of the forbidden primitive tendency. When the distance is too great, that is to say when the resemblance is excessively faint, the affective interest is slower in displacing itself; when the distance is too small, the repression of the primitive tendency is liable to influence the new tendency, and interest is inhibited thereby. producing an impression of intellectual incapacity. In my opinion it is likewise essential to bear in mind the degree of intensity in repression, the violence of the sense of guilt in relation to the primitive (forbidden) object; for the more violent this emotion, the more liable is it to become generalised and to place impediments in the way of intellectual development.

Nor must we fail to ask ourselves whether certain types of children are not more prone than others to block up the roads leading to certain branches of study. Why does one child transfer the prohibition on to problems in general, whereas a boy like Karl will concentrate upon such concrete sciences as geography and physics, and are peculiarly gifted for mathematics? I am inclined to

[1] Sigmund Freud, Leonardo da Vinci, p. 14.

98 THE MIND OF THE CHILD

believe that in the latter case the children are extroverts whose repression of the forbidden topic is linked up with direct observation; the former, on the other hand, are probably introverts who ruminate upon the object of their curiosity, and turn the problem over in their minds.

In any case, the way in which the conflict is solved contributes, at an early age, and to a wide extent, towards determining the lines along which mental development will take place. Isadora, for instance, was obsessed by a complex connected with veils, and her passion for seeing was immense, for did she not want to become an "initiate"? Yet this passion of hers was by no means an intellectual one. She was far more inclined to be interested in mysticism and theosophy than in the sciences, since for the latter she felt herself lacking in aptitude, and her passion consisted less in the search for truth than in an adoration of Isis of the three veils. Thus it is not only a damming up or a development of the intelligence which comes as a consequence of the "forbidden curiosity" complex, but the whole mental tone depends upon how this complex is resolved; a preference for the exact sciences, for the concrete sciences, for knowledge in general, for mysticism—all these are different sublimations of the same complex. It is, therefore, absolutely necessary to intervene at the proper moment so that the child may find the happiest solution of this complex.

The discussion has led us to a fresh problem: that of sexual enlightenment. Freud maintains that a child's interest in sexual matters begins at an early age.[1] Jones, for his part, insists that children are a good deal more intelligent than grown-ups are apt to imagine. A boy

[1] Sigmund Freud, Introduction à la psychanalyse, p. 341.

DISPLAY AND MYSTERY

of fourteen who came under Sophie Morgenstern's care, was obsessed with sexual desires and declared frankly: "Children see much more than grown-ups suppose. Many a thing is engraved upon a child's memory."[1] Often a most promising child fails to fulfil its parents' hopes because a sense of guilt in respect of "forbidden curiosity" hinders its mental development. The first thing to avoid is that a child should ever feel guilty because of gratifying its curiosity; we should invariably answer its questions without hesitation and never make it feel ashamed of itself by replying "one must not speak of such things." Secondly, if a definite and full answer concerning the sexual life cannot be given, we must at least see to it that, no matter how tender its age, it is not put off with a lie.[2] But we must avoid going to the other extreme and prematurely giving our children explanations concerning the sexual life. Sophie Morgenstern is perfectly justified when she expresses astonishment because, reading Miss Searl's book *Flight into Reality*, she comes across the following passage: A child of three, wanting to know how its electric heater worked, was informed that its real desire was to be told how its father's penis worked within its mother during the night. Such unnecessary "explanations" are very detrimental to psychoanalysis. Sophie Morgenstern, while admitting that sexual curiosity underlies most of the interminable questions asked by children, wisely suggests that we do no good service to the sexual enlightenment of children when we give them details which they have not expressed any wish to know and which they are too young to understand.

The general rule should be never to talk to a child

---

[1] Sophie Morgenstern, La psychanalyse infantile et son rôle dans l'hygiène mentale, p. 71.

[2] Cf. Ernest Jones, Papers on Psychoanalysis, p. 644.

100   THE MIND OF THE CHILD

about such matters until it asks for information, and then to confine our answer to the limits imposed by the question in point. Nevertheless, as Jones writes: "If a child does not ask spontaneously by the age of four or five it means that something has gone wrong, that it has indirectly gathered from its parents' attitude that this is a forbidden subject which must not be approached; it then becomes desirable to take more active measures, with, of course, the necessary tact."[1]

On the whole Jones does not think that the school is the best place for imparting the necessary knowledge concerning sex, except in so far as this end can be gained by means of lessons in anatomy and physiology. A teacher must merely be prepared to give explanations in individual cases, and these are extremely rare. Pfister considers that it is the parents' duty to enlighten their children if need be, and to inspire them with respect for the laws of nature. He refers, moreover, to Rank's and to Sachs' warning that we must avoid giving unasked for information concerning the sex life, even if such information is wholesome and well-considered beforehand.

Experience shows that children do not easily understand the explanations given them concerning the sexual life; they may appear to assimilate the information, but they prefer their own fantasies and fall back upon these individual theories and upon the stories they have been told about the cabbage patch and storks and so on. There are many reasons to account for the fact: first of all we have to consider the stage of development to which a child has attained—but this applies to any and every information given to the young, for a child may verbally repeat what an adult has said and yet retain its own theories and explanations; in the second place

[1] Ernest Jones, Papers on Psychoanalysis, p. 644.

DISPLAY AND MYSTERY

it is necessary to take the individual affective factors into consideration. We saw in an example given earlier in this book how a little girl, moved by jealousy, refused to admit that her younger sister had ever been inside her mother's body. But a sense of guilt undoubtedly plays the leading role in this refusal to understand; the tabus imposed by children upon certain subjects are generally encouraged by the attitude adopted by the parents at the outset. When, later on, a candid explanation is furnished, the child, having accepted the tabu, tends to ignore the explanation; and this refusal must by no means be interpreted as signifying that the information has been prematurely imparted; it may be that it has come too late, namely after the establishment of a very strong tabu. I knew a boy, Georgio by name, who was already eleven years old when his mother brought him to me for the treatment of certain disorders, such as backwardness in his studies, absent-mindedness, bed-wetting, and so on. It was necessary to make a direct assault on the subject of his tabus, which were intimately connected with forbidden interests. When I tackled him on these matters, he became even more obviously distrait. Then he said: "It's funny, but ever since you've been talking to me about these things it seems as if I could not understand and as if I could not hear." These words are an admirable illustration of the tabu. The boy was certainly better informed than he himself suspected; but what he had learned had been taught him by his schoolfellows and had been expressed in terms repugnant to his sensibilities, thereby reinforcing the tabu, so that his knowledge of the sexual life had been repressed, to reappear as a sort of symbolical shadow thrown upon a screen. "Some friend of mine once told me about a toad one finds in South America. It is supposed to secrete

THE MIND OF THE CHILD

a kind of whitish liquid—but I don't know how much of all this is true."

Taking one thing with another, we have everything to gain by never making a mystery of the difference existing between the sexes, by never making innuendoes on the subject, and by giving the child sound information regarding maternity. Questions relative to the part a father plays in the business necessarily arise later. Odier considers that by the time a child is nine to twelve years old it should have been fully initiated into the whole problem of the generative process. He does not deem the parents to be the best persons to impart such information. A doctor, gifted with tact, or a psychoanalyst, would be more competent to perform so delicate a task. Once a child has reached the age of puberty, such enlightenment comes too late; explanations prove enormously more difficult to phrase since they are liable to excite the youngsters' sexual desires—a disadvantage which does not occur at a more tender age. As a rule, and because of our present-day outlooks, such information usually comes too late, when a child has already been clandestinely told.

At this point we shall do well to ask ourselves whether frank explanations concerning this thorny subject, while preventing the unfortunate accidents discussed above, may not at the same time hinder the transference of childish curiosity on to more satisfactory avenues of knowledge. As a matter of fact, such transferences are inevitable, for, be our answers as sincere as possible, they will never completely satisfy the inquisitiveness natural to all children. Every intellectual fact is a function of activity of one sort or another. As Janet expresses it: "To understand is to know how to invent and to make," and later on in this book we shall make the acquaintance

DISPLAY AND MYSTERY 103

of a boy who would like to be a little girl because women "make" children. Experience shows that theoretical explanations as to the sexual life, comparisons with the pistil and stamens of flowers, and the like, are unsatisfactory and do not satiate a child's curiosity. If enlightenment is not to prove utterly futile, it must give due credit to the pleasure and the joy and the caressive side of love.[1] This is precisely the point where educators need to exercise the utmost tact. Behind every form of curiosity there lurks not merely the desire to know but likewise the desire for action; and behind a child's curiosity as to the sexual life, there is incontestably a desire to participate in the sexual life of adults. Since the latter desire is unattainable in childhood, there invariably remains an element of dissatisfaction in the child's mind, and this suffices to bring about transferences of affect and various forms of sublimation. But if we refuse to give the information a child asks for, we run the risk of forcing it to find enlightenment elsewhere and of succumbing to precocious or perverse sexual experiences.

Since the child's inquisitiveness can never be completely gratified, it will not be able wholly to avoid resorting to tabus and it will suffer from a certain sense of guilt in relation to the subjects of its tabus, which form part of our primitive ancestral heritage, inborn and inescapable. Our duty is to lighten as far as possible the child's burden of guilt instead of, as is usual, making it almost unbearably heavy and thus bringing evil consequences in its train.

Just as tabus seem to rise spontaneously in the child mind, so likewise do fantastic theories as to the sexual life. Here the attitude of the parents is nowise to blame, for we have to do with a very primitive instinct, one

[1] Cf. S. Ferenczi, Die Anpassung der Familie an das Kind.

104 THE MIND OF THE CHILD

which personal experience is incompetent to cope with. These theories form part of child psychology, and all we adults can do in the matter is to avoid reinforcing them by our refusal to give the child the explanations it demands. One of these theories concerns the difference between the sexes, and lies at the heart of the mutilation or castration complex; another concerns the origin of a baby, and introduces us to the birth complex. Each of these complexes will have to be dealt with separately in the sequel.

PART TWO

COMPLEXES OF THE EGO

CHAPTER FIVE

MUTILATION

THE theory which accounts for the anatomical difference between a boy and a girl as being the outcome of a mutilation performed upon the latter is almost universally met with among children of both sexes, but each child may have its own reflections as to the manner and form of the operation. A boy is usually proud of possessing an organ which he deems to be of superior value, and this initial sense of superiority then becomes condensed in his mind with other attributes with which his environment, rightly or wrongly invests the male sex. A girl is humiliated in proportion as the boy is esteemed, and she reacts, as we shall see in due course, by having recourse to the Diana complex. Some little girls fancy that the organ "will grow." A small child called Maud was constantly seeking comfort from her brother by insisting that the latter assure her it would grow, and she would often look at herself in a mirror to see if it had grown. When no growth took place she was so disappointed that she burst into tears. A boy holds keenly to his superior position, and fears only that he may be thrust down from his pedestal. But there are boys who have special reasons (which we shall study later on) for relinquishing this favoured position, looking upon it as an injustice to girls, and desiring to become members of the opposite sex. The reactions manifested by each individual child in respect of this inevitable comparison, or in other words the aspects of the "castration complex," are repeated over and over again in even graver forms and are definitely related to specific types

108 THE MIND OF THE CHILD

of character. Virility symbolises strength, influence, brain capacity, a special class of Christian names, personality, an affirmation of the ego, a sense of superiority under any and every guise. Mutilation, on the other hand, unconsciously connected with femininity, is a symbol of weakness, of inferiority, of death and decapitation, of punishment. To chastise and to castrate have certain etymological similarities which come to confirm their kinship, for both words are primarily derived from the Latin *castrare*.

The complex is one of primary importance, and has ramifications everywhere. Together with the Oedipus complex, the castration complex is one of the fundamental premises of Freud's theories. Adler has made the castration complex the very centre of his system, naming it variously the inferiority complex and the masculine protest. I do not propose to join issues with the two schools of thought as to which aspect of the complex is fundamental. It seems to me that a study of the complexes as such should form the starting-point of all psychoanalytical investigation. The question as to which component of a complex is the most important is a very secondary matter. The word complex implies that there must exist several ingredients, and it is precisely this plurality of components which makes it a complex. When discussing the mutilation complex, the protagonists of the various schools want to know whether the inferiority fantasies arising out of it are nothing more than disguised symbols of castration or whether, on the contrary, the word castration is merely a *modus dicendi*, a concrete way of expressing the abstract idea of inferiority. The question does not seem to me to be of primary importance; it is, moreover, clumsily put, for the complex consists in the grouping of these disparate elements, and not in the choice of one among the many.

MUTILATION

It is, therefore, invariably wiser to speak of the complex by a synthetic term capable of expressing this plurality of components. Thus the word "mutilation" would appear preferable to either "castration" which is wholly sexual in significance or "inferiority" which is too abstract.

Memories of this infantile comparison between boys and girls are sometimes found to persist on into adult life. For the most part they are disguised, or thrown upon a screen as it were, so that scenes bearing a certain resemblance to the forgotten (repressed) facts are remembered, whereas the actual occurrences are only dug up in the course of analysis by means of associations connected with the screen memories. Freud cites the case of a young man who recollected the following scene from childhood's days. His aunt was teaching him the alphabet; he asked her to tell him the difference between "m" and "n," whereupon she explained that an "m" had a piece more to it than an "n." Now this subterfuge memory really masked certain other childhood scenes having to do with the differences between men and women.

At other times we find the patient's mind occupied with distinctions between analogous objects such as hemp and flax, or between two similar words one of which has an extra letter. Sometimes the screen shows no true recollection at all: in such cases the "memory" is nothing other than a symptom, and serves as an association of ideas.

In the course of an analysis I was making of a girl named Irma H., she would frequently refer to a friend of hers, Olga, and would then go on to speak of the river Volga. I asked her to give some associations she might have concerning these two words. "Olga is pale, has a

THE MIND OF THE CHILD

flabby, white skin, and these are signs of weakness; the Volga is a mighty river, it is untamed, and birds are free to fly over it; I'd like to be a bird like that." The V, which alone differentiates the two names "is a thing which enters into another thing."

Fernand, another of my patients, was possessed of a wish to mutilate himself, so that he might identify himself with femininity. The boy's condition of mind found expression in a high degree of moral refinement, and later led to his refusing to undergo military service. Until he was analysed, Fernand invariably confounded the words "coassement" [croaking] and "croassement" [cawing], and in general was wont to introduce the letter r (a symbol of virility where he was concerned) into words where it nowise belonged.

If we observe a child closely, we may catch these reactions at the very moment when they begin to take shape. A boy between the ages of five and six was lazy about the pronunciation of the letter r, the guttural sounds, and explosive consonants; during the same period, his mind was dominated by ideas of mutilation, so that he dreamed fairly often that an ogre was cutting out his tongue, and he spoke of "dressing up as a girl" so as not to have to go to war.

Mutilation anxiety, in a boy, frequently takes the form of a dread of being punished; especially is this the case when the child habitually masturbates. Certain instances might lead us to believe that in a child's mind masturbation looms as the sin of sins and that this sin above all calls for specific chastisement—the total suppression of the organ which gave rise to the sin; "if thy hand offend thee, cut it off" as the Gospels advise. A small boy will fear lest he be deprived of the organ which determines

MUTILATION

his sex; a little girl will fancy her like organ has been cut off because she has been naughty or that it refuses to grow because she has touched herself there. Furthermore, this disaster, this dreaded or supposed mutilation, is, in the child mind, symbolical of the loss of all the types of superiority associated with virility. Varying from case to case, the dread may attach to this type of superiority or to that. Frequently, the dread finds expression in some morbid symptom.

Zulliger cites some very interesting observations he has made in respect of the mutilation complex. A boy's whole character suddenly changed and he became very absent-minded. Here are two of his dreams.

1. I lift up my left thumb with my right hand; my thumb gets all red and swollen; then it bursts and a white worm comes out; then I can bend my thumb again.

2. I am in a railway station; I am carrying a saw and some planks tied together with a cord ["tying together" is often met with in this system of ideas, simultaneously as a punishment for sin, i.e. impotence equivalent to mutilation, and as a protection against one's own actions, i.e. binding the hands, etc.]. Suddenly I cut my left leg with the saw, but this does not hurt me.

The associations which arose out of these dreams showed that the child was engaged at that time in a struggle against masturbation, a struggle in which the analyst was able to help him to victory. All his troubles were related to this conflict. In this connexion I may say that when children are absent-minded or scatter-brained it is frequently found to be an unconscious equivalent of mutilation. We find the same idea conveyed in the myth of Osiris who was cut up into fourteen pieces. Again, in Jacques, one of my own cases, I found that the child's

112 THE MIND OF THE CHILD

concentration of mind was associated with being "entire," and his absent-mindedness with being "mutilated."[1]

Another of Zulliger's cases concerned a boy of thirteen who could not resist crumbling bread in order to feed the ducks and fowls. When Hans was younger he had been alarmed by ducks and fowls, for his mother told him they might gobble him up. He dreamed: "I took off my jacket and my shirt, and mother came in and asked angrily why I was going about half-dressed. Then a drake flew on to my back and bit me in the neck." Here are some of the associations this dream called up: he liked walking in nothing but a pair of trousers, but he never went without his socks; he had once seen a goose peck a girl who was bare-legged. Associations with the "neck" are: "when I am caned I drop my head so as to protect my face and eyes." One day, when he had stolen some hazel-nuts, a gentleman cuffed him. He thought that the drakes treated him as if he were a duck. He was given an essay to write, the teacher allowing him to choose his own subject. This is what he wrote: "When I was a very little boy my knickers were always open in front. My mother used to say that the chickens would peck it all away. I thought this is what had already happened to little girls and I did not want to be a girl. So I carefully buttoned myself up again." To complete the story, the boy added that a neighbour who was the owner of the ducks threatened to cut off Hans' organ if the child showed it again and continued to play with it. In the present case, not only was the punishment to apply directly to the masturbatory act, but also the act of exhibition (spectacular complex).

The mutilation complex, as I have earlier defined it,

[1] Cf. Hans Zulliger, Psychoanalytische Erfahrungen aus der Volksschulpraxis, p. 90.

MUTILATION

is all through made manifest: the dream about the drake's pecking the neck is a condensation of the ideas of punishment, of mutilation, and of humiliation. The obssession which constrained Hans to throw bread-crumbs to the fowls and ducks is likewise linked on to the same complex; the boy gives these animal bread in order that they may not take from him a part of his body. Again, such behaviour is a repetition of more primitive behaviour, which in its turn is connected with the mutilation complex, i.e. the act of propitiation. The propitiatory act consists in inflicting upon oneself in the presence of the adversary or the all-powerful deity a mutilation in effigy, in order to avoid having an actual mutilation performed. I have shown elsewhere that the signs of greeting, such as raising the hat or bowing the head, are relics of this primitive behaviour. It seems to me that Hans exhibits various elements of such a system of ideas, and the dropping of the head in order "to protect my face and eyes" is not unconnected in this respect with the throwing of the crumbs. Nor would it be difficult to prove that, so far as neurotic persons are concerned, many an obsessive act, many a mania for finding protection and security, have their origin in this system.[1]

Another, and very picturesque, case given by Zulliger is that of a glutton. Max is a splendid trencherman and is everlastingly eating. His pockets and his desk are always filled with fruit, cheese, bread. Sometimes he even steals money in order to buy food. In spite of all his guzzling the lad is thin and looks sickly. This stupendous appetite of his appeared when Max was thirteen. Max's feelings had been overwrought by a series of operations: his mother had had a goitre removed, and the boy himself had had adenoids cut out. While recalling these two operations

[1] Cf. Hans Zulliger, Gelöste Fesseln, p. 99.

THE MIND OF THE CHILD

he remembered one that he had completely forgotten: at the age of three he had been circumcised and, with tears, he recalled how the doctor had said: "We snip all that off." He thought that the loss of blood on each occasion would prove fatal, and when he was asked why he ate so much he answered "in order to make blood to get fat, to grow tall," though he was tall enough for his age. Further examination of the case showed that Max masturbated, and he was haunted with the idea that this practice crippled him, undermined his strength, and so forth. At all costs he needed to fortify himself. But the supposed loss of strength was, in the unconscious, identical with the loss of blood during the various operations and with the mutilation he had been threatened with when three years of age.[1]

In general, people are inclined to exaggerate the dangers attendant upon the practice of masturbation. Especially is this the case as regards adolescents; and the authors of popular works dealing with the problems of sex often tend to reinforce this dread of the results of masturbation by writing foolishly upon the subject or in a spirit of self-interest. The soil is already prepared for the reception of these bad suggestions by the spontaneous work of the complexes. Fear lest the practice of masturbation may be followed by a loss of vital energy is, in some, nothing but another way of expressing the dread of punishment by mutilation. The dread, which is instinctive and not rational, runs the risk of proving detrimental to the young person's development and should on no account be encouraged. If a child practises "self-abuse," it must not be made to think or be allowed to fancy that it has committed an exceptional and horrible sin, and is, therefore, a lost soul. Children are only too

[1] Hans Zulliger, Gelöste Fesseln, p. 89.

MUTILATION

prone to believe this of their own accord. An adult in charge of such a child should speak to it loyally and simply, avoiding any reference to sinfulness or culpability. If an educator would act for the best in this matter it is necessary to remember that the practice of masturbation is extremely frequent at puberty and only becomes a danger if it is allowed to instal itself as an incurable habit. In any event, nothing is gained by inspiring terror.

Further, we have to recognise that long before the appearance of genuine masturbation, which is usually met with at puberty, a child has practised a larval kind of masturbation which goes by the name of "infantile masturbation," and which is practically universal. Psychoanalysts even maintain that this infantile form of masturbation goes through two quite distinct periods: the first period dates from the earliest days of babyhood and is simultaneous with the period of thumb-sucking, etc.; the second, and more important, period starts between the ages of three and four, to disappear under normal circumstances, towards the sixth year, at the time when, according to Freud, the most radical repression of infantile sexuality takes place, and when the "latency period" (which continues until the onset of puberty) is beginning. Now it is during the second phase of infantile masturbation, i.e. between the ages of three and six, that, according to psychoanalytical experience, the fear of castration becomes implanted in the child's mind. At puberty, this system of ideas is reawakened, but the infantile fear takes another and more recondite form, such as a dread of losing one's strength, or of ceasing to grow, or of dying, or of being morally lost. At puberty, the educator is faced with a situation which is already of long standing, only renewed under another guise, so that no matter how this situation is tackled the root of the

THE MIND OF THE CHILD

trouble cannot be reached. As a matter of fact the problem is already set as soon as a child arrives at the second period of infantile masturbation.

Psychoanalysts, applying their special methods, have gained a great deal of knowledge concerning this almost forgotten period of life. They advise that all those who have young children in charge should desist from everything which might prematurely excite the genital zone (care should be taken when bathing the child and cleansing those parts, excessive fondling must be avoided, the child is better served by not being given a rocking-horse or other playthings which necessitate a see-saw movement, and so forth). Nevertheless, despite every conceivable precaution, psychoanalysts maintain that infantile masturbation seems to them inevitable. All they can recommend is that, at the outset of this period, parents and guardians should refrain from treating children with the severity usual under the circumstances. They adduce two reasons for following this counsel: first of all, since this infantile form of masturbation is almost universal, it is absurd to look upon the manifestation as abnormal or vicious; secondly, doubtless in consequence of some primitive and hereditary mechanism, a child is inclined to interpret any form of severity concerning this habit as a threat of castration, and such a menace invariably awakens, in the primitive unconscious, the most appalling terror and the most poignant suffering. Everything is to be gained, it would appear, by explaining rather than by severity at this tender age. Marie Bonaparte even goes so far as to say: "Grown-ups once having their minds enlightened by the data of psychoanalytical discoveries, should cease to imagine that they hold a monopoly in affairs of sex. The child, too, has a sexual life of its own and has every right to possess such a life. This is in the

MUTILATION 117

natural order of things, and is neither exceptional nor sinful. . . . First of all, instead of looking upon infantile masturbation as the sin of sins, a child should not be made to feel ashamed of itself, but, rather, it should be encouraged, at suitable times and in suitable circumstances, to talk freely about this habit to its mother or to any other person in charge of its upbringing. . . . Undoubtedly we should not be acting in the child's best interests were we to encourage it to masturbate to excess. But a child is more apt to go to extremes in this matter, despite the feeling of guilt which attaches to masturbation, if it is forbidden to touch its organs than when it is left to do as it pleases. Forbidden fruit. . . . Sometimes we meet with cases where masturbation has become so ingrained that the habit persists on into adult life when sexuality ought to find expression in union with the beloved. In such cases, one cannot but ask whether the masturbation is not the outcome (as are certain other psychical fixations of childhood which are retained in the unconscious) of a kind of defiance natural to rebellious and obstinate spirits in respect of the veto of our educators. . . . What attitude are we, then, to adopt in relation to infantile masturbation? We must neither forbid, nor encourage; all we can do is to watch, . . . and to recognise that the act is a normal one and must be tolerated." The author goes on to say that in this matter she is merely expressing her personal convictions, and that "even psychoanalysts can differ as to the amount of freedom it is wise to allow a child in respect of its sexual activities."[1]

All things considered, the problem of masturbation must be studied in conjunction with the wider problem of sexual enlightenment as a whole. If the educator deals

[1] Marie Bonaparte, Prophylaxie infantile des névroses, pp. 40–42 and 47.

118 THE MIND OF THE CHILD

wisely with the latter, the former becomes a far simpler proposition, for when a child is sanely enlightened it is preserved from most of the troubles contingent upon the sexual life. The two problems intersect at several points. Thus, for instance, we saw above that lying was often associated with curiosity concerning forbidden topics; so, too, with masturbation, for it is a habit the child will tend to conceal because, despite severe reprimands, it continues to indulge.[1]

When we first begin to investigate the nature of a child's desire to be superior we fancy that the field of enquiry is totally different from those we have just been considering. On closer study, however, the situation is found to resemble those already enumerated.

Adler has intimately discussed this "desire to be the first," this effort at rising superior to those with whom the child comes directly in contact. This desire is evident wherever several children live together. A child wants to be the first to taste a particular dish, it will run ahead in order to be the first to reach the goal, it will endeavour to outstrip the pace of a cart or car; indeed many a childish game is the fruit of this competitive passion.[2] Among highly strung children this passion reaches the point of exasperation. Green, following Adler here, shows us the many forms the desire to be first may take among more or less neurotic children. The desire may find its realisation in day-dreams, or a child will work hard in order to win good marks but it will be unable to take part in examinations lest it fail to come out top (it will fall ill at the last moment, and so forth).[3]

---

[1] Cf. Marie Bonaparte, Prophylaxie infantile des névroses, p. 43.
[2] Alfred Adler, Le tempérament nerveux, p. 295.
[3] George H. Green, Psychanalysis in the Class-room, Chapter III.

MUTILATION 119

Here we are faced by an interesting fact: the desire to be first is shadowed by the dread of not being first. The desire to be superior and the feeling of inferiority go hand in hand and, as Adler has shown countless times in his analyses, the superiority complex is above all a reaction to the feeling of inferiority. When one or other of the feelings is unduly pronounced, the contrary emotion becomes exacerbated, and this brings about a situation characteristic of all neuroses. Indeed, so far as Adler is concerned, it is the situation of all others which furnishes the best soil for the growth of neuroses. The desire to be superior—which may in the end bring the person concerned to a situation of genuine superiority—is, primarily, a desire for compensation, and would appear to be the outcome of the search for security which we discussed when considering the "propitiatory act."

The feeling of inferiority is mixed up with the knowledge that such and such an organ is below par, so that the child feels humiliated. Adler has shown that the desire to be superior is rooted in the knowledge of some physical lack, and that the child endeavours to compensate itself for some very definite inferiority of its person. If it stutters, it will dream of being a fine public speaker (compensation), and if it happens to be Demosthenes it will become a great orator (over-compensation).

Curiously enough, the organic inferiority which humiliates and tortures a child is not always the one most in evidence to those around it. Often it is some trifling defect, such as too long or too stubby a nose, ears sticking out, or what not, that the child feels to be intolerable. Blanchard tells of a girl who suffered from a neurosis (with a strongly developed sense of inferiority, and a morbid desire for admiration, etc.) caused by a negligible facial disfigurement in the form of a peculiar

THE MIND OF THE CHILD

birthmark.[1] If one asks for associations connected with the particular sore point of each patient, one frequently finds that the sentiment a child has in regard to the failing in question is actually symbolical of its observation of its own genital organs. Most of the "inferiorities" from which children suffer would seem to be of this nature.

According to a peculiar mechanism consisting of association by contrast, the motif "a little too much" or "a little too long" is treated by the unconscious as equivalent to the motif "slightly too little" or "slightly too short." Irma, whom I analysed, was profoundly humiliated by the fact of being a girl when, on examination, she found that her bodily structure differed from that of a boy; her whole life was dominated by a lively protest against this injustice (Diana complex, women's rights, and so forth); moreover, she remembered that as a child she had felt wounded in her natural vanity by having too long a nose. I found the same mechanism at work in Linette, whose Diana complex was highly developed; she suffered from an unconscious feeling of "having too little" (lack of the male organ) and by a conscious feeling of "having too much" (hairy arms and legs). The "too much" hair on her limbs annoyed her in the conscious because it upset all her estimates as to what was ideally feminine, whereas at bottom and in the unconscious she had an overmastering desire to be a boy. This case throws light upon the strange mechanism which is at work among girls and women, and which presides over the psychological motives for cutting the hair short. To cut is equivalent to mutilation: but to have the hair cut short like a man's is to correct the primitive mutilation so grossly resented by women folk and one which is caused

[1] Phyllis Blanchard, The Care of the Adolescent Girl, p. 68.

MUTILATION 121

by the mere fact of being a female. The wish to be a man, exasperated by the social conditions following immediately upon the war of 1914-1918, settled the question of close-cropped heads and furnishes sufficient explanation for the passionate and quite disproportionate disputes the new fashion of hairdressing aroused. But no sooner was the fashion well established and all our young women had their hair cut short, than we saw little girls fired with the ambition to let their hair grow long as an unconscious protest against the mutilation from which all women are forced to suffer. The underlying motive for this protest was identical with that which had determined the action of the older generation of girls and women when they made up their minds to got short-cropped. Another fact, which runs a parallel course to the above observations is this: if a boy has, on medical or hygienic grounds, to be circumcised, he feels this to be equivalent to castration; yet if it should happen that a little Jew is not circumcised as are all his other co-religionists, analysis has again and again shown that the fact of being uncircumcised is then interpreted as a mutilation!

I do not feel that this strange equivalence of two contradictory situations has as yet been sufficiently studied. Now, if my presuppositions as to association by contrast are correct, if this association of "ideas" is, like all others, an association of tendencies, if the association by contrast reveals the existence of a mechanism which I may call "reversion," i.e. a game of see-saw between two contrasted tendencies, we have to conclude, in view of the above-adduced examples, that the mutilation complex is peculiarly subject to "reversion." This would explain (at another level) the amazing solidarity which exists between the inferiority and superiority complexes, for

122 THE MIND OF THE CHILD

these are invariably found side by side in the same individual, exciting one another, so that bashfulness is always backed by pride, while, as Bergson has said, "there is much modesty underlying vanity."

However this may be, the link between the feeling of inferiority and the fear of (or desire for) mutilation is perpetually making itself evident. We shall do well to note that this link, so differently explained by Freud's school of thought and by Adler's, is fully recognised to exist by both schools—and this harmony of observation is of far greater importance than the many disputes and premature judgments wherein animosity is more likely than not to prevail and which arouses a most unfavourable impression among the general public. One thing is firmly established and that is the existence of the complexes, and we can discuss these very freely without embarking upon invidious discussions. From the practical point of view, analysis has proved most fecund in that it brings the elements forming the complexes in relation one with the other, and renders the subject conscious of their continuity. Now, we have found over and over again that such a continuity exists between the various forms of "mutilation," ranging from castration proper to the most abstract feeling of inferiority.

I had to do with a youth of seventeen. Ever since he was a child he had been obsessed with the desire to be the head of his class—and, in actual fact, so far he had succeeded in keeping this place. Now he had to matriculate, and was faced with competitive examinations in order to enter the university. He left the provincial town where he had so far pursued his studies, and went to Paris to join a class of students who form the élite of the youthful aspirants of France. Here, he lost his premier

MUTILATION 123

position. Consequently he fell ill, became depressed, and was unable to put in an appearance at the examination. This is precisely in conformity with the theories of Adler. At the same time, the young man's dreams are typically Freudian, dreams concerning mutilation which he carefully described in his diary before the analysis was made and before he had the slightest notion of Freud's ideas.

Adler, again, tells of a man suffering from an inferiority complex which he endeavoured to compensate by obstinacy, but which in the end brought him nothing but anxiety, headaches, a dread of examinations, and so forth. This man was rather too fat and his companions were wont to poke fun at his corpulence, comparing him to a pregnant woman. He suffered from the fear of losing his virility. A governess had threatened that if he continued to touch his body in certain spots, he would become a girl. All these data are explained by Adler along the most orthodox Freudian lines.[1] In this case we have, as in those previously mentioned, the peculiar equivalence of the "too much" and the "too little." The fact of being "too fat" is felt by the subject to constitute an inferiority of physique; the "pregnant woman's" enlarged proportions express the idea of femininity which is secretly associated with the idea of mutilation.

I think we can without hesitation accept this strange and important symbolical system according to which castration, mutilation, punishment, and inferiority of every sort are interchangeable terms and are unconsciously held to be equivalents one of the other. Recognising the existence of this system, we may propound the following formula, which, though excessively simple, has rendered

[1] Adler and Furtmüller, Heilen und Bilden, p. 69.

124 THE MIND OF THE CHILD

good service in practice: "A conscious feeling of inferiority is usually the mask of an unconscious feeling of guilt." We have to analyse the latter in order to relieve the former. Furthermore, it must be remembered, that the bridge between the two is formed by ideas of mutilation.

CHAPTER SIX

DIANA

WOULD YOU RATHER BE A GIRL OR A BOY?

IT is easy to see that the mutilation complex is capable of attaining serious proportions where little girls are concerned. Indeed, it may lead to the most serious and unexpected disturbances. Zulliger tells of a girl of thirteen, Anna by name, who had not yet learned to read and whom every one considered abnormal and incurable. During treatment, the analyst discovered that Anna understood what she read but was incapable of pronouncing the words. It was as if the words got strangled in her throat ere she could utter them. Further, on analysis, she was found to have a great dread of men; in childhood she was told stories about "wicked men" who inveigled little girls into the woods in order to kill them or strangle them. While Anna recounted this memory, she placed her hand on her neck at the spot where there was an old scar. She said: "They cut out something there." Henceforward she was able to read out loud, but stopped dead before words beginning with the letters A, B, and W. One day she spoke of a certain butcher who had threatened to cut off her nose, and (again carrying her hand to the scar on her neck) she said that "they cut out my adenoids." Dr. B., who had performed the operation, had made her say "Ah" and had hurt her ("hurt" in German = "Weh"). Thus, the recollection of this scene of violence had left behind it a fear of those three letters. The analysis had to be continued some time along these lines before the lack of reading facility could be remedied. At the time when a

126 THE MIND OF THE CHILD

little brother was born, Anna's people noticed that the difficulty in reading became more pronounced. After the birth of the baby, Anna had been greatly frightened at the sight of the blood-stained linen used by her mother, but she had not ventured to ask any one for an explanation. Then, while the baby was being washed, Anna had noticed and examined its genital organs. She would like to have possessed similar appendages, and at the same time she was sorry that the little brother was not a little sister instead. Anna fancied that by cutting off these organs, boys could be transformed into girls. As soon as she was told the truth concerning this matter, she began to read quite fluently.[1]

The mutilation complex in a girl is perhaps less marked by its intensity than by the quality it assumes, for a young girl has her own particular way of reacting to the infantile theory concerning the differences between the sexes, and this reaction was especially in evidence in the concluding passages of the case just recorded: the wish that a boy might be deprived of his virile organs, and the counter desire to possess those organs herself.

It would be foolish to ascribe the system of complexes we are about to study entirely to "penis envy," as we might do were we to accept all the deductions of certain authors. Nevertheless, we have to admit that among a certain number of little girls this "envy" takes precedence. My patient Maud who used to contemplate herself in a mirror in order to see "if it was growing," remained for a long time humiliated at the thought of this anatomical difference between herself and her brothers. At one phase of her life this "envy" found expression in the following picturesque form: her father had an arch-

[1] Hans Zulliger, "Revüe Française de Psychanalyse," vol. iii, p. 743.

A GIRL OR A BOY?

bishop as friend, and the family sometimes went to visit this dignitary who was wont to smoke a huge cigar, much to the child's amazement; she frequently dreamed that she possessed a cigar of the kind and stuck it between her legs; one day she plucked up sufficient courage to ask the archbishop to give her one of his cigars; alas, he only replied with the fatal words, "but women don't smoke"; all the following night she spent in weeping; she told her father that she wanted to play with the cigar, and when asked "what sort of a game do you want to play with it," she became confused and did not know what to answer not wishing at any price to tell a lie; then she reflected that the simplest thing to do was to take a cigar from the archbishop's box, but since she hated the idea of being a thief, she thrust the temptation aside; for three years she was tortured by the thought of how to obtain the cigar she coveted, until at last she got over her obsession. Naturally enough, her "envy" took on other and less obvious forms in the sequel.

A little girl who becomes aware that "it isn't growing" seeks to explain her deficiency by ascribing the failure to masturbation, thus adding a sense of guilt to her troubles and intensifying the situation. In general until early childhood is over and done with, a little girl never quite gives up hope of becoming a boy. One of my pupils is a teacher in an infant school. A girl of four is to leave Geneva and spend the holidays in the country. The teacher explains that when her little pupil returns she will be four and a half years old. To which the child makes answer: "Oh, I'll be quite big by then and perhaps I'll have turned into a boy." When a girl at last resigns herself to her fate she still continues, quite unconsciously, to find all sorts of equivalents for virile attributes. Adler calls this the "characteristic form of the masculine

128 THE MIND OF THE CHILD

protest"; in Freud's terminology it is "female psychical homosexuality." Marie Bonaparte terms the psychological reaction among women "the virility complex."[1] For my part, I usually refer to it as "the Diana complex."

As soon as a girl begins to go to school we have ample opportunity for studying the important role played by the Diana complex in female adolescent life. Karl Pipal furnishes us with the results of a most ingenious investigation made by a teacher who set the boys in his class to write an essay entitled "I would like to be a girl" and the girls "I would like to be a boy." Out of the twenty boys, eighteen declared they would rather be anything in the whole world than a girl; whilst out of the twenty-two girls, nineteen replied that they would prefer to be a boy or would willingly accept being a boy. We need make no further comment.[2]

The children forming the class described by Pipal ranged in age from twelve to fourteen years. It is worth our while to study in detail the answers given by these forty-two girls and boys. One boy wrote, "girls are not normal," another "I want to remain a boy so as to be free" and he adds "God preserve me from ever having to mind brats!" As for the girls, Melanie declares that boys are nicer and will not have to suffer so much as women. Frederika thinks that if only she had been a boy her mother would have loved her more. Leopoldine thinks that a boy's work in life is of greater interest, and she exclaims: "But it's all Mother's fault! Why did she not make a boy of me?" Marianne would rather be a boy because she would be cleverer at her lessons.

[1] Marie Bonaparte, Prophylaxie infantile des névroses, p. 13.
[2] Karl Pipal, Er möchte ein Mädchen sein.

A GIRL OR A BOY? 129

Milna, if only she were a lad, would frighten the girls! Lucy, on the other hand, would like to be a boy because then she would no longer be afraid of boys.

I, myself, undertook to make enquiries along the same lines at a school in Geneva. The children were less numerous and their ages varied from six to sixteen. This is how the question was phrased: Are you satisfied with being a boy; would you have preferred to be a girl, and why? Thus for the boys. For the girls I turned it the other way about: Are you satisfied with being a girl; would you have preferred to be a boy, and why? The results I secured go to confirm those obtained by Pipal. Out of seven boys, six are positive that they want to remain boys. Out of four girls, three would like to be boys, though one of the three has her reservations. The fourth girl starts her essay with the words: "I am very contented with my fate"—but this declaration must not lead us astray; in a moment we shall see what she really means.

Here are the boys' answers: "I am so happy at being a boy," writes a youngster of eleven, "that I am wondering why they have asked me why I like to be a boy better than being a girl. First of all, a girl has no power of observation. . . . You will never see a girl admiring something because it is beautiful. . . . All great geniuses have been men. A girl will always think first of her dresses rather than give herself the trouble to create works of permanent value for the good of mankind. . . . A girl is so shy, and never feels at her ease. One never can tell what she is thinking about. The only thing they really like to do is to sneak into a corner and whisper secrets or tell one another sly tales. Truly girls are not at all interesting. . . . I am so glad to be a boy that for nothing on earth would I consent to be a girl even for five

130   THE MIND OF THE CHILD

minutes." A little chap of six tells us that he wants to remain a boy, but he does not know why. A lad of twelve and a half considers that boys are much freer than girls. Another, eleven and a half, prefers to remain as he is because he has never been a girl. Yet another, eleven years of age, opines, "Since I was born a boy, what is the use of preferring to be a girl? . . . A boy is frank and strong, but a girl is a sneak and cowardly and she has no strength. . . . A man is free!" He winds up his essay with a harangue on coquetry among girls. Another lad of the same age, starts off with: "Thank God for making me a boy and not a girl!" His arguments (which we shall find repeated in the girls' essays) are as follows: "First of all a skirt is not practical, one can't twist about freely and kick up one's leg in a skirt, it's a great hindrance. Girls are frail. . . . No, quite seriously, it is not practical to be a girl, they can't possibly climb trees. When they are riding a bicycle they have constantly to be seeing to their skirts for every time they move their skirts rumple up. . . . They fancy themselves men's superiors, but they make a threefold mistake. . . ." Fresh paragraph: "I am very glad I am a boy." Another new paragraph: "I am thoroughly happy to be what I am."

Now for the girls' compositions. One girl, eleven years old, considers that boys are "better treated," and "so far they have done everything"; nevertheless, she prefers being a girl because they are better able to look after themselves and are gentler. (As a fact, this child has a brother who is two years older than she, and she reaps her revenge on him by managing things better than he does.) A girl of fifteen is satisfied with her lot, but gives the following reasons: "The greatest happiness, in my view, is to remain a young unmarried girl because then

A GIRL OR A BOY? 131

she never becomes the slave of her husband; she is free." Thus we see that she is, like all the others, up in arms against the fate of women. Then she tells why, on the whole, it is preferable to be a man, and contrasts man's stability with woman's waywardness. A girl of sixteen writes that she would rather be a boy "because he is free," and is not bothered with skirts and things when climbing trees or doing gym; boys' games, too, appear to her more interesting. In the fourth girl, fourteen years old, we again encounter the skirt disability, only the grumble is couched in a very simple-minded way considering the writer's age. Indeed, her naivety of language would be incomprehensible were it not for the unconscious symbolism it expresses. "I should love to be a boy, because girls have to worry about their clothes. If anything is spilled on a light-coloured dress it looks dirty at once, or if a girl is wearing a flimsy kind of frock she has to take care all the time lest it gets soiled. Now boys and men always wear dark clothes."

From the point of view of the unconscious, the argument just recorded is not lacking in good sense. It masks a motif which is constantly met with in the course of psychoanalysis, the motif of defloration. The "soiled gown" or the "torn gown" is not merely found with great frequency to occur in dreams. It is likewise encountered in legends and folk-lore. We have a beautiful illustration of it in the story of Tristan and Iseult. The defloration motif inevitably awakens the infantile motif of castration. One of the boys' answers bears on the same theme when he writes, "girls are frail." There is likewise a direct reference to an unconscious motif connected with the same complex, and this reference is made over and over again, namely that men are "free" and girls are "shy." Sometimes the "freedom" or the "shyness"

THE MIND OF THE CHILD

are to be understood from the angle of moral conduct, and at other times they must be interpreted in the physical sense. "Shyness," being "ill at ease," "cumbered by a skirt," etc., are in actual fact intimately related to the motif of being "bound," "tied up," "ligatured," and this latter motif as I have already shown is an equivalent of mutilation. The other arguments adduced by my young people represent conscious elaborations of these themes, elaborations which are mere variants and in some cases more explicit.

The answer given by the fourth girl is worthy of closer examination. This young person, having expressed herself clearly as to the light-coloured dresses worn by members of her sex, consoles herself for the fate imposed upon women by the following childish reflection: "I am very fond of little children and I am pleased that I shall always be able to have them near me. Men, of course, cannot always be with children, because they have to go out to work. A woman would do everything for her baby; she is so fond of it that sometimes when she is tired of life and thinks she will kill herself she changes her mind when her eyes fall on her children and then she says: 'It is for you that I am going on living.'"

This argument is a faithful reproduction of what goes on in the unconscious. Frequently, in the course of analyses, a woman or a girl suffering from the Diana complex will find compensation for the mutilation indignity by the idea that she has or may have a child. Analysts express this by the rather simple but none the less effective formula: an unconscious equivalence is set up between the phallus and the baby. A girl, and in later life a woman, can always compensate herself for the inferiority imposed upon her by her sex when she

A GIRL OR A BOY?

recalls that no man can have a baby. This is why the girl who would fain be a boy is able to renounce this desire once she has become aware of her maternal role, and this explains such an answer as the following, which was given me by a young woman of twenty-two: "When I was ten years old I wanted to be a boy, for above all I admired their bodily strength. Also I would like to have been a doctor, and it seemed to me almost impossible that a girl could ever succeed in such a wish. At fifteen, I changed my mind, and ever since that I have been quite content to be what I am." The desire to become a doctor is very significant, and is typical. A doctor, so far as a child is concerned, is more often than not the person who procures the baby for the mother. In addition, he knows all there is to know about birth.

These considerations will help us to understand why another investigation among a different class of pupils produced what seemed at first sight contradictory results. Here we had to do with the children in M. W. Perret's co-educational school at Neuchâtel. Dr. G. Richard undertook to make the investigation, and to furnish me with a report. In this establishment the young folk must be living in a veritable paradise, for nearly all expressed themselves as satisfied with their lot. This is how the question was put: "Some boys say they would like to be girls; some girls say they would like to be boys. Some declare they are quite satisfied to be what they are. If you could choose, if you could be born again, which would you choose to be, a boy or a girl?" Out of nine boys, eight preferred to remain as they were. Out of eleven girls, nine were satisfied, one wished to be a boy, and one declared "it is all the same to me." No one can say for sure that the conscious answers thus given

134 THE MIND OF THE CHILD

correspond to the unconscious desires of these young people! Nevertheless we may be permitted to express our contentment at such universal satisfaction on the part of these boys and girls, and to declare that such a state of mind signifies a very fine result from an educational point of view. It will be of interest to the reader to learn what the master himself thought about the environment he had succeeded in creating for the children under his charge.

In this class [he said, in substance], the balance between the female element and the male is well established both as regards intellectual ability and physical development. The children have never been forcibly segregated on account of their sex; the girls have not been made to sit at desks on one side of the class-room while the boys were relegated to the other. Lads and lasses have invariably worked and played shoulder to shoulder in the most spontaneous and natural way. Animal breeding, anatomical questions, social considerations, all have gone to show (without any interference on the part of grown-ups) the important role played by the female in nature. When the girls approached the age of puberty, the phenomena of growth merely served to enhance the notion of the creative mother, whereas the utility of the father was never mentioned simply because no questions were asked regarding this matter.

It seemed to him [he went on], that this state of affairs, this sort of co-education—which might perhaps have to be modified when the children were somewhat older—, was eminently desirable; and, indeed, that true education was only possible when the above-described spirit was general. Beyond question this attitude towards the sexual problem could not arise under the conditions that

A GIRL OR A BOY? 135

prevailed in schools where the sexes were segregated in the traditional manner. However that may be, let us turn to consider the children's answers.

The boys' answers are similar to those already reported from other sources, the only difference being that they express no disdain for the girls. Boys' games, and masculine occupations are preferred by the lads; some wish to travel (to be free from ties); another is content merely to wear breeches because they are more practical; yet another is proud that at some future date he will be a voter. The girls' answers are more novel. Among the nine girls who express satisfaction with their lot, one is pleased at being able to do "more delicate kinds of work," a second admires "feminine gentleness," a third thinks that "long hair is beautiful." But the remaining six base their preference upon the idea of motherhood. Some of them add to these desiderata a liking for housework; one says that she has the privilege of not having to go to war. Still, the baby occupies the first place: a girl may become a mother or a grandmother, "because a grandmother can pet and spoil her grandchildren and may even manage things so as to take care of little babies."—"I would like to have babies and to be a mother."—"I would like to have the whole charge of small children," and so forth and so on.

The girl who said she would like to be a boy wanted to be a peasant so as to milk the cows. The one who expressed indifference, writing "it is all the same to me," kept the scales evenly balanced between being a girl "so as to have a baby" and being a boy "so as to be strong in order to work hard." Nay more, this constant preoccupation with motherhood comes out even in the boys' essays. One of them gives among his reasons for preferring to remain as he is, "I shall not have to suffer on account

136 THE MIND OF THE CHILD

of a baby," whereas one lad who wished to be a girl wrote, "a girl manufactures, . . ." then corrected this to "a girl makes little girls and boys. Men do not make children."

In the master's summary of the matter, one reason he mentions for the attitude taken by the children under his care is especially worth emphasising. He says that when girls approach the age of puberty, the phenomena of growth enhance the notion of the creative mother. These youngsters, the boys as well as the girls, are obviously impressed with the idea; and it is this, more than anything else, which seems to reconcile the girls to their allotted sex. Nothing could fit better into the psychoanalytic system, which posits the equivalence of virility on the one hand and childbearing on the other: "being a girl so as to have a baby," and "being a boy so as to be strong . . . ; it's all the same to me."

And yet this can never really be a matter of indifference to a girl. If it be true that a girl can find consolation (a compensation of the simplest and most natural kind) for her presumable inferiority, it is none the less true that maternity with its attendant pains and enslavement may appear to her as an added insult to her sex. Which aspect of the situation is going to predominate? Doubtless much depends upon circumstances. If the second is predominant, the Diana complex, far from finding its solution in the idea of motherhood will be intensified by that idea.

The dread of motherhood may be aggravated by the attitude of the parents. A mother said to her little daughter of five: "If you children knew what it was to be a mother, you would be a great deal more appreciative of your mother, and would think twice before becoming mothers

A GIRL OR A BOY?

yourselves."[1] The dread of motherhood thus implanted became a persistent terror. In many girls, and in many married women, the fear we are now considering is practically identical with a flight from womanhood, and is one of the typical symptoms of an unresolved Diana complex. We often find that a woman is equally averse from motherhood and from marriage, both of which are regarded as aspects of the same degrading servitude. That was the case with Isadora who, speaking of marriage, remarked: "I shall never be such a fool as to marry." Her Diana complex had been intensified by various conditions. She was one of a large family, and her mother had always worked very hard. Isadora, being the eldest daughter, had to help in mothering the younger children. This kept alive the enmity which, during infancy, she had conceived against her little rivals, and it accentuated her hostility to the idea of herself bearing children. Furthermore, the prospect of having to lead a life like her mother's came into conflict with the girl's strong spectacular and aesthetic trends. (The reader will recall her motif of the veil.) The motif of "the woman with a grievance," which will subsequently be discussed, was also well-marked in this girl.

After the onset of puberty, the Diana complex is a common cause of menstrual disorders, which in such cases must be interpreted as a refusal of womanhood. In some instances we shall note a delay in the establishment of menstruation, in others the flow will be irregular and painful. In addition, during the monthly periods, there may be fits of ill-temper, malice, and so on. These, likewise, can mainly be accounted for as the expression of an unconscious protest against the slavery, the bleeding wound, of womanhood, which infallibly renews the

[1] Crichton Miller, The New Psychology and the Teacher, p. 110.

138 THE MIND OF THE CHILD

buried memories of the castration complex of earlier days.

The Diana complex is, in a way, responsible for kleptomania and petty thieving among girls. Any kind of theft has to be interpreted as being an act of assertion of one's claims on society (a "taking what belongs to you by right" as the anarchists would say). A child who steals is one who fancies it has been wrongly deprived of one thing or another. In a little girl, the proneness to steal can easily be accounted for by her claim to virility, which her sex has deprived her of. The objects she steals are very often those which are associated with virility and even with the male organ. This would explain why kleptomania is more frequently encountered among female patients.[1]

Characteristic of the Diana complex are the tomboy manners of certain little girls, their independent behaviour accompanied by a certain pig-headedness. One of Adler's cases, from earliest childhood, was boyish in all her gestures, preferred to play boys' games, invariably acted the male part in charades, etc., was domineering, and so on. In addition to these traits, she had the habits of wetting her bed and sucking her thumb, habits which Adler interprets as being special signs of obstinacy. At puberty, her mother's explanations of what was happening to her, in conjunction with what she spoke of as a dread of "falling," induced alarm lest she should have to give up her "virile" role. Her anxiety in this respect was intensified by her ignorance of the true facts of the sexual life. Later, she refused to get married, or rather, she refused to "accept" the idea of marriage, became neurotic and had palpitation of the heart and various other forms of nervous anxiety,

[1] Cf. Hugo Staub, Psychoanalyse und Strafrecht, p. 449.

A GIRL OR A BOY? 139

so that she was thus guaranteed against having to take a husband. Her bad state of health gave her an excuse for never encountering men, or at least, since she did not leave the house except when accompanied by her sister, she felt herself protected from male advances and from sexual temptations.[1]

The motif of being "protected against male advances" is often met with when our patients suffer from the Diana complex, and may take very various forms. Sometimes it would appear as if the girl found a refuge in her own virility so as to protect herself against man's assaults. Crichton Miller shows how this mechanism was at work in a girl of ten who came under his care. In other respects she was normal, but had a strong personality and totally lacked any feminine attributes. She dreamed that she was out walking with a man; she saw a lorry crowded with "wicked men" coming towards her; she was frightened and clung to her friend for protection. Miller interprets this dream as follows: the "friendly man" is her own masculinity which the child is endeavouring to develop in herself, and which is to be her safeguard against men.[2] The interpretation is a plausible one, though it in no way is exhaustive, for this male protector may possess certain attributes of the father, and the effort to be "virile" reveals a desire to become "identified" with the father (identification in the psychoanalytical sense of the term). But the whole case as recorded by our author is in keeping with one of the answers furnished during our investigation among schoolchildren, the case of the girl who would gladly be a boy so as no longer to be afraid of boys.

[1] Adler and Furtmüller, Heilen und Bilden, p. 70.
[2] Crichton Miller, The New Psychology and the Teacher, p. 108.

140 THE MIND OF THE CHILD

The motif of protection becomes exaggerated, naturally enough, if the girl has been the object of an assault. Such is the position of affairs in another case recorded by Miller. The child had been exposed to an unrighteous act by a man when she was nine years old. Later in life she became a trained nurse, which was a means of gratifying her maternal instinct without having to marry —but an additional attraction, no doubt, may have been the notion that a nurse's uniform is, more or less, a safeguard against male aggression. There can be no doubt that the various societies for the protection of young girls are, in part, organised by persons in whom the Diana complex has taken a kindred form. (There is, of course, a relationship between this motif of protection and the mental attitude of the woman with a grievance.)[1]

It would be extremely interesting to follow up the development of these two girls, and to watch the evolution of the "imago" of the protector. A fairly normal method is that after the girl has sought to develop her personal virility, to become her own protector, she goes on to project this idea on to a man who is to play the part of "bosom friend." Such a projection must often take place at the moment when the girl begins to fall in love. Thus the Diana complex would find a satisfactory issue, and a projection of the sort may play an important part in the psychological genesis of the family.

Though I may be reproached for referring to homosexuality as a derivative of the Diana complex, we have nevertheless to recognise that the complex is capable of finding expression in more or less latent homosexual tendencies or it may accentuate these tendencies. Fear

[1] Crichton Miller, The New Psychology and the Teacher, p. 106.

A GIRL OR A BOY?

of men conjoined to an unconscious desire to play a virile part in life may lead the adolescent girl to fall passionately in love with other members of her sex. Such "flames," whether the object be a schoolmate or one of the teachers, are of so frequent occurrence as to have become regarded as "common form" in the psychology of girls in their teens. Young persons of this age are often moved to write epistles like the following: "Why, dear Miss X., are you ashamed of writing to me? You know that a word from you makes me happy. If only we had been alone, I hardly know what I would have done. Really, and without exaggerating in the least, I believe I would have hugged and kissed you to death. . . ." Or again: "If you could know all your eyes tell me in their dumb language, and how eloquent their silence can be. . . . There are but two places in the world where I feel I am not being watched: in church and in bed. I can then do what I like. Well, I just cry my eyes out, and let my heart go its own way. . . . Dear Miss R., if you wish to comfort me a little, do please continue to look at me from time to time with those loving eyes of yours. . . ."[1]

There comes a point at which such "flames" are not free from danger and when sensuality puts in an appearance. Then the girl will have dreams similar to one cited by Crichton Miller in his book on *The New Psychology and the Teacher* (p. 115): "I dreamed that Mrs. X. was holding up a bunch of roses of transcendental beauty. She took them out one by one and dropped them to the ground. As each touched the earth it burst into flame. I was fascinated by the miracle, until suddenly I realised that I was surrounded by flames, and I woke

[1] These letters are quoted by Antoine Marro in *La puberté*, p. 64.

142   THE MIND OF THE CHILD

in terror." Such flames of adolescence do not always scorch or burn; indeed, they are often quite harmless; but they may, nevertheless, forebode the development of homosexual relationships. The fact that homosexuality is more frequent among women than among men is due to the Diana complex. This fact merely recapitulates, on another plane it is true, the results of enquiries made during the school age, i.e. that the female is more prone than the male to desire a change of sex. I have in mind the case of a young woman who, like the girl spoken of by Crichton Miller, was induced by the Diana complex to become a sick-nurse—while, thanks to this same complex, she entered into a homosexual liaison. When she had been psychoanalysed the homosexuality vanished, and with it the desire for a nurse's vocation.

Sexual inhibition (frigidity) is also more often met with in women than in men, and this phenomenon, too, is usually an outcome of the same complex. It has been said that frigidity results from a latent homosexual trend; but, to my way of thinking, frigidity and homosexuality are both of them consequent upon the Diana complex.

If this complex does not find an issue during the years of adolescence by such simple ways as "desire for a baby," "protective love," etc., or if, on the other hand, it does not result in declared homosexuality, a neurosis will be the most probable result. I have already instanced several forms such neuroses may take. The feeling at the root of them all is that of an irreparable lack, of incompleteness—an idea which is embodied in the legend of the Danaids and analogous myths. Adler records a case which admirably illustrates this connexion. His patient was, as a child, inspired with the ideal of "suffering everything" with great fortitude "like an

A GIRL OR A BOY? 143

Indian"; next she wanted to become "like Joan of Arc"; later on, she refused to marry, and at this period she was incapable of completing any sort of work. Specially troublesome was a piece of needlework which she felt compelled to unpick as soon as done. Her associations showed plainly enough that her affective life was dominated by what psychoanalysts have termed "the Penelope myth" (this lady being merely another kind of Danaid who had to unravel every night the tissue she had woven in the daytime, in order to keep suitors at bay). Such encounters with old-time myths and legends are very general and disclose a situation rooted in the "collective unconscious."[1]

I do not wish to imply that the situation we are studying is incurable. Quite otherwise! A girl may find release through sublimation, by means of certain activities which as a rule are more in a man's province than in a woman's; she may set herself to learn Latin, for instance, or she may go in for a medical career, or take up a sport, or become a Girl Guide. Cecilia, a girl whose Diana complex forced her to be in constant rebellion against her environment, vacillated between medicine, gymnastics, and aviation as a profession. "Women's rights" and the struggle for "the vote" constitute a more or less happy outlet for certain feminine natures. Sometimes the activities verge upon the neurotic, but in a fair number of individuals they constitute a genuine form of sublimation. Such activities, which are undoubtedly an outcome of the Diana complex, tend to act as corrective to the conditions which would otherwise become aggravated by this complex. Adler considers that the inferior position of the female sex in our present-day society cultivates the "masculine protest" among women, and is mainly

[1] Adler and Furtmüller, Heilen und Bilden, p. 114.

144 THE MIND OF THE CHILD

responsible for the neuroses from which so many of them suffer.[1]

Whatever the cause, we find that the Diana complex exists universally among women, though in some cases it is more marked and in others less. Where it is most obvious, the subject is not always as conscious of its presence as in less developed cases. The sense of guilt may mask it, as in the case of girls who have been made to feel ashamed of their tomboy ways, or when homosexual tendencies have come to play a leading role, or when the young person has got accustomed to look upon her desires for virility and independence as an equivalent and a symbol of forbidden fruit and as opposed to the normal. Thus the most precise aspects of the complex may be repressed, may be masked by the assumption of a completely contrary attitude, and they may only peep out from time to time so disguised as to be hardly recognisable. Linette, from earliest childhood, suffered from a very marked Diana complex. When, at the age of seventeen, she was asked whether she would like to be a boy, she protested that on no conceivable pretext would she choose to be a boy. But when I asked her, "Which animal would you prefer to be?" she answered without hesitation, "A stag," and went on to justify herself by saying that "a stag is so free!" The stag has been described as a phallic emblem, and this explanation seems peculiarly appropriate in Linette's case; in addition, it leads us straightway into the Diana myth. Later in this book I shall deal more fully with Linette's symptoms and their intimate connexion with the legends surrounding this goddess of the woods and the chase.

The Diana complex, a fundamental trait of feminine

[1] Adler and Furtmüller, Heilen und Bilden, p. 114.

A GIRL OR A BOY? 145

psychology, manifests itself throughout the works of women authors. In these works, transpiercing "screen memories" and other elaborate symbolisms, we are confronted with the infantile situations which constitute the bases of this complex, such as: comparisons between boys and girls, early curiosity aroused by the sexual life, mutilation, or the quality of femininity looked upon as a punishment, and so forth. In illustration, I will quote a passage from Colette's book *Sido* (p. 45), which is an admirable example of my contention, and one which I can leave the reader to interpret without further comment on my part.

"My mother . . . put all her ingenuity to the test while questioning me:

" 'It is most annoying . . . but I cannot remember whether I have planted a family of crocus bulbs in this bed or the chrysalis of a hawk-moth . . .'

" 'You need only dig them up to see . . .'

"Quickly her hand thrust forward, arresting mine:

" 'On no account must you do that,' she cried. 'If it turns out to have been the chrysalis, it will die on being exposed to the air; if what I planted were crocus bulbs, the tiny white shoots will wither, and our labours will have to be started all over again. You quite understand? You are not to touch them.'

" 'All right, Mother.'

"As she spoke, her face which had been flushed with the ardours of faith and of universal curiosity, disappeared behind a mask at once older, more resigned and gentle. She knew well enough I should not resist the desire to know, any more than in her childhood she had been able to withstand such a temptation. Was I not her own little girl, already, child though I was, on the look out for the shock of a new discovery, already seeking that

K

146   THE MIND OF THE CHILD

accelerated beating of the heart, that catch in the breath, that lonely intoxication of the treasure-seeker? . . .

"I went off on the quiet, and grubbed about in the garden until I found, arising out of the seed-leaf, the virile shoot which the springtide was forcing out of its sheath. I interfered in the blind destiny the rusty black chrysalis was following, and I hurled the creature from its deathlike slumber into final destruction.

" 'You don't understand. . . . You can't understand. . . . You are nothing but a little murderess, eight years old. . . . You don't understand anything about the feelings of creatures that are craving for life. . . .' "

Another example is culled from a charming book of child verses written by Madeleine Ley. The collection is entitled *Petites voix*, and the poem in question goes by the name of "Chanson de juillet."

> J'ai tant regardé la rivière
> et le soleil
> et le doux ciel
> que j'ai laché mon roseau vert.
> Il est allé dans l'eau si claire,
> il est allé jusqu' à la mer !
>
> J'ai voulu cueillir aussitôt
> un autre roseau si beau,
> mais je me suis coupée aux herbes,
> mes cheveux ont traîné dans l'eau . . .
> (Ah ! rendez-moi donc mon roseau
> et ma prairie et ma rivière !)
>
> J'ai vu passer le fils du roi ;
> il m'a dit : "Ma belle, pourquoi,
> le long de la jolie rivière,
> pourquoi pleures-tu là ?"
> Ha ! ha !
> C'était le fils du roi.

A GIRL OR A BOY?   147

Il m'a dit: "Viens avec moi,
et si tu veux tu seras reine.
Tu auras pour filer la laine
un rouet d'or et un fuseau
aussi leger qu'un os d'oiseau!"

Las! je suis reine et prisonnière
dans un royaume merveilleux.
Mon coeur, mon coeur a tant de peine,
pleurez, pleurez, mes yeux.
Ou sont mes soeurs et ma rivière?
J'ai perdu mon roseau vert.

[I looked so long upon the river
and up to the sun
and the quiet sky
that my green bulrush slipped from my hand
and floated away on the limpid stream,
floated away to the far sea strand!

At once I wished to gather
another rush as fine,
but I cut my fingers on the blades,
my long hair was caught by the waters . . .
(Ah, give me back my bulrush
and my meadow and my stream!)

The king's son came riding by;
he said to me: "My Pretty, why,
along this lovely river bank,
why is it that you cry?"
Ha! ha!
He was the king's son.

Again he said: "Come, live with me,
and, if you will, my queen shall be.
If you would spin I'll give you woo
and a golden wheel and a spool
as light as a birdie's wing."

THE MIND OF THE CHILD

Alas, I am queen and a captive
in a realm of faëry.
But ah, my heart, my heart is heavy,
weep, weep sad eyes.
Where are now my sisters and my river?
I have lost my bulrush green.]

CHAPTER SEVEN

BIRTH

1. *Children's Theories*

A CHILD guesses or is told at a very early age that the mother is the giver of life; but children have theories of their own in this matter. It cannot understand where the father comes in; nor does it attach any significance to the part the genital organs play. This twofold lack of knowledge is made up for by children forming their own theories, such as that the mother brings a baby into the world after eating certain food—this supposition arising out of reading (or being told) fairy tales. Erna, a girl of six and a half years wonders whether the baby is expelled by way of the mouth or the breast. Of one thing she is certain, however, and this is that would-be mothers have to drink milk and eat white bread. During the war her mother had no babies, and this Erna can only explain by attributing the fact to the lack of suitable food.[1] Many children fancy that birth takes place through the navel or the anus. A boy of six was given a full explanation of the phenomenon of birth. The information seemed to come as something quite new to him. When asked, "Did you not already know about it? " he answered, "Oh yes, but I thought it came out of the bottom." The excretory and the genital organs often get confused into one single cloaca. Truth to tell, the child's imagination never gets seriously to work on the subject, so that identical theories are met with time and again. Those enumerated above are, according to Freud, the most prevalent.[2]

[1] Ernst Schneider, Zur Sexualforschung des Kindes, p. 203.
[2] Freud, Trois essais sur la théorie de la sexualité, p. 93.

THE MIND OF THE CHILD

These birth theories, so general among children, are usually forgotten as the youngsters grow up, or, rather, they are repressed. Psychoanalysis had first to come to the rescue in order to bring them back to the surface and to discover how almost universal they are among the young. The recollection of them is often masked behind a screen memory.

Isadora, for example, tells me the following anecdote from her earliest years. Her family had removed to another home, away in the country. The village could be approached from two sides; by a little wood, and by a stretch of open country. Isadora had always been convinced that the first time the family had come to the village to settle into the new house, they had taken the open-country road, and she was greatly astonished when in the sequel she was told that she had made a mistake, since they had come by way of the little wood. Her younger sister, too, laboured under the same conviction, and the two girls had frequently talked the matter over. This memory always makes Isadora vibrate with a strange and inexplicable emotion. As a matter of fact, the two means of access to the village symbolised respectively the anal region and the genital parts. The screen memory merely served to disguise an anal theory of birth which in subsequent years was shown to be inaccurate. From the content of this screen memory, I thought myself justified in inferring that the little sister had been Isadora's chosen companion for investigations into the mystery of birth. My surmise was confirmed by subsequent revelations.

Zulliger gives a similar instance of two girls, aged eighteen and sixteen respectively, who up to those ages had been deliberately kept in ignorance of the sexual life. The mother wished now to enlighten her girls, but

BIRTH 151

to begin with she asked the elder tentatively, "How do you think babies come into the world?" The girl answered that she thought the child was brought by an angel. Touched by so much innocence, the mother got no further that day. Some weeks later, the girl confided to her mother that she could not get any sleep at night for worrying as to which way the angel entered a house. "Do, please, tell me whether it comes in by the front or the back, by the kitchen or the hall."[1]

Infantile theories may not merely be held after childhood in the form of screen memories, but may also continue under the form of symptoms, for the content of a fantasy may be a theory that is highly tinged with affect. Thus Wilfrid Lay, quoting one of Pfister's cases, tells us of a "girl, sixteen years old, who suffered regularly at her menstrual period from vomiting. It was found that, when a child, she had believed that children were born through the mouth. After enlightenment in this particular the symptom immediately ceased."[2]

From the earliest days of childhood, the queerest conclusions concerning birth may be encountered at every turn. Bleuler had to do with a boy of three who showed a special dislike for the word "yesterday" and habitually replaced it by the word "to-morrow." The child's mind was preoccupied with the enigma "something is happening to-day and to-morrow it will have happened yesterday." Further examination made clear the fact that the above problem was closely related in the boy's mind with the riddle of birth. He asked: "Mummy, do tell me, doesn't the evening grow out of the morning?" He knew nothing as yet about animal reproduction, but he had learned about plant life, and, basing his theories upon

[1] Hans Zulliger, Eltern, Schule und sexuelle Aufklärung, p. 230.
[2] Wilfrid Lay, Man's Unconscious Conflict, p. 254.

THE MIND OF THE CHILD

this knowledge, he concluded that man propagated his kind in similar fashion and the days likewise. These ideas were mixed with magic in his mind—as is suitable to that stage of the thinking process at which he had arrived by the age of three. He very much wanted to be a big boy, and one day he discovered a means for the attainment of his desire: he would become a magician and then he would simply have to say: "Open, button!" All these preoccupations are masked behind his uneasiness in respect of the word "yesterday."[1]

This case makes one realise how very early in life the great questions concerning origins and causes, those perennial mysteries of childhood's days, are associated with the enigma of birth. This association of ideas is never solved, for in adult life we tend to react in regard to metaphysical problems in precisely the same way as in childhood to the problem of birth. The transition on to the metaphysical plane is, indeed, likewise effected at an early age. My own son, the eldest, was between five and six years old when he asked me off-hand: "What was there before there was anything at all?"

Anxiety and fear are also close associates of the birth complex. The enigma of birth is, unaided, impressive enough to cause a sense of anxiety in those who try to solve it; and from the heart-searchings it arouses, the subject insensibly passes on to those dreams and fantasies wherein he finds himself in a confined space which is a more or less faithful representation of the maternal womb. From this confined space the subject has to pass by a narrow passage and with difficulty into the open, and this act is invariably accompanied by a sense of dread. Are we to interpret such dreams and fantasies as being a kind of dim recollection of that initial fear which must affect

[1] Bleuler, Natürliche Symbolik und Kosmogonie.

BIRTH 153

every one of us at the hour of birth, a fear so eloquently described by Lucretius in a few lines of his celebrated poem? There is no denying the fact that a baby directly it is born presents all the physiological symptoms of dread, and Freud has emphasised the existence of this particular phenomenon in his *Introduction to Psychoanalysis*. Rank, pushing the idea to its ultimate conclusions, attributes a decisive role, in the psychology of the unconscious, to the birth trauma; other authors, again, interpret the very frequent allusions to birth as a "symbolical expression." However this may be (and it is a thorny point to decide), there is no denying that the fact exists, solid and irrefutable: birth and dread are inseparable companions.

Nor is it only in the dreams of adults that the typical "birth-dream" is encountered in the course of analysis. Sophie Morgenstern reports a very fine example of a birth-dream told her by a lad of fourteen whom she had under observation. This dream often recurred and caused him great fear. He saw himself in an enormous room from which he could not get out except through a tiny hole hardly large enough for a mouse to creep. Sometimes the exit appeared to be fairly big, but as soon as he advanced towards it, he found it getting smaller and smaller. What makes this case specially worthy of note is that the interpretation of the dream was innocently furnished by the boy himself and not by the analyst. He opined that "the enormous room must be the female organ where the child lies before it is born; the little opening, the opening through which the baby is born." He is the same boy whom I quoted above, as having said that children see far more than grown-ups are apt to suppose."[1]

[1] Sophie Morgenstern, La psychanalyse infantile, p. 71.

THE MIND OF THE CHILD

This typical dream and its variants, again comes to the fore when the subject finds he has to break with his previous way of living and start afresh upon a new and dreaded career. The maternal womb continues to be a symbol of refuge in time of need, as a place to which one can flee from unpleasant duties or too strenuous a life; whilst birth itself, "the narrow passage whence it is difficult to get out," is a symbol for action, audacity, victory over oneself.

Even better than dreams are a child's games, which are strangely analogous to its dreams. A child loves to play at making castles, tunnels, grottoes in the sand, and to creep into these constructions. Of course such games may be nothing more than unconscious memories of the life of our primitive ancestors. Nevertheless, psychoanalysts attribute a symbolical significance to this form of play, finding therein analogous situations to those found in the dreams which are their counterpart: dreams of "birth," or, on the other hand dreams of "taking refuge," of "returning to the mother's womb." Pfeifer, among others, has drawn attention to the shape children give to their various forms of shelter, to the openings they make in these buildings, and have thus shown anatomical similarities, which are at times of dubious worth while at other times they are incontestable.

The whole system we have just been discussing seems to be activated in the lower planes of the unconscious by this search for a refuge, a shelter from the disagreeables of life. Many an obsession (cautiousness pushed so far as to become a mania, excessive punctiliousness, etc.) is traceable to the search for a refuge as described above; in general, many modes of behaviour, both among children and neurotics, may be derived from the same source. In a great number of cases we have good warrant

BIRTH

155

for giving a preference to this interpretation of certain troubles, and for all practical purposes it suffices to accept the interpretation without more ado. Janet as well as Adler look upon this unconscious "search for a refuge" as a matter of supreme importance. Nevertheless, if the analysis is carried a stage further, we soon become aware that in yet deeper layers of the unconscious this hunting after security is a symbol of the search for the mother, the maternal refuge, i.e. the mother's womb.

Let us consider one of Adler's cases. This author is content with the "search for a refuge" interpretation; but I would go deeper. A boy of thirteen has been suffering for three years from a strange inclination to idleness, and has, therefore, not made the progress expected of him in his studies. Adler shows that as the lad approached puberty he felt as though he were surrounded by snares whose nature he could not understand—which only served to frighten him the more. He was, consequently, thrown back upon himself, and, so to speak, set up barricades between himself and life. A passion for reading which became manifest about the same date, was regarded by Adler as part of the "research after security," for, the boy's anxiety in relation to the dangers inherent in puberal development made him seek in encyclopedias for a solution, which in its turn aroused a passionate love of books.

In view of the relatively conscious plane to which Adler deliberately confines himself in this case, the interpretation he arrives at is perfectly feasible. But it is easy to complete the picture by having recourse to a deeper explanation based upon the birth complex. Adler reports this case with a most commendable wealth of detail, and I cannot but urge other authors to follow so admirable an example, and not to be content with merely adducing such facts as go to corroborate their particular theories. In a science as youthful as psychoanalysis, detailed observation is of far greater value than any amount of theory. Precisely because Adler gives us a conscientious and detailed description, we are able to bring to light many characteristic traits which his personal theories fail to take into account, and yet these same traits are, to my way of thinking, of very great interest. First of all, in the course of Adler's investigation, we come upon the fact that the boy was a sleepwalker. Now, in the light of many other observations, we know that somnambulism is usually the symbol of a yearning, of a nostalgia, or, to be precise, of a craving for the mother, for the mother's bed which is gropingly sought for, or, in the last resort, a longing for the mother's womb into which the subject hopes to creep. In the case we are now studying, this typical interpretation is, once again, found to be true. Our young somnambulist wakes up one morning to find himself in the cook's empty bed! The cook, thus chosen to symbolise the mother, is by no means a haphazard choice. A cook, a milkmaid, and so forth is often found, in the course of analyses to represent the mother who tended her baby in earliest childhood, for the mother's function is essentially that of feeding the young. Some analysts have applied the term "mother-food" to this symbolical personage. On the other hand, the lad's study of the encyclopedia is related (almost unquestionably) to another branch of the birth complex, namely curiosity as to the origins of life. These two tendencies—that of flight, or of a "return to the mother's womb," and that of curiosity—tendencies between which no ties could have been foreseen to exist so long as our consideration of them was confined to the plane of the logical consciousness, are here disclosed to be associated,

BIRTH 157

forming an inseparable integer. Birth has been the starting-point of them both, and that is why we can speak of a complex.

The same association is very plainly shown in a case I have reported on elsewhere, that of a boy of fourteen, Bertrand by name, suffering from kleptomania. Analysis disclosed that he had frequent dreams about underground passages, volcanoes, etc. In these dreams, he played the part of a detective, hunting down a thief who on one occasion took refuge in a "mummy's coffin"—the mummy being the image of a foetus. In other dreams, which came in succession to those just mentioned, Bertrand was an explorer in remote parts of the world, such as the North Pole and Central Africa. To sum up, he studied the world, both its surface and its interior; and the associations showed clearly that his actions in such dreams, over-determined, represented at one and the same time his investigations concerning birth and his longing to return to the mother's womb.[1]

This brings us back to our starting-point, the questions a child asks about birth and its theories on the subject. I have given an account of those theories which, in Freud's view, are the commonest. But this is not to say that some children may not entertain other theories than those mentioned. G. H. Graber, for instance, refers to a great number of such hypotheses: that children come from God, from the sky (an angel, the moon, storks), from bushes, a spring, the sea, a forest, or, finally, from the mother's body (breast, back, mouth, anus, navel, vagina).[2]

We can classify all these hypotheses under three heads, as follows:

[1] Ein Fall von Kleptomanie, p. 309.
[2] G. H. Graber, Das Geburtproblem, p. 249.

THE MIND OF THE CHILD

1. the child theories enumerated by Freud;
2. grown-ups' answers to children's questions;
3. an imaginative elaboration of repressed theories.

Theories belonging to these different groups may, moreover, be combined in various ways. Those of the third group, which I am about to consider, are especially apt to be outgrowths of those of the second group. It seems probable, indeed, that some of the answers made by adults to a child's questions, provide the little questioner with materials for the imaginative elaboration of its previous theories, which it has never wholly discarded, but has repressed into the unconscious from disgust, shame, or a sense of guilt. Thereafter, as with every repressed system of ideas, they are replaced in the conscious by fancies of a more acceptable nature, which are sometimes extremely poetical. The reader will recall Zulliger's case previously quoted, when a girl let her fancy run upon thoughts of an angel which came into the house, and wondered whether the visitor entered by the back door or the front. This is obviously an imaginative elaboration in which a primitive child theory is easily recognisable as substratum. In the fancies of the little boy mentioned by Crichton Miller, "sure that the Holy Ghost was a huge gasometer," we cannot fail to recognise the vestiges of an anal theory of birth.[1]

2. *Rebirth: Explanation and Compensation*

Birth fantasies, like all creations of the fancy, have their trend determined by wishes. Barbara Low has pointed out that these fantasies fulfil two functions, that of explanation and that of compensation.[2] Like primitive

[1] The New Psychology and the Teacher, p. 58.
[2] The Unconscious in Action, chapter i.

BIRTH 159

myths, they do not merely serve to gratify curiosity, but also to satisfy other urgent wishes in so far as they provide an escape from some disagreeable reality. This twofold function enables us to understand better the significance of the two lines of thought we are now tracing, and to mitigate our surprise at finding them lead to the same point. A page or two back, when we perceived that the birth complex was the expression of curiosity and at the same time was an attempt to find a harbour of refuge— when I pointed out that Bertrand was simultaneously eager to explore the depths of the maternal world and to return to his mother's womb—there were already disclosed the twin aspects which are to be discovered in every birth fantasy: the explanation of an enigma, and compensation for a disappointing or cruel reality.

Most typical among birth fantasies is that of a second birth, in which the child reinvents the mythologies of ancient days. It is identical with the legendary hero's birth which has been studied by Rank.[1] The desire for rebirth, as embodied in this birth fantasy implies a belief that the reborn will live under happier conditions than those actually experienced. In part it is determined by the wish with which we are already familiar—to return to the mother's womb; but to this is superadded a second longing, that for rebirth into an existence that shall be better, more beautiful, more glorious. The symbolism varies from case to case, but the fundamental motif remains unchanged, and the two successive movements are always recognisable. We shall never find any difficulty in detecting the compensatory character of such imaginings.

Anna Freud records a case of a little girl who was

---

[1] Cf. Baudouin, Psychanalyse de l'art, p. 29; and Otto Rank, Der Mythus von der Geburt des Helden.

160 THE MIND OF THE CHILD

very much upset by the birth of a sister who seemed to her a usurper. "I would much rather have never been born," she said. (This was merely an elaboration of the motif of a return to the mother's womb.) Then she imagined her own death, and her subsequent rebirth as an animal or a doll. She knew of a little girl whom her nurse had visited on one occasion, and she had become this child's doll; there she was given her bath and was made much of; her little mother loved her more than anything else in the world, and she would be the favourite doll even if another doll were to arrive at Christmas.[1] Here we have an extremely simple and typical fantasy whose compensatory nature is obvious at the first glance. Even this brief account of it will have reminded the reader of some of the characteristic motifs of the "collective unconscious." Christmas is one of the commonest of such motifs, and the reason is not far to seek, for it crops up so naturally when the birth complex is stirred, whether in the investigatory sense (the enigma of birth), or in the compensatory sense (rebirth, miraculous birth).

In the free essay of a boy named Max, recorded by Zulliger, we discover a fantasy of rebirth which conforms strictly to the classical myth. A shepherd lad has very strict parents. One day he learns that his father so-called is not really his father. A queen appears to him in a field, and recognises him as her son, for she knows him by a birthmark on the chest (a birthmark which Max himself had). She has for some time been seeking her son, stolen years before by gypsies.[2]

Day-dreams of this sort are extraordinarily common in children, some of whom give free rein to the

---

[1] Anna Freud, Introduction to Psychoanalysis for Teachers (London: George Allen & Unwin Ltd.).

[2] Hans Zulliger, Gelöste Fesseln, p. 58.

BIRTH 161

imagination, whilst others believe more or less in their own fancies. In respect of many of the hard facts of life, the day-dream provides compensation, or, if you like, consolation. By giving free flight to fantasy, the child is able to enjoy the idea of emancipation from paternal authority, and also (through the motif of illustrious descent to indulge the will to power. Moreover, in many such day-dreams, we can hardly fail to discover (as Rank has discovered in the corresponding myth) elements of the Oedipus complex, thoughts of the elimination of the father.

All the same, we should never forget that in the birth complex, compensation and explanation are always closely intertwined. The two factors go hand in hand in so far as the fantasy of heroic birth supplies an agreeable correction to child theories of birth (birth through the anus, etc.), or to a knowledge of the actual facts of birth which has been conveyed in an improper way. The emotions of disgust and shame arouse in the child a wish to forget these unsavoury details, and it therefore substitutes for them its own pretty fancies. Consider the following instance, which I quote from Pierre Bovet.

"My patient was a girl of thirteen whose behaviour was intolerable so long as she was with her mother. I asked her about her dreams, and in the course of her associations I learned that 'a nasty servant we had, disobeying Mamma's orders,' had told her 'some horrid things.' The servant had said that babies came 'from a horrid place.' This revelation was a torment to the girl's subconscious. She wrote essays for her own amusement, and showed me one of them. It was a story, the hero of which was called Médicos. I recall the central theme. His father brought him, for a sister, a girl of seven, found in the desert, on a sunny beach. My readers will notice

L

162 THE MIND OF THE CHILD

that this tale transfigures reality into its opposite. An increase in the family is effected by the father" [the name of "Médicos" would suggest the collaboration of a theory commonly held in childhood, for many a youngster believes that the doctor has a mysterious power of giving life] "who, in a 'lovely' place, discovers a child which is already several years old."[1]

A kindred though more complicated train of thought can be followed up in the case of Isadora whose exhibitionist and inspectionist trends have already been alluded to, and who (as we discovered) cherished a theory of anal birth. Then the realities of birth were disclosed to her crudely and brutally, the net upshot being that all such matters were felt by her to be hideous and repulsive. When she was sixteen, Isadora had some inclination to embrace a form of Catholic mysticism, which was rather unorthodox, for she tinctured her Catholicism with theosophic elements. But despite this comparative freedom of thought, there was one point of Catholic dogma which she regarded as unassailable. It was sacrilege to discuss or to cast a shadow of doubt upon the Immaculate Conception.

In young Bertrand, whose investigatory tendencies made common cause with his desire to seek asylum in his mother's womb, both culminating in the same dreams of exploration, detective work, underground passages, etc.— the movement of flight to safe harbourage was speedily supplemented by a second movement, that towards rebirth, elaborated, as often happens, in the form of rescue work. The explorers were lost in the Polar regions, and were then saved by Swedes (the pupil to whom I had entrusted the task of studying Bertrand's case was a young Swedish woman who had been temporarily adopted

[1] Pierre Bovet, La psychanalyse et l'éducation, p. 27.

BIRTH 163

by the lad as a second mother). On another occasion, the youth followed the myth even more closely. In the course of his dreams of adventure he was swallowed by a whale, which subsequently spued him forth. Furthermore, we know that Bertrand suffered above all because he considered he had been evicted by a younger brother, just as the girl reported on by Anna Freud had been ousted by a younger sister. In both cases, the fantasies of rebirth were compensatory.

Birth fantasies may take other forms than that of rebirth or that of the birth of the mythical hero, but they always betray a desire for compensation.

Adler speaks of a "fiction of primogeniture" which may be present in the younger members of a family. Bluntly reversing the natural order of succession, the younger plays at being the eldest, cherishing the ambition which the same author has shown us to be a common ingredient of the mentality of the younger children.[1]

This reversal of the natural order of events becomes even more emphatic in certain remarkable fantasies to which Ernest Jones has drawn attention. Here there is a "reversal of the order of generations." A child begins by imagining that its parents will grow small again when it grows up. A girl of three said to her mother: "When I am big, you will be small, and I shall beat you the way you beat me now." A boy aged three and a half said to his mother: "When I am big, you will be little; then I shall carry you about in my arms, undress you, and put you to by-by." By degrees the child comes to imagine that it can give life to its parents, that it is their father or their mother. One more step leads to an identification with the grandfather or the grandmother (to whom the

[1] Adler, Le tempérament nerveux, p. 293.

THE MIND OF THE CHILD

child, moreover, is prone to appeal against its parents). This identification may have a repercussion upon character, the child setting itself to imitate the grandfather or the grandmother.[1]

This fantasy may be combined with other birth fantasies. My patient Bertrand, over and above his expeditions into remote countries, manifested an obvious identification with the grandfather. Besides, the two motifs were linked, for he had a longing to be with his grandfather who lived in a far-off land. His grandfather was a painter; Bertrand aspired to become a painter; in the course of the analysis he took to drawing, and seemed to find in this art a successful sublimation. A similar fact was observable in a lad under the care of Madame A. Tamm. She does not stress it, but I am impelled to do so by its kinship with what I observed in Bertrand. Madame Tamm's patient was likewise a kleptomaniac. One of the boy's grandfathers was a pedlar, and his supreme desire (manifested in dreams) was to accompany the old man in the latter's rambling life.[2] In both cases we have thievish impulses, fantasies of distant regions, and identification with a grandfather. It seems likely enough that in both cases all the symptoms derived from the same source—a longing for compensation in a boy who felt himself balked by his parents.

In connexion with the theme of distant lands, let me make an apt quotation from Pierre Bovet: "Fugues (running away) often depend upon memories of a happy childhood. Living in the country with ample freedom, surrounded by an atmosphere of affection, the child

---

[1] Ernest Jones, Generations-Umkehrungs-Phantasie, published in English as Chapter XXXVIII of Papers on Psychoanalysis, 3rd edition.

[2] A. Tamm, Drei Fälle von Stehlen bei Kindern.

BIRTH

enjoyed a happiness which, since then, life has denied it. It wants to revive these lost delights, and heedlessly runs away from town in an attempt to escape from the present."[1] I should add that, at deeper levels of the unconscious, this interpretation can be supplemented by invoking the birth complex. First of all, the longing to recapture the vanished joys of earlier childhood is usually coincident with a longing for the mother, for a return to the mother's womb. Secondly, we know that nature ("Mother Nature") on the one hand, and a far country on the other, are frequent symbols of the maternal womb, the strange "land" whence one came.

The simple fugue passes readily into vagabondage, and this in turn is the borderland of theft which we have just been studying. In young offenders,[2] it would be well to take note of such symptoms at the time of their first onset and to study them in relation to a longing for the mother and to the birth complex. Perhaps from this outlook vagabondage might come to be regarded as a sort of somnambulism in the waking state. Apart from this, it is very remarkable that gypsies, the most representative nomads among civilised nations and popularly reputed to steal children, play a considerable role in birth dreams and birth fantasies. A child, for example, will imagine that it is not the offspring of those who give themselves out to be its parents, but that it had been stolen by gypsies, and subsequently adopted into its present home. Obviously this idea shades off into or combines with the myth of heroic birth. The child dreams that it is of royal origin, or at least of noble lineage. Victor Hugo's *L'homme qui rit* is a fine elaboration of this theme,

[1] Pierre Bovet, La psychanalyse et l'éducation, p. 28.
[2] Aichhorn has been a pioneer in the psychoanalytical treatment of youthful criminals. Cf. his fine book Verwahrloste Jugend.

166   THE MIND OF THE CHILD

and like all variations of the same motif brings us back in a few steps to classical and mythological tales. We think, for instance, of Moses "saved from the waters" in an ark of bulrushes.

A notion with which analysis must familiarise us is that there often occurs a collaboration of two groups of factors, one group belonging to a fairly conscious and logical region of the mind, whereas the other group works in the abysses of the unconscious and primitive. However unlike, however disparate, these factors may seem at the first glance, they nevertheless join forces for the production of one and the same over-determined phenomenon. The explanation of what happens as the outcome of the factors belonging to the first group is the obvious one, and is sound as far as it goes; but it can be supplemented by reference to factors belonging to the second group. We have seen this in respect of the mutilation complex, showing that feelings of inferiority, which may seem adequate explanations of many facts, are usually a mask for castration fantasies which can be discovered by a more far-reaching analysis. At an earlier stage of the present study we saw that identical relationships obtain between the hunt for safety and the fantasies of a return to the mother's womb.

There are the same relationships between compensation and fantasies of rebirth. We have just been noting the compensatory character of the various birth fantasies. Conversely, if we study cases obviously dominated by the desire for compensation, we shall very probably unmask allusions to birth fantasies.

Consider the case of a girl whose brothers and sisters are very rowdy and are all of them older than she is. She compensates for her feelings of inferiority by fancying

BIRTH

herself God and engaged in the creation of living beings. (Compare with this my own remark in connexion with an instance illustrating the Diana complex, where in the idea of motherhood the subject found compensation for her alleged castration which had aroused a sense of inferiority.) Subsequently she had obsessions, an intense dread of everything connected with the sexual life, and above all a fear of giving birth to a child.[1]

A boy of fourteen, whose mother, a widow, had instilled into him a feeling of superiority, was then bitterly disappointed at school because he could make no headway with his studies. How did he compensate? In a document found in his possession he identified himself with an imaginary friend who was supposed to be in the confidence of the Almighty. He had a brother who had been born in heaven, and heaven had become his country. He would repay God by continuing on earth to work as schoolmaster and doctor.[2]

In this connexion I must remind the reader of Green's case, that of a little boy who, after the birth of a brother, found compensation in the histories of kings and heroes.

To make a child aware of its search for compensation, and to guide that search in a favourable direction, may yield excellent results. This was well shown in Green's case. But when circumstances permit of a profounder analysis, this should be undertaken, and the analyst will probably discover fantasies of rebirth, or of heroic birth, royal or divine descent.

[1] Mary Chadwick, Le phantasme d'être Dieu chez les enfants.
[2] Crichton Miller, The New Psychology and the Teacher, p. 52.

PART THREE

COMPLEXES OF ATTITUDE

CHAPTER EIGHT

WEANING

A CHILD's life consists of successive stages; passing from one stage to the next involves an expenditure of energy; each transformation requires a willingness to renounce the gratifications of the preceding phase, a willingness to take risks and to dive into the inhospitable unknown—presupposes, to express the matter more comprehensively, an adaptation which, like all adaptations, is a "costly" action (in Pierre Janet's sense of the term[1]).

The first of these metamorphoses is, unquestionably, birth. Here the crisis of adaptation is primarily physiological, but it would be an error to suppose that the physiological changes have no psychological accompaniments. Besides, there is no sharp line between physiology and psychology, for they shade into one another; and no rigid distinction can be drawn between the shock of birth and the other shocks of transformation, all of which have affinities with birth. It is because of these affinities that the various difficult metamorphoses continue (as shown in the preceding chapter) to find expression in birth symbols.

Are we to infer that the initial trauma, that of birth, is, psychologically no less than physiologically, the most important of all the traumas of transition, and the prototype of the rest? Such would seem to be Rank's view.[2] Freudians in general are more cautious in their statements, and do not go further than to declare that weaning is the first psychological trauma of transition

---

[1] Cf. Pierre Janet, *Psychological Healing.*
[2] *Le traumatisme de la naissance.*

172 THE MIND OF THE CHILD

which is definitely accessible to observation. The shocks attendant upon weaning (which are mentioned also by Rank) have been emphasised by Laforgue and Codet. Ferenczi, criticising Rank's thesis, holds that the psychoanalyst's attention should be brought to bear upon weaning rather than upon birth; then upon the training into cleanly ways; then upon the opening days of school life, upon the abandonment of infantile masturbation, and later upon all the phases characterised by an advance in the process whereby the child breaks away from the family.[1]

These successive shocks contain, one and all, an element of "weaning," and therefore tend to resemble in various ways what is known as weaning in the strict sense of the term. The emotions they arouse are intertwined with the emotions which were aroused when the child was taken away from the mother's breast. We have, then, to do with a complex. In its turn, this complex is closely linked with the birth complex—a fact which must be recognised, however we may choose to interpret it. The interlinking of the two systems is made evident by the simple reflection that weaning, like birth, is a separation from the mother. We are entitled to regard them as two successive phases of one single process of separation which will be carried still farther when the child begins to go to school, and accentuated by the subsequent breaking away from the family, etc. The separation, even if purely physiological to begin with, is continued later upon the psychological plane. In accordance with the principles and the methodology I have adopted, I shall not here enter into the problems of interpretation. Suffice it to point out the aforesaid interconnexion between the birth complex and the weaning complex, the latter seeming to branch out

[1] Ferenczi, Die Anpassung der Familie an das Kind, p. 239.

WEANING 173

of the former. The branch is a thick one, and deserves independent examination.

It must not be forgotten that in the suckling the buccal zone is pre-eminently the zone of pleasure, for at this stage of life the anal and genital zones, which will awaken in due course, still slumber. I agree with Freud that, for practical purposes, taking the breast (or its substitute, the bottle) is the infant's only pleasure—and a pleasure so intense that the suckling finds it difficult to renounce.[1] When the infant ceases to take suck, it substitutes some part of its own body for the mother's nipple, sucking vigorously at its tongue, its thumb, etc. In the growing child there are gradual transitions from these habits of sucking to masturbation. When masturbation is prevented, sucking habits readily reappear in one form or another. It would be hard to say with precision where one begins and the other ends. Freud's remarkable discovery of the continuity of the phenomena in question enabled him to make certain generalisations on the subject which are apt to be considered repugnant by those who come across them for the first time, but which are always instructive and concrete, even when Freud's terminology seems open to criticism. K. Pipal has described, as phenomena forming a continuous series, the habits of nail-biting, scratching, chewing a penholder, or continually thrusting the same object into the ear. All these habits are common among children, Pipal and other psychoanalysts usually regarding them as "masturbation equivalents." It will be noted that many such habits are associated with the act of sucking, and in later life the sucking habit is revived in the form of smoking. Such relationships recur again

---

[1] Freud, Introduction à la psychanalyse, p. 337; Trois essais sur la théorie de la sexualité, p. 74.

174 THE MIND OF THE CHILD

and again the deeper we penetrate into the realm of the unconscious; and the originality of psychoanalytical methods is precisely this discovery of unsuspected continuity among apparently disparate phenomena. Perhaps it might be wiser to avoid such terms as sexuality and masturbation when speaking of infants. But it really matters little what terms are used so long as we realise that there exists a continuity—I do not say an identity—among the facts which have been repeatedly observed.

Confining ourselves, for the moment, to the act of sucking, we note that a child is inclined to cling to the habit more tenaciously if, for one reason or another, the weaning process has been resented. The habit of sucking goes hand in hand with other symptomatic traits. For instance, my little patient Françoise, aged six, persisted in sucking her thumb with the utmost assiduity. If some other interest turned her thoughts elsewhere for a while so that the habit was momentarily forgotten, when she remembered it once more she would hurl herself upon her thumb with extraordinary violence, like an eagle upon its prey, in much the same way as an infant will seize its mother's breast if in the course of its feeding time the nipple has escaped from its lips. Françoise must have been too suddenly weaned, and must have suffered a good deal in consequence. Other characteristics would lead one to suspect the existence of a weaning trauma in this little girl's case. She bolted her food, and despite being scolded and reasoned with continued to gulp down her meals without chewing the food at all: as a matter of fact she persisted in treating every comestible as a liquid. True, Françoise at an earlier date made use of her teeth —but this was merely to bite her elder sister in the course of their quarrels. This misuse of the teeth was likewise a sign of the very important part the buccal zone played

WEANING 175

in the girl's life. Further, she was greedy and difficult to please where food was concerned; all the more so because she had been put upon a strict diet owing to enteric disturbances—which in their turn were not wholly unrelated to her particular complex. Among other things she was absolutely forbidden to take any milk, and it requires no very deep penetration to grasp why the child was so readily displeased with the meats placed before her, why she refused to eat one dish and clamoured for a serve of another. One day the doctor who was attending had the excellent idea of prescribing "dried milk" to be added to her diet. Françoise was transferred to the seventh heaven of delight. Nothing pleased her palate more than "my milk" which she demanded at each meal. One of her favourite games was to feed the bottle to her dolls. I encouraged her in her play and endeavoured to guide her towards the game of weaning, for in play a child acts the traumas it has incompletely surmounted and in this way it is able to free itself entirely.[1]

Jean Paul, four years old, was brought to me for treatment. In this boy the weaning complex had assumed an unwontedly violent form. The whole condition of the youngster's life was abnormal. He was the illegitimate son of an unmarried girl who had lived with her baby and given him the breast for two months after birth. Then he was suddenly and completely severed from his mother, the girl having been persuaded by her father to give up the child. A few months later the baby was adopted by the woman who brought him to me for examination. Having resigned himself to the bottle, when the time came for him to take his food from a spoon or a

[1] Cf. Freud, Essais de psychanalyse: Au delà du principe de plaisir, pp. 19 et seq.

176 THE MIND OF THE CHILD

cup he showed very positive resistance, and it was extremely hard to get the child to submit to this stage of his development. When, in due time, solid foods were introduced into his dietary, Jean Paul flatly refused to have anything to do with them, and he took three hours to finish a meal consisting exclusively of slops. He was for a while placed in a New School where he began to eat what the other children ate; but no sooner did he return to his adoptive mother's home than he once more insisted upon a liquid diet. Concurrently with this refusal to accept solid foodstuffs there developed a hesitation in his speech amounting to a definite stammer. This, too, betrayed the importance the child's unconscious attached to the buccal zone. It seemed as though he were treating words as solid substances and was refusing to accept them, or would only tolerate them in a liquid form; whereas the stuttering symbolised for him the gratification of sucking at the mother's breast. In actual fact this stammer in Jean Paul's speech was already overdetermined. Like many other forms of impediment in speech it appeared to be related to forbidden curiosity, for it had become worse during his fourth year, just at the time when his curiosity had been aroused. He wanted to look into the boxes in my study, to open my files, to peep into my stationery. His favourite question was: "What's inside it?" This question had first been asked by him one morning when, on entering his adoptive mother's room, he had caught sight of her breast as she lay in bed. Jean Paul had contemplated this object with an expression of rapt ecstasy; the moment was for him a sort of illumination, appealing no doubt to his unconscious memory, and forcing him to say in his baby language that he had never seen anything so beautiful before. Thus his curiosity was concentrated upon the

WEANING

region whence had come the initial shock in his young life. The boy had probably already fathomed the mystery whereby his existence was surrounded, thus realising why his position was an abnormal one. Thereby the tabu placed upon curiosity as to our human beginnings became aggravated in Jean Paul's case. This little boy invented a very original form of weaning game. When he was four, his adoptive parents thought it would be a good thing if they were to "give a little sister" to Jean Paul, so they adopted a girl baby of nineteen months. No adult could invent the words spoken by the boy when he was shown his new sister: "She'll belong to me. I'll teach her to eat."

In this matter, as in others, we note a continuity between the reactions dependent upon a particular physiological function, and kindred reactions which have no direct connexion with that function and are purely psychological. Thus the greediness which a child that has been injudiciously weaned shows at mealtimes tends to influence the whole character. We see the same sort of continuity between regret for the loss of the mother's breast as the physiological instrument of giving suck, and regret produced by severance from the mother—a longing for her presence or for close contact with her.

One day Friedjung was called to see a boy aged sixteen months suffering from whooping-cough. While examining the baby, he found a woman's stocking in the cot. Making enquiries the doctor learned that for several months (probably since weaning) the little boy could not go to sleep unless he was sucking his thumb and clasping in his hands either a bust bodice or else a stocking which his mother had worn. When not allowed his way in this matter, he burst into a furious rage. Underclothing clean

178 THE MIND OF THE CHILD

from the wash or that worn by his father, would not serve his turn. The grandmother and the nurse told Friedjung (when the parents were out of the room) that in the early days of this obsession the child was only interested in his mother's nightgown. The nightgown was still a fetish, but a stocking or a bust-bodice was preferred. When his mother was not present, the little boy refused to eat his soup unless he held the stocking in one hand.[1]

Underclothing fetishism and other forms of sexual fetishism are common in children. In a previous chapter I referred to the case of François, one of "cannibalism," in which the little patient had also strong buccal trends which were probably vestiges of a weaning trauma. For a time, when his father was away from home, this boy could not sleep unless he had in bed with him his father's photograph, without a glass, so that he could finger it to his satisfaction. Like fetishistic reactions are met with in animals. A dog I knew, having been left by his mistress for some time in the care of friends, was lucky enough to find in one of the rooms a glove which the mistress had dropped, and he would not go to sleep unless he had this glove between his paws.

Apart from the forms of protest at severance from the mother which I have just been discussing, children find many other means of expressing dissatisfaction at being deprived of the maternal breast. Freud long ago drew attention to the dread aroused by this separation, emotional states which find expression in a fear of being in the dark and other forms of fear which are mere substitutes for the resentment caused by the forcible weaning. He tells us moreover that he owes his knowledge concerning the origin of infantile fear to a little boy of three who

[1] Joseph K. Friedjung, Un cas de fetichisme concernant le linge chez un enfant d'un an.

WEANING 179

declared: "If you speak to me, it isn't dark any more."[1] Fear is then, declares Pfister, a child's means for attracting to itself that care and fondling of which it has been deprived. But all these fears, dreads, and anguish caused by the severance from the mother quickly bring us back to the birth complex.

Ilona, whose exhibitionist trends were discussed earlier in this book, has her own special way of protesting against enforced separation from her mother whose profession as an actress makes it impossible for her to bring up her little girl herself. The child has, therefore, been boarded out, and she compensates herself as best she may: she obviously preserves a poignant regret for the days when she could follow her mother from the dressing-room to the wings at the theatre; she endeavours to live once again in that happy period of her life, and this effort on her part certainly serves to promote her strong exhibitionist inclinations. In the following chapter I shall further discuss this yearning for the mother, together with the drawing in upon oneself and the regression it may bring about.

One very significant and characteristic trait of the weaning complex is the greediness and even avidity it arouses, so that the sufferer is never satisfied and is sometimes so unreasonable as to pass all measure.

Berthe F. was brought to me at the age of thirteen because she still wetted her bed—a symptom almost invariably connected with the infantile longing for the mother's care and affection, and fairly closely related with the weaning complex. The girl was treated by psychotherapeutic suggestion and was soon cured of her bad habit. Fifteen years later she came to me again.

[1] Freud, Trois essais sur la theorie de la sexualité, p. 185.

180 THE MIND OF THE CHILD

Now she was a married woman, and was suffering from acute depression which brought out certain character traits that had always been peculiar to her since early childhood, and had not, of course, been resolved by the simple treatment I gave her to cure the bed-wetting. These traits gave ample evidence that Berthe was still suffering from the weaning complex. Directly she has a wish she wants it gratified: she sees a hat or a frock which takes her fancy; immediately her desire must be gratified or she knows no peace. She herself is distressed because of these unreasonable impulses, considering them utterly silly; but she cannot overcome them. "I get into a terrible state of nerves if I cannot have what I want," she declares. "I am furious if I am prevented from going out in the evening when the fancy takes me." Furthermore, she eats too quickly, "I gulp everything down." If she is sent away to the country for a rest, she becomes so bored that she feels she "simply can't stand it." Recollecting certain events of childhood she says: "When I was between six and seven years of age I was sent to school, but I cried all the time, so that they had to let me go home to Mother whom I could not bear to leave." Later on, she tells me: "I was weaned at fourteen months, and was taken to stay with an aunt in the country; but I could never feel at home there." Distaste for life in the country can be traced back to this incident of babyhood, and persists even now when Berthe is twenty-eight years old. It finds its place in the same complex as do her other symptoms. In addition, Berthe is an only child, is aware that she was rather spoilt, and this undoubtedly makes it more difficult for her to forgo her unreasonable demands.

Greediness, which (in the widest sense of the term) is characteristic of the weaning complex, may develop into

WEANING
181

ambition so fiery that it is apt to consume its host. We have a conspicuous and tragical instance of such a development in a famous journal, that of Marie Bashkirtseff, who began to write this document at the age of twelve, and continued the record until her premature death at the age of twenty-four.

In the preface the writer finds it expedient to tell us that she continued to take the breast much longer than is customary, and in this connexion she goes on to speak of the birth of ambition: "Ever since I began to think, from the time I was three (I took the breast until I was three and a half) I have had overwhelmingly great aspirations. My dolls were always kings or queens; my thoughts, and what I noticed in the conversations between my mother and her friends, seemed always to bear upon the great destiny which awaited me."

Let me note here that a belated weaning may have similar effects to one that is premature. When a child is taken from the breast too early, it adapts itself with difficulty to the new situation and clamours for the old one. When the period of suckling is unduly prolonged, then will have arisen an inveterate habit of taking the breast in a child which has already developed a mental life of a fairly complicated kind. Here, once more, the child finds renunciation extremely difficult, and the unwillingness to renounce is extended to other domains, is universalised. It was upon the foundation of these ambitious longings in conjunction with avidity that the remarkable talents of Marie Bashkirtseff were established. Though she was not fond of painting, she longed for the fame of a great painter. Nay more, she went so far as to say that: "I want to go on living for the very reason that others may not enjoy and may not triumph" (March 31, 1877). We have good reason to infer that this

THE MIND OF THE CHILD

utterance embodies an echo of the rivalries of childhood (the Cain complex).

As she grows older she becomes ever more aware that death is threatening her, and is increasingly conscious that her ambition passes all bounds. The most suitable term to apply in her case is "avidity." What precisely is she longing for? She wants to have everything, at once, and is driven to despair because the fulfilment of her desires is impossible. At one point in her diary she seems to soar above her writing and her life, giving brilliant expression to her thoughts and feelings.

"Look back at the diaries I kept in 1875, 1876, and 1877. I am perpetually on the grumble, but I don't know what it is I want; aspirations towards something indefinable. I felt bruised and discouraged when evening came, exhausting myself in a vain search for the thing I should do. Furious and despairing search. Shall I go to Italy? Stay in Paris? Marry? Paint? What was to become of me? *If I go to Italy, then I shall not be in Paris, and I thirsted to be everywhere at once!!!* " The italics are the diarist's own.

"Had I been a man, I should have conquered the whole of Europe. But since I was merely a girl, I frittered away my days in useless writing and eccentric behaviour. Oh how wretched I was!

"There are moments in life when one naively believes oneself capable of doing anything and everything. If I had leisure I should be a sculptor, a writer, a musician.

"It is like a fire eating you up. Death awaits me at the end, inexorably, whether I consume myself in vain desires or not.

"Yet, if I am a nonentity and am doomed to be nothing

WEANING   183

better, why have I dreamed of personal glory ever since I began to think? [i.e. since the time she was weaned. Here we have the identical words she made use of above.] Why am I devoured by these mad aspirations towards personal eminence, towards grandeurs which I at first conceived of as wealth and titles?

"Why since the age of four, when I was able to think consecutively, do I yearn after glorious things, things magnificent and confused, but immense? How innumerable were the roles I played as a child. I was a celebrated dancer in St. Petersburg, worshipped by the whole town. Every evening I wore a low-cut dress and a crown of flowers on my head; then, with the utmost gravity, I danced before the household assembled in the drawing-room. Then I became a world-famous singer. I accompanied myself on the harp, and I was carried in triumph—but I do not know by whom or whither. Later, I electrified the masses by the eloquence of my public oratory. The tsar of Russia married me in order to keep his throne, and I lived in direct communion with my people, speaking to them and explaining my policy so that empress and people were moved to tears.

"Thereafter I loved, but the man I loved betrayed me—or, if he did not betray me, he died of some accident, usually a fall from his horse, just at the moment when I felt my love for him to be at the lowest ebb. I would then love another, and all would be arranged in seemly fashion with due regard for the moral code, seeing that the men died or played me false. I soon consoled myself if death overtook them; but if they betrayed my love I felt an unquenchable disgust and was so filled with despair that I died.

"In everything, in every branch of activity, of human feelings and satisfactions, my dreams were magnifications

184 THE MIND OF THE CHILD

of natural possibilities. If my desires could not be realised, it was better to be dead." (June 25, 1884.)

This is the point where matters take a tragical twist, for avidity seems, more than any other sentiment, to correspond to the law of "all or nothing"[1] which is the hall-mark of the great primitive urges that have not passed from the savage state. Marie Bashkirtseff, from very early in life, is swayed between the two poles of all or of nothing; if she is to have nothing, she interprets this as a presage of death. The tuberculosis which laid her low seems in her case to have ratified the subsequent findings of psychoanalysts, who often discover reasons for supposing that the onset of this disease masks a secret desire for death,[2] a desire whose importance is obvious in the case of a malady wherein the whole course depends upon the condition of the "soil."

This desire, which for Marie is nothing other than the obverse of ambition, manifests itself at an early date, and its growth may be traced throughout the pages of her diary. In 1878 she is already writing: "Death? That would be absurd, and yet it seems to me I am going to die young. I cannot live; I do not seem to have been properly fashioned from the start; I've got too much of certain things, and yet there are a lot of others that I lack; my kind of character is not made to last. Were I a goddess with the universe to wait upon me I should find the work ill performed. Never was there so fantastic, so impatient a creature as I, nor one so hard to please. . . . I am convinced my life will not be long . . ." (February 12, 1878). "When I am twenty-two I shall either be famous or dead." (April 13, 1878.) This is an

---

[1] Cf. W. H. R. Rivers, Instinct and the Unconscious. Also Charles Baudouin, La psychologie et l'action, Chapter II.

[2] René Allendy, L'orientation des idées médicales.

WEANING   185

even more whole-hearted resolve than that uttered by Victor Hugo at the age of fifteen: "I shall be another Chateaubriand or nothing."

The desire for death, which in other cases of phthisis has been described as an "unconscious" trend, does not escape Marie Bashkirtseff's vigilant eye. With her it is more than a desire; it is a resolve. "If I cannot soon win to fame as a painter, I shall kill myself and that's the end of the matter. I made up my mind to this some months ago." (January 10, 1879.) This reaction is traceable to another reaction of earlier years—to love's disillusionment when her supposed lover played her false: "I grabbed a handful of cigarettes and my diary, and went off intending to poison my lungs while writing inflammatory pages. . . ." (June 24, 1876.)

Death-dreams and superstitious presentiments produce a profound impression upon her mind. But she is "quite surprised at not being alarmed by the prospect of dying." (July 16, 1879.) Later, when more than one specialist had been called in consultation, so that she suspected that her condition was pretty bad, she wrote: "What a wry face auntie pulled! For my part, I am merely amused. . . . I would like to have a really serious illness, and have done with it all. Auntie is horror-struck; I am triumphant. Death does not frighten me; I should not dare to take my own life, but I should like it to be over and at an end. . . . If you only knew! . . . I am not going to wear flannel, nor do I intend to stain my skin with iodine. I do not want to get well." (September 10, 1880.)

Towards the last, when she knows that death has obeyed her summons and stands at her elbow, she has a moment of revulsion; but her pride makes her stiffen her sinews, so that she cries with mingled triumph and distress:

186   THE MIND OF THE CHILD

"Ah, I have always said that I would die young. God has not found it possible to grant me that which would make life endurable, so he is getting out of his difficulty by killing me. After showering wretchedness upon me, he is killing me in order to be rid of me. I have always said that I would die young; my life could not go on the way it had done. I thirsted to have all, my aspirations were gigantic—it could not last. I told you so long ago, years ago, at Nice, when I vaguely glimpsed all that I needed to make life worth living. . . . Others are given more and they do not die!" (December 28, 1882.)

"Others" have accepted the fact of "being weaned" —the current term among psychoanalysts to describe this situation. But Marie Bashkirtseff could never make up her mind to accept it. We must not, of course, go so far as to assume that the whole of this tragedy was merely the outcome of the weaning trauma; nor would I venture to maintain so exclusive an opinion, for only too well do I know that where human psychology is concerned everything is over-determined. Many other complexes are present in this remarkable girl: strong exhibitionist trends, narcissism (to which we shall return in the sequel). Nevertheless, the weaning complex is the most obvious in Marie's case, and takes precedence. It evolves along typical lines, and so mightily that it cannot fail to leave a deep impression upon the reader of her diary. All along one feels its unfailing presence in the incurable avidity which consumes her, and at last deals her the death-blow.

CHAPTER NINE

RETREAT

In our previous studies, we have encountered various phases of regret or retreat in which the child longed to return to some previous condition. The two complexes we studied last of all, the birth complex and the weaning complex, brought us, more especially, face to face with such trends. Fantasies of a return to the mother's womb, the difficulties of adaptation to each new stage of development, the shocks of transition, a clinging to an outgrown phase and the difficulty of consenting to be "weaned" from it—such have been the various phenomena leading us towards the consideration of the cases with which we shall be concerned in the present chapter, cases in which a movement of retreat dominates the picture.

If we are to survey these phenomena of psychological retreat in all their amplitude, we shall find it necessary to do what I have done in an earlier essay of my own,[1] namely to distinguish clearly between simple regrets, in the first place, secondly regressions, which are revivals of the behaviour proper to an antecedent phase, and thirdly introversions, which are a retreat from action and a seeking of a refuge in oneself. But, having drawn these distinctions, it is then necessary to become aware of the solidarity among the phenomena in question, which are all (however great their differences in nature and importance) constituents of one and the same retreat complex, embodying the inclinations to retreat, to take flight, to seek asylum, inclinations which may be observed also in the lower animals.

[1] La regression et les phénomènes de recul en psychologie.

188 THE MIND OF THE CHILD

A state of affairs that seems to me fairly common in children, and one it is very important for the educator to recognise, is that which arises when a regret for the last days of early childhood (a regret justifiable enough by the shocks which are plain even to a superficial observer) leads to a more or less well-marked regression of the intelligence, the character, and the behaviour towards an infantile stage. We have to remember that the child is a being in process of development, and that if it regrets a lost past it is necessarily regretting an earlier phase of that development. Hence regret easily culminates in regression. The child, it would seem, longs to return to the paradise of infancy, and is to some extent successful in fulfilling its wish.

Graber has described a typical case of retreat in a boy of nine. Kurt was submissive to a degree which transcended the limits of the healthy and could only be regarded as morbid. Incapable of independent action, of manifestations of will or energy, at school he was extremely backward (intellectual regression). His dominant character trait, submissiveness, sufficed to render probable the existence of a strong retreat complex. Submissiveness is one of the symptoms of this complex, and mental backwardness is another. Kurt would have liked to remain small, saying: "When one gets bigger, one is not so much loved" (regret). Besides this, he liked to be shut up in a very warm room during rain or a thunderstorm, "for then nothing can happen to me" (refuge); he also was fond of being in a church, or in a shut motor car, and added, when questioned about this taste, "I don't know in what thing I was shut up when I was quite little because of course I was not anywhere before I was born" (fantasies of return to the mother's

RETREAT 189

womb). Kurt's dreams at this period were mainly concerned with similar topics.[1]

As regards undue submissiveness and regression in Kurt's case, I have already insisted, when studying regressive phenomena, upon these couples of complementary trends, one active and the other passive, between which oscillation goes on upon the instinctive plane. Among the most typical of these couples are those of domination—submission, attack—flight, and sadism—masochism. In my view, the association of the passive components of these three couples (flight, submission, and masochism) is the foundation of the retreat complex.

Very numerous cases of enuresis nocturna (a matter on which I have previously touched) have been interpreted—though there may be over-determination at work—as an expression of regret for the first years of childhood. The child that wets its bed is a child playing baby. It is going back to the period when, night after night, it was the object of the most assiduous care, and the shock which has induced the regret is often plain.

I have previously recorded a case of bed-wetting wherein the regret and the regression were outcomes of a sense of rivalry against a younger sister. In another case, that of Berthe F., the enuresis was the expression of a refusal to accommodate herself to weaning. Cases of bed-wetting have been described in which this symptom appeared to be a regressive compensation for masturbation.[2] One of my pupils had under observation a girl of six, Gail, who habitually wetted her bed and her underclothing. She was an affectionate child, but markedly introverted. Having been sent to a boarding-

---

[1] G. H. Graber, Unterwürfigkeit, p. 53.

[2] Ernst Schneider, Die Abwehr der Selbstbefriediẑung, p. 145.

THE MIND OF THE CHILD

school at this early age, she only saw her parents once a fortnight. There were various indications that she felt forsaken. She stole dainty little objects, and also fruit from the garden, such thefts being typical of a child which considers itself bereft of parental affection and wants to assert its demand for restoration. In her games, she endeavoured to override this trauma, playing the mother who abandons her offspring. One day she ran away from school with three other small children. They were all found together in a field, the others sitting on the ground in tears, whilst Gail had tied her stockings to a tree as a sort of flag, in order to show her companions that they would have to stay out all night. Elsewhere I have given a detailed account of the case of James, which I will now merely summarise. He was brought to me at fourteen, when he still had the habit of wetting his bed. Very small for his age (he was piqued by this), he always chose much younger boys as his chums. He stammered, suffered from night-terrors, bit his nails, and was untruthful; very backward in class. The initial shock which had brought about the regression was easy to discover. His mother died when he was six and his father married again. It was then that he had begun to wet his bed, and he became at the same time a sleep-walker.

Here is the first dream he told me in the course of analysis: "I am in a hotel in front of a ravine. At the bottom of the ravine there is a river. Across this I can see the other side of the ravine. My chum Jean Louis is climbing this other side, hoisting himself by clutching huge primroses. After he has pulled up some tufts of grass, the dinner gong suddenly sounds at the hotel. He rose into the air like an airplane and then fell into the water crying, 'Mother!' While he was climbing the

RETREAT 191

bank his hair was short, but when he fell with a cry his hair was long."

The associations to this dream were significant. They related to his mother and to the happy days when he worked under her supervision. Now he works at school, which "I do not like so much." Jean Louis is not backward at school, and excels above all in those subjects where James proves a dullard (arithmetic, for instance).

James has a strong mother-fixation. Craving for this lost mother, he would like to go back to the early days of childhood. There is a conflict. In the unconscious he would like to remain small, weak, and with long hair like a girl. His conscious wish to get on as well at school as his chum does is shown in the dream by his impersonation of Jean Louis. On the other hand, the regressive wish finds vigorous expression at the end of the dream. We may suppose that "the other side of the ravine" represents virility and the reality principle, whereas the hither side represents the pleasure principle and his mother-fixation (the mother who provides him with nourishment, the dinner gong).

We know that those who have to get up at night to minister to a child's needs often reappear as ghosts in the latter's fantasies. James says that he is always afraid after dark. He recalls a remarkable fact to explain how it was he began to wet his bed. "I woke all right when I wanted to wee-wee, but I would not get up because I was afraid of ghosts." What he really wanted was to be petted and cared for by his mother as in the old days. To conclude, the reader will note that there are links between the symptom of enuresis, the dream of the river into which "Jean Louis" falls, and the standard fantasies of return to the waters in his mother's womb.

The somnambulism from which James suffered as

192 THE MIND OF THE CHILD

well as enuresis is equally characteristic of the complex with which we are now concerned. I have, indeed, already pointed out that sleepwalking has often been explained as the expression of a longing for the mother.[1] In the case of Herbert, aged fifteen, which I classified as an instance of "regret and regression," somnambulism was likewise one of the symptoms.[2] Pfister records the case of a girl of twelve who, while sleepwalking, was in the habit of taking down two pictures from the wall and hiding them under a chair or beneath the counterpane. The subject of the pictures in question, one of which showed children being fed, and the other showed some little birds, and the associations they called up in the analysis, were extremely significant of the feelings by which the girl was moved: a craving for the caresses of which she felt herself deprived, the desire to be fed by her mother.[3]

Here is another very instructive case reported by Graber. Fred, a boy of ten, got out of bed at the same hour every night, went into his parents' room, walked up to his mother's bedside, and then went back to his own bedroom. The following day he had no memory of what he had done during the night. In the waking state, he was calm and composed; when other children were playing, he would stay in a corner (a typical motif of retreat) looking on; he had no interest in other boys, liking to play with girls. (Let me note in passing that when a boy inclines to identify himself with girls, as we see here, and as we saw in James, we generally have to do with an attitude of retreat.)

---

[1] Charles Baudouin, Leidvoller Verlust und Regression im Kindesalter; also Freud et la psychanalyse, Introduction II, 7.

[2] Same references as in previous note.

[3] Oskar Pfister, Die Behandlung schwererziehbarer und abnormer Kinder, p. 58.

RETREAT

Fred had dreams of the following sort: "Mother is asleep in her room; I get up, and open the door; but Mother is no longer there; a large dog comes towards me; I cry out, and Mother appears." Here we have plain expression of a longing for the Mother. In another dream, he finds a nest in the desert and lies down in it; a giraffe comes with its little ones. Then we have a dream which reminds us of James's. He is flying through the air with a lady (the mother) but he falls. Next he sees himself in a balloon (the mother's womb); the balloon has a restaurant (nourishment supplied by the mother); and so on. We may surmise that the analysis, if pushed a little further, would disclose a weaning complex.[1]

The regression which ensues upon the feeling of being forsaken may lead to the mental backwardness which we have noticed in several of the foregoing cases. Now I want the reader to understand clearly that in such instances the backwardness is apparent, not real. We are concerned with an affective trouble, and there is nothing wrong with the child's intelligence. Still, grown-ups are apt to make a mistake about this matter, and to treat as defectives children in which psychoanalysis would restore the mental capacities which seem to be lacking. All the same, a backwardness that is at first apparent merely, may in the end become real, just as, on the other hand, the intellectual superiority which a child's complexes lead it to desire above all things may become an actual superiority—the reason, of course, being that a function develops when it is exercised and atrophies when it is neglected. We have noted this before in the case of another kind of backwardness due to affective causes, that which depends upon the over-stressing of a tabu

[1] G. H. Graber, Aus der Analyse eines nachtwandelnden Knaben.

194 THE MIND OF THE CHILD

relating to curiosity aroused in connexion with certain forbidden topics.

Let me seize this opportunity of repeating that the regression which occurs in a child as the outcome of the feeling that it has been forsaken may affect the moral life just as easily as the intellectual life. In such cases, it will return to the anal-sadistic stage, becoming dirty or naughty, or both. The shades of behaviour vary. One child will be careless; another, harum-scarum; a third, idle; a fourth, rude; a fifth, untruthful; a sixth, disobedient; a seventh, aggressive.

The upshot of a regression, in fact, is never a simple return to the past, but a composite formation, a mingling of the behaviour characteristic of the stage at which regression occurs and the behaviour proper to the actual age of the child in question. For instance, a boy in whom anal tendencies recur will not necessarily have the faecal incontinence of a baby, but will soil and mess his clothes, be slovenly in appearance, untidy in his work, and so on.

The fact is that the majority of disorders of behaviour and faults of character in children fall within these categories. We do not exaggerate in saying that troubles of the kind, which are of supreme interest to the educator, frequently arise from an affective shock in consequence of which the child believes, rightly or wrongly, that it has been robbed of its parents' love. I developed this thesis in a paper on *Psychanalyse et l'éducation morale* which I read at the Fifth International Congress for Moral Education held at Paris in 1930.[1]

My patient James, who wetted his bed, exhibited signs of moral regression as well as mental backwardness,

[1] The paper was published in "Action et Pensée," vol. vi, no. 11, 1930.

RETREAT

and, in truth, the mental backwardness seemed to be the expression of the boy's general slackness. But all his troubles followed upon his mother's death and his father's remarriage. In this same connexion I may refer to various cases which have been previously mentioned as illustrations of one complex or another: to young Franz, under the care of Aichhorn, whose character became intolerable from the day when his mother married again; and to various children whose "character changed for the worse" after the birth of a younger child.

In regard to cases of the latter type, which are so common, it is well to reiterate the formula enunciated in the last paragraph but one. Rightly or wrongly, the child believes itself forsaken. When a younger brother or sister is born, the elder child will feel robbed of its mother's love, and yet will have no objective ground for complaining of the latter's conduct. In like manner a "spoiled" child may react just like a child which has really been robbed of parental affection, for it will be exacting, and, from its own point of view, will invariably be in a state of privation. The stoics were right when they said that things in themselves counted for nothing: what mattered was what we thought of them. Although, in certain instances, as in James's case, there has been a grave and obvious trauma (here, the mother's death), in other instances the event has, substantially, been far less tragical. Yet the affective shock may have been no less severe, and the consequences no less disastrous. For some little boys, the birth of a younger brother may be tantamount to the death of the mother.

I spoke of carelessness and slackness. In other cases the term "indolence" would be more appropriate. The child gives expression to its desire for retreat by

196   THE MIND OF THE CHILD

slowness; when out walking, it lags in the rear; its actions are sluggishly performed. The boy of thirteen under Adler's care, mentioned above as an instance of the search for an asylum (retreat in face of the dreaded puberty), was noteworthy for his habitual sloth, and for the length of time he needed to dress in the morning. Graber's little sleepwalker was likewise sluggish, remaining "in the corner" while other children were at play.

But when we look into matters more closely we find that in many instances this reduction of objective activity is compensated by internal activity in the form of reverie or thought. When a child remains in a corner or lags behind others during a walk, we must not assume without further enquiry that apathy is the only or the chief cause of such behaviour. Perhaps the child in question merely wants to isolate itself to day-dream and to think. Thus, by gradations, we pass to introversion, which would seem to be in all cases a compensation (more or less successful) for suppressed objective activity.

The reader will remember that in the case cited from Adler's practice, a passion for reading developed contemporaneously with indolence and slowness of movement. The boy therefore resembles the other little fellow of nine mentioned by Green, a case I have referred to several times as typical of introversion. After the birth of a younger brother, this lad took to going to bed every afternoon at four. There, like a king enthroned, muffled up and surrounded by books, he devoured tales of the heroes. Round his waist he wore a broad belt which, in his fantasy, was the train of his royal robes, and he held one end of this belt in his hand whenever he spoke to anybody.

I need not recapitulate here all that I have said in

RETREAT 197

another publication regarding the value and the dangers of introversion.[1] Enough to say that, far from introversion being essentially morbid, it may be the starting-point of a rich and fruitful inner life. Still, the onset of conditions of introversion among children must be carefully watched, for the reason that they may be associated with retreat in general and with affective regression. Descriptions of typical introversion are full of details indicating a wish for isolation which, when pushed too far, is dangerous.

I recently referred to the boy who retired "into a corner." Others of the same nature have a fancy for games in which they barricade themselves behind three chairs; and games of taking refuge or seeking shelter readily tend towards games in which isolation is sought. Now, although we must not forget that inclinations to seek asylum or shelter have their good side, and are no less vitally necessary than inclinations towards attack and the running of risks, their undue accentuation may be far from wholesome for the individual at whose safeguarding they aim. The same may be said of inclinations towards isolation and introversion, which are linked with the foregoing in real life as in play (for play, like dreams, manifests only trends which find expression during ordinary life). This connexion, which is a general one, is seen with especial plainness in certain analyses. Adler's case which was mentioned a page or two back, that of the boy whose introversion took the form of immersing himself in books, has, it will be remembered, been depicted from another outlook as a typical instance of search for an asylum. I recall the case of one of my patients, Gustave, who from early

---

[1] La régression et les phénomènes de recul en psychologie; also Mobilisation de l'énergie, Part II, Chapter 5.

198 THE MIND OF THE CHILD

childhood developed a number of minor safety-manias which were the starting-points of obsessions. Subsequently, he sought in insomnia protection from the dangers to which anyone who allows himself to sleep is exposed. Simultaneously he became keenly aware of the prestige of persons who withdraw from the public gaze: monarchs who dwell apart in palaces; patients shut up in sick rooms; elderly recluses who have lost their mental balance; strange beings who sleep in the daytime and keep the watches of the night (in passing let me say that this discloses itself as one of the motifs in the over-determination of insomnia). But to this lad, the thinker, the man of science working into the small hours by artificial light, also seemed one of the "watchers of the night"; and these imaginings were connected with the peculiar development of this patient's intellectual life. He was especially fond of Puvis de Chavannes' fresco, *Sainte Geneviève veillant sur Paris*, which gave expression to one of his guiding fantasies. Thus his protection complex contained elements differing as widely one from the other as obsessions, insomnia, and a vigorous intellectual life. The last was sincerely regarded by him as a safeguard against the dangers of a concrete existence; and this was apparent in his tendency to substitute a comforting formula for that reality which eludes us all and is invariably disquieting. Thus, in history, he inclined to memorise dates rather than facts. In another of my patients, Jacques, I have shown with abundant detail how the intellectual life served as a refuge from and a defence against life properly speaking.[1] Jung has drawn attention to the protective role of formulas and of intellectualism. The fact is that, in these instances, there comes under our direct observation what seems to be the

[1] Mobilisation de l'énergie, Part I.

RETREAT 199

normal biological function of the intellect, although in "patients" we perceive it in more or less morbid distortions.

The tendencies grouped together to form a complex are of very varying worth, for some are wholesome whilst others are pernicious. Nevertheless all these trends may be intimately related, and it is this which makes education so difficult an art, needing both tact, and adaptation to each particular case. Introversion, for example, may be the prelude to a most happy development of the mind and of the inner life, but it is always verging upon a strong affective regression, a danger which goes by the name of narcissism.

The danger is readily understood once one realises that introversion isolates the individual, detaches him from objective life, saps his interest in the world around him, and concentrates his affective attention upon his own person. Narcissism and a desire "to return to the mother's womb" are at a first glance obviously related one to the other. But when we undertake the practical observation of each case we perceive that the kinship is more complicated and more intimate even than we imagined. Psychoanalytical methods invariably show that interrelated elements are connected in various ways and in various senses.

Again I shall refer to Green's case of the boy of nine who wished to pose as king. When the introversion fit was upon him and he withdrew to his room because he was disappointed in his mother's love (birth of a rival baby), we may deem that he metaphorically sought refuge in his mother's womb by shutting himself up in solitary grandeur. On the other hand his behaviour may be interpreted as meaning that, by a play of his introversion, he reconstituted within himself an equivalent

THE MIND OF THE CHILD

for the beloved object (his mother) which he had been forced to renounce ("introjection of the object"). He sought his mother, therefore, among the queens whose stories he was reading, in his fantasies, in his own self, so that finally the affection that had been alienated from her fell back upon himself—and this is precisely the reaction of the narcissistic impulse. In my patient Gustave, this reaction is even more definite. The prestige attaching to persons who lead solitary lives withdrawn from the world is connected with a longing for enclosed spaces, for a cosy room, both of which are equivalents of the desire to rest for ever in the shelter of the mother's womb. From his associations we learn that the protectress whom he symbolises in Sainte Geneviève watching over Paris is nothing other than his mother watching over her little boy. When, however, he himself becomes the "watcher," it is obvious that he has "introjected" the mother figure into himself. Gustave's whole life is, indeed, dominated by identification with the feminine principle.

Connected with the regression to narcissism, with lack of interest in the outside world, with a depreciation of objective reality in favour (simultaneously) of fantasy and the ego, we find a peculiar and illusory over-estimation of the mental life, a belief that thought, that ideas, are all-powerful. Such a belief, which has a flavour of magic about it, has been described as con-stituting a characteristic stage of narcissism. To my way of thinking, the relationships between introversion, fantasy, magic, and narcissism have not hitherto been fully established. But such relationships do undoubtedly exist, and in actual fact the transition from one of the phenomenon to the other is made easily enough.

Zulliger records the case of a boy who carefully avoided walking in the tracks made by the feet of his

RETREAT

teacher (Zulliger himself) in the snow, believing that by walking in another's footsteps one ran the risk of killing the individual who had made them. Here we see "magic" at work. Such survivals of magic have frequently been observed in children, but the point of interest in the present case is their relationship with a child's withdrawal from the world of reality into a realm of fantasy and narcissistic love.

The relationship is fairly precise in the case of the little girl reported on by Mary Chadwick. She compensated her feelings of inferiority by fancying herself to be God and engaged in the creation of living beings. Subsequently, this child suffered from obsessions, such as a dread of influencing others by her ideas, and above all a fear of giving birth to a baby. The relationship between the obsessions of later life and her earlier fantasies are very clearly defined. Both tend to substitute magical relationships for natural ones, and at the same time to attribute to the ego a kind of omnipotence.[1]

This same child was fond of writing plays, thereby providing herself with a further illusion of creating things. Here I may be allowed to refer to the connexion of art with magic and narcissism, a connexion to which Freud has drawn attention.[2] Indeed, art furnishes the ideal avenue for the sublimation of the tendencies we have just been studying. But art does not invariably suffice. In Marie Bashkirtseff, whose case I instanced above, we witness a strong narcissistic regression consequent upon a violent weaning complex. Her unbounded ambition forced her to develop in a high degree the fine talents with which nature had endowed her, and yet

---

[1] Mary Chadwick, Le phantasme d'être Dieu chez les enfants.

[2] See also Charles Baudouin, Psychanalyse de l'art, part I, chapters 2 and 5.

202   THE MIND OF THE CHILD

this did not suffice to re-establish her vital contact with the world of reality and with her fellows, nor did it compensate her for an all-devouring narcissism. When she was thirteen she wrote the following lines, which go to show that even at that tender age she was already heading for this danger: "I love to be alone in front of a glass." [We could not have a more perfect translation into words of this narcissistic complex.] "Perhaps it is silly to praise oneself so much, but writers always describe their heroine with the utmost care, and I am my own heroine. . . . Happily (or unhappily!) for me, I look upon myself as so great a treasure that no one is worthy even to glance up at me; those who dare to do so are hardly worth my pity. I fancy myself a divinity. . . Even a king would be difficult to treat as an equal. It seems to me that I am quite right. I look down upon men, and since they are such lowly creatures I treat them charmingly. I look at them as a hare would at a mouse." (July 17, 1874.) In her diary of the following year, Marie complacently quotes the philosopher who wrote: "If man, directly after birth and when he was making his first movements, failed to encounter resistance as he came into contact with the things forming his immediate environment, he would never succeed in distinguishing between himself and the outside world, but would suppose that this world formed part of himself, of his very body; when he was getting into touch with it, he would persuade himself that the whole of the outer world was nothing but a dependency and an extension of his personal being; he would confidently declare, 'I myself am the universe.'" She naively added: "Well, that is precisely how I dreamed of living, but contact with things of the outer world has produced very painful bruises." (October 1, 1875.) Unfortunately she was no

RETREAT

more able to learn the lesson of these "bruises" than she had been able to accommodate herself to the "weaning." She went on thinking "I myself am the universe"—and this, far from signifying "a taking possession of the world," denotes its negation, denotes an affective regression to an infantile phase in which the notion of "the object" has not yet come into being. We must not take things at their face value, and, although it may be true that "there is much modesty underlying vanity," it is no less certain that narcissism carried to an extreme at which it appears all-conquering represents one of the last phases of retreat, where death is ambushed round the corner.

As regards this matter of death, I am inclined to differ somewhat from Freud who has recently put forward the impressive hypothesis of "death instincts." Before accepting any such hypothesis, I think it would be well to study every longing for death which may present itself, from another outlook; to consider it as a possible expression of one of those instincts of retreat which are fundamentally defensive, but which, when exaggerated, are harmful. I believe that death may often be interpreted as the supreme refuge. The matter is discussed more fully in my *Mobilisation de l'énergie*, part II, chapter 8.

PART FOUR

RELATIONS AND REGULATIONS

CHAPTER TEN

POINTS OF INTERSECTION OF THE VARIOUS COMPLEXES

IT must never be forgotten that our tendencies or trends are interconnected like various railway systems, so that energy can be shunted from one to another—meeting, however, more resistance here and less resistance there. A "complex" is a region where the railway system is close-meshed, where the resistance is minimal, where energy flows with peculiar ease. This is what we mean when we say that the elements of the complex are interlinked. Throughout the mind, however, the elements are interlinked, are "associated"; it is merely a question of more or less, merely a question of whether the railway network is wide-meshed or narrow-meshed. In the introduction to my *Psychanalyse de l'art* and in *Mobilisation de l'énergie* (part II, chapter 3), I compared the aspect of a complex to that exhibited on a map by the routes of communication in the neighbourhood of a great city. Thus, no complex is isolated so as to form a State within a State, or so as to form an enclave. There is interlinkage between the complexes by means of wider-meshed lines of communication. The reader would form a false picture of reality if, after distinguishing between the various complexes and studying them in isolation, I were to refrain from drawing his attention to this wider-meshed lines of intercommunication.

When we analyse a disorder, a symptom, we are usually able to refer it definitely to one complex or another. But there is invariably over-determination, always multiple causation, and the various causes may belong

208   THE MIND OF THE CHILD

to different complexes, among which the symptom constitutes a point of intersection. Here are some examples.

We have learned that rivalry between the children in a family becomes exceptionally acute when the difference in age is about five years, and especially between an eldest child and a second child born after the lapse of five years. The probable explanation is that the Oedipus conflict reaches its apogee towards the age of five. At this epoch, when a child is engaged in the difficult task of trying to overcome an exclusive and jealous affection for one of its parents, naturally enough the appearance of another rival is extremely inopportune, and is likely to give rise to much perturbation. The emotional explosion apt to occur in such cases is attributable to a convergence of the Cain complex and the Oedipus complex. A clash between these respective complexes would also seem to be the invariable explanation of a brother's hostility towards an elder brother and of a girl's dislike for a sister older than herself. These feelings, which prolong the familiar rivalry between brothers and between sisters in early childhood, are likewise fed from an Oedipean source, the Oedipean enmity towards the father being transferred to the brother, that towards the mother to the sister. Shaw says somewhere that if there is any one whom a girl hates more than her mother, it is her elder sister.

There is another very interesting link between these two complexes, interesting because it shows the regulative activity which one complex can exert upon another. If brothers and sisters succeed in overcoming their primary mutual hostility, this is largely thanks to their Oedipean feelings. What happens is that two forces which have hitherto been collaborating, now counteract one another.

INTERSECTION OF VARIOUS COMPLEXES 209

A brother falls in love with his sister because he discovers in her an image of his mother; and in like manner a sister will love the father in the person of the brother. Finally, a brother may come to be fond of a brother, or a sister of a sister, because the loved parent makes a point of it, and the old rivalry is discarded in order to be worthy of parental affection.[1] However this may be, the feelings of affection between brothers and sisters are secondary rather than primary. Such were the mechanisms of which I was thinking when, at the close of the first chapter (in which I discussed the Cain complex), I pointed out that the feelings of sympathy indispensable to social life are far more strongly buttressed by filial than by fraternal affection.

There are two points of intersection between the Oedipus complex and the spectacular complex (inspectionism, etc.). Adler describes a girl of seven who had a keen sense of rivalry with her mother (imitating the latter, for instance, by suffering from attacks of headache). Adler also found indications of the aforesaid rivalry in the child's questions about birth; she could not bear that her mother should know more about it than she did.[2] In my own patient Karl, who originally had a passion for the concrete sciences, but in whom this interest was subsequently annulled by the growth of curiosity concerning forbidden topics, the position was complicated by a parallel repression founded upon the Oedipus complex. When Karl was a very little boy, he had wanted to be a doctor like his father, but somewhat later this profession seemed to him the most undesirable in the world. The Oedipus tabus had come into action, one of these being a prohibition to behave like his father

---

[1] Cf. Pfister, Love in Children, pp. 200-201.
[2] Adler and Furtmüller, Heilen und Bilden, pp. 44-54.

210 THE MIND OF THE CHILD

or to take his father's place in any conceivable way. Over and above this, the doctor is a person who knows forbidden things. Medicine, pre-eminently, is concerned with the concrete sciences of life. Here, then, in the prohibition of the concrete sciences, we recognise an interlocking of the two systems (Oedipus and curiosity).

In Jean Paul, who furnished a fine example of the weaning complex, we came to the conclusion that his stammer was a resultant of the weaning motif and the curiosity motif. He treated words as he treated the slops on which his elders were trying to feed him; but at the same time (like so many children who acquire a stammer) he was beginning to realise that his origin was being concealed from him, and that there are things "of which one must not speak." We saw that a lively curiosity was at work.

Furthermore, the weaning complex may be complicated by fraternal rivalry. I once had under observation a woman who since early childhood had suffered from severe attacks of enteritis, but these attacks always became more distressing after she had been visited by a younger sister. Her first words when she came to consult me ran somewhat as follows: "It is not surprising that I am ill, for my mother poisoned me with her milk. She was still nursing me when she was expecting my sister. Because she was with child the milk became bad, and I had to be weaned." Obviously, many years afterwards this patient still found it impossible to forgive her sister.

Pfister's young sleepwalker who used to hide under the counterpane some pictures that symbolised her conflicts was also, it is evident, animated by fraternal rivalry in addition to her longing to be fed by her mother and her longing for an asylum. One of these pictures was of six

INTERSECTION OF VARIOUS COMPLEXES 211

children, of which the eldest was giving food to the youngest while the others were demanding a share. Among the associations came the avowal: "I know that Father and Mother would rather have had a boy than me; my sisters said that it would have been better if I had never been born"; and so on.

Relationships between curiosity and the anal system (destruction) are plainly visible in the "cloacal" theory of birth—which seems so obvious to children.[1] The reader will remember that, following in the footsteps of numerous authorities, I have explained stammering, sometimes as the outcome of the repression of anal trends, and sometimes as the outcome of the prohibition of enquiries concerning the sexual life in general and birth in particular. Are we concerned here with radically different types? They do not differ so much as they may seem to at first sight. The link between the two motifs is the cloacal theory of birth. In certain cases a far-reaching analysis, bringing to light this cloacal theory of birth, may disclose a linkage between the two situations.

Graber had a boy of nine as patient. The child, Willi, stammered, and on analysis the defect was interpreted as a result of the anal complex. In this case, Graber furnishes us with some very interesting data: when the lad evacuates his bowels he suffers from the same difficulty in breathing as he does when he endeavours to speak; in like manner, if he is trying to utter a word, he hops from one foot to the other just as when he is "waiting to do wee-wee" or to go to stool; when the stools are "easy" or of the right consistency, Willi does not stutter, but when he is slightly constipated and they are "difficult" the impediment in his speech is pronounced; and so forth. He dreams of a deep pit, of a subterranean cave

---

[1] Ernest Jones, Papers on Psychoanalysis, p. 695.

212   THE MIND OF THE CHILD

full of precious stones. The associations aroused in connexion with the underground places lead straightway to
anal subjects, and also, though veiled behind cloacal
fantasies, to the maternal womb. As the work of analysis
proceeded, Graber was able to note that Willi subconsciously established an identity between the absorption
of food and conception, and between defaecation and
childbirth.[1]

Since we have seen that there exists a bridge linking
anal tendencies with curiosity, and that there is an even
closer tie between anal tendencies and sadistic trends
(destruction complex), it is not hard to grasp that there
should likewise exist a kind of partnership between
curiosity and cruelty. The last-named is met with in
children who wilfully tear their dolls to pieces, whether
the pretext for such an act of destruction is to cut them
up or is merely a desire to see how they are made—a
pretext behind which we have no difficulty in discerning
inquisitiveness regarding human beings. Pfeifer reports
a case which admirably illustrates this point when he
records the games of young Hans.[2] Again, Zulliger's
story of a little girl named Greti is instructive. This
child not only rips up her doll, but secretly cuts out all
the female organs depicted on a coloured plate in a
work on physiology. Violent sadistic trends manifest
themselves at this period against her mother and against
the baby which Greti knows to be on the way, and it is
in connexion with this latter fact that her curiosity has
become more accentuated. In a word, this case is a
demonstration of how closely related are the three trends:
rivalry, cruelty, and curiosity.[3]

[1] G. H. Graber, Redehemmung und Analerotik, p. 363.
[2] S. Pfeifer, Aeusserungen infantil-erotischer Triebe im Spiele,
p. 243.   [3] Hans Zulliger, Gelöste Fesseln, p. 73.

INTERSECTION OF VARIOUS COMPLEXES 213

François, the little cannibal whose case I cited in Chapter Three, is a further example of how intimately cruel impulses are related to curiosity concerning forbidden topics. With this idea in mind, let us recall some of his sayings: "I love stories about people who are killed. . . . When they're going to kill some one, I'll hide behind some planks and then I'll see everything." At the same time he becomes greatly interested in his father's nakedness. He declares one day: "If you die before me, I'll be able to eat you; I'll cook your brain, and then your eyes and your ears. . . . If you die, I'll open your skull and your tummy to see what it looks like inside. Oh, yes, I'll do that." When he tells his aunt that as soon as she is dead he will "plough" her body and "keep the skeleton," the first-mentioned prospect expresses a sadistic impulse, whereas the second is, rather, a form of curiosity.

One cannot help feeling that this combination of trends represents a typical attitude of mind which may be met with under differing circumstances and at various degrees of sublimation. For instance a strong leaning towards vivisection and surgical operations may be taken as a form of sublimation on the scientific plane. In a yet more subtle form we meet with it in the ultra-analytical type of brain, in the effort to understand and pierce through the nature of an object by dissecting and disintegrating it. Indeed, all intellectual activities can be placed in the same category of sublimations. Here, however, we have to admit that the sublimation of the trends we are studying has reached a very high level.

In our search for points of contact between these systems of complexes we have been faced with certain situations wherein more than one of these systems has played a part: such as, for instance, rivalry and cruelty

THE MIND OF THE CHILD

and curiosity. This fact will in no way surprise those who have already realised that a complex does not constitute a circumscribed system. Some cases, in especial, serve to illustrate the convergence of a multiplicity of springs. Thus Anna Freud introduces us to a girl of six who, after passing through an Oedipean phase of the most pronounced character, retraces her steps to the anal-sadistic stage of development when a younger sister is added to the family group. The consequent hatred she felt towards her mother was due, according to our authority, to an over-determination of several motifs, some of them related to fraternal rivalry ("my mother has forsaken me so as to look after the baby"); others to the Oedipus complex ("my mother has deprived me of my father's affection; she has given birth to a child which I would have liked to give to my father;" etc.); while yet others seemed to depend on the Diana complex ("Mother did not make me a boy").

Little by little, as we approach the realm of what I term "complexes of attitude," we become aware of the presence of systems where the associations with other complexes are enhanced to a peculiarly high degree.

There are many kinds of shock which determine a regressive movement, leading the subject to seek an asylum. Many children seek such a refuge because of the birth of a younger brother or sister; which means nothing more than the acknowledgment that rivalry has given place to a desire for "retreat." This is exemplified by cases wherein regression has ended in bed-wetting, or by Graber's case of the introvert, Willi, or by Anna Freud's case of the little girl who wished she had never been born and who rounded off her desire to return to the mother's womb by fantasies of rebirth ("I'd like to

INTERSECTION OF VARIOUS COMPLEXES 215

be born again so as to be my favourite doll"). Fantasies concerning rebirth invariably contain a compensatory element, and we can readily understand, therefore, how it is that such fantasies are called up by situations which, being felt as rebuffs, immediately call forth an effort at compensation. Now, such situations are very varied and may have their point of contact in all the complexes.

It has been pointed out earlier in the book that the "search for a refuge" forms an important connecting link between the birth complex and the various "attitudes of retreat." In Kurt (Graber's little patient, the boy who was so extraordinarily submissive and who exemplified in an exceptionally typical fashion the "attitude of retreat"), with his desire to be in a church or in a closed car, etc., this attitude found an issue in fantasies concerning the asylum of the maternal womb. In my own patient, Jacques, we saw that the various regressive movements, the various "retreat tendencies," and so forth, were indisputably associated with mutilation. The reader will not have forgotten the dream wherein, assuming the aspect of his chum Jean Louis, this little boy did his utmost to climb the bank of a ravine, which symbolised an endeavour to achieve action, to attain to reality and success, only in the end to fall into the waters of the stream below, crying "Mother." One detail of this dream needs to be emphasised: while scrambling up the hill he had "short hair"; as he fell, he had "long hair, like a girl." The "attitude of activity" is, therefore, subconsciously interpreted by Jacques as representing virility; whereas the "attitude of retreat" symbolises for him femininity. Elsewhere in our present study we have seen how certain infantile theories presuppose an identity between femininity and mutilation. In the example furnished by Jacques' dream we have yet

216 THE MIND OF THE CHILD

another demonstration of the childish theory of "somewhat too little" and "somewhat too much": a girl has something less than a boy, a fact which in the realm of symbolism is expressed equally well by the image of something too much—in Jacques' dream by "long hair, like a girl." Furthermore, this young patient of mine told me several other dreams, each of them concerned with an accident, which in its turn was a veiled allusion to the mother's death, the greatest accident of his life. All these accidents were associated with characteristic mutilations: "A river in winter; blocks of ice are being broken up; one chum is carried away by the current [cf. "Jean Louis's" fall into the river in the previous dream]; another schoolfellow has his head crushed and his legs fractured." In this lad, one of the motifs of the over-determination of his troubles by means of bed-wetting (as in so many other cases) would seem to be the unconscious equivalence between the enuresis and castration, so that the bed-wetting symptom may be looked upon as the precise spot where the complexes of mutilation and retreat converge.

Such a synthesis is by no means rare. Gustave, whose case was alluded to in Chapter Nine, not only had a well-developed tendency to seek a retreat, but likewise presented a strong mutilation complex: identification of himself with the feminine principle, feelings of inferiority dating from earliest childhood, while later in life he definitely refused to accept any kind of sexual activity. In Jacques and in others of my patients the same phenomena are found at work.[1]

This attitude of retreat is associated with the Oedipus complex in Graber's young sleepwalker, Fred. This child

[1] Cf. Charles Baudouin, La régression et les phénomènes de recu en psychologie; also, Mobilisation de l'énergie, Part II.

INTERSECTION OF VARIOUS COMPLEXES 217

dreams that he is seeking his mother, but a huge dog stands in the way and terrifies him. On analysis, the dog was found to symbolise the father. It is easy to understand, in the case of this little boy whose "attitude of retreat" is conditioned by a longing for his mother, why the Oedipus complex should play so obvious a role.

The transition from the Oedipus complex to the attitude of retreat and to narcissim is effected (so far as boys are concerned) in a way that is very understandable and precise. We have seen that the two main components of the Oedipus complex (attachment to the mother coupled with hostility towards the father) may converge so as to determine a flight from social life and the reality principle. The constraints imposed by social activities and reality become assimilated to the father, and participate in the hostility which the boy harbours in respect of his father; meanwhile, the child who thus flees from reality takes refuge "in the mother's womb." Let me remind the reader of Zulliger's patient Hans, who could never write on the line but always above or below it. Analysis showed that "the line" symbolised the world of actuality, regulations, paternal decrees; "beneath the line" meant "in the earth," "above the line" meant "in the sky." This "in the earth" and "in the sky" (or "in heaven") was the place where Hans's little sister had "taken refuge" body and soul when she died; now the girl has become "an angel, and can do anything she likes," so that Hans envies her fate because "Father won't let me light a fire." Here we see, in the germ, the flight from reality which is the sequel of a refusal to accept paternal decrees, on the one hand, while on the other hand there is the search for an asylum "in the mother's womb" ("in the earth" and "in the sky"). There is likewise a trace of fraternal rivalry: the younger

218   THE MIND OF THE CHILD

sister has found a refuge in death; Hans envies her; and so on.[1]

Whenever one engages upon a thorough-going analysis of any kind of symptom, one invariably encounters elements belonging to other groups of complexes. All the lines of communication seem to start vibrating directly some central zone is set in motion. But we needs must identify this centre of commotion before we can follow up the avenues of activity it has opened up.

The reader will already have realised that the conjuncture of two or more complexes is not brought about by chance. Such a meeting of complexes can only take place along certain routes which resemble one another in case after case. We may, therefore, detect a kind of intermediate complex hyphening, as it were, two main complexes, and possessing a physiognomy of its own. Thus, without running this topographical or linguistic simile too hard, we can locate certain forms of the search for a refuge *between* the retreat complex and the birth complex, and certain forms of flight from social constraints *between* the Oedipus complex and the retreat complex.

A system composed in part of the Oedipus complex and in part of the mutilation complex may be termed the "Prometheus complex," and it is by this name that I usually speak of it: a son desires to mutilate his father, to steal from him the power which goes hand in hand with adulthood and paternity (stealing the forbidden fire); by virtue of the law of retaliation, the father in his turn will mutilate the son; this form of mutilation is often replaced by its equivalent, ligation ("Prometheus

[1] Hans Zulliger, Psychoanalytische Erfahrungen aus der Volksschulpraxis, p. 100.

INTERSECTION OF VARIOUS COMPLEXES 219

bound"). I must insist upon the importance of this Promethean system, for it comes so frequently into play when little boys addict themselves to the practice of masturbation (forbidden fire) and subconsciously interpret the act as the theft of paternal power, a theft which will bring punishment in its train. Zulliger's patient Max, the "glutton," presents us with a picture of the Prometheus complex. That explains why he dreams that he is tied down in his bed while a man comes towards him with a knife in order to cut off his leg.

Such an intermediary system, just like all other systems of complexes, has a way of finding expression for itself by means of highly individual fantasies, and by typical motifs, each of them more or less related to the parent myth. From the Promethean motif it is but a step to that of the hero in general. Since Rank's and Jung's explorations along these lines, it has been recognised that the hero motif is a compost of the spectacular complex (illustrious hero exposed to all men's gaze) and the rebirth motif.[1] This shows that the role played by "heroic fantasies" is essentially a compensatory one. Thus fantasies of "heroic birth" appear readily in a child as the sequel of the idea, "I am not the child of my parents."

When these hero-fantasies become entwined with masochistic trends, with desires for chastisement, and so forth, we get another combination: the hero-motif is allied to that of the martyr. In Ilona's case we witnessed something of the sort. This little girl, whose imitation of a mayoral address had so amused her audience, was an almost perfect example of the spectacular complex

---

[1] Otto Rank, Der Mythus von der Geburt des Helden; C. G. Jung, Wandlungen und Symbole der Libido, part II, chapters 4 to 6; Charles Baudouin, Psychanalyse de l'art, p. 29.

220   THE MIND OF THE CHILD

(her case was dealt with in greater detail at the beginning of Chapter Four). Ilona gave herself up to strange reveries: she was a fairy; she lived in a beautiful castle; she wore transparent draperies; she wanted to do good among mankind, but no one understood her; she was imprisoned as a witch and was persecuted; finally, she was condemned to death, dragged to a public square, and burned at the stake, "before a large crowd." The hero-theme (solar myth, etc.) frequently enough ends in some such solution. It is the funeral pyre of the demigod Hercules.

CHAPTER ELEVEN

TWO TYPICAL MOTIFS

1. *I am Shut Out*

IN the previous chapter we came to the conclusion that there exist certain typical motifs wherein the convergence of several complexes is effected in a fairly definite manner. The present chapter will be devoted to a closer study of two of these motifs, concerning which I myself or other investigators have been able to collect an abundance of valuable material, and which, intrinsically, appear to be among the most important.

One such motif may be summarised in the formula "I am shut out." This motif originates as the outcome of fraternal rivalry. When a younger brother or sister is born, the elder child runs the risk of feeling that it is cold-shouldered. Thereupon, the phenomenon of over-determination appears upon the stage. First of all the ubiquitous Oedipus complex makes its presence felt; furthermore, the advent of a younger child almost invariably stimulates the elder's curiosity as to birth; this curiosity, in its turn, comes into collision with the parental veto, with the parents' hemming and hawing concerning so "indelicate" a topic, with their lies, so that in the end the child feels it is being fobbed off and excluded from its parents' confidence in a twofold manner, for it is excluded from the love which is now lavished upon the baby and it is simultaneously excluded from acquiring knowledge of an important truth. Thus, since it suffers a double-edged disappointment in its parents, it loses its trust in them. The convergence of

222 THE MIND OF THE CHILD

these two streams (fraternal rivalry and curiosity) may suffice to create a situation heavily charged with affect.

A hint at the existence of this system occurs in the case of Anna (cited above) who out of jealousy refused to admit that her younger sister could have been formed inside the mother's body. But a more obvious example is furnished by a boy of seven years and six months presented to us by Sophie Morgenstern. This child was very intelligent, and, previous to the birth of his sister, had been of a gentle disposition. Since the advent of the baby, however, his character had undergone a complete transformation. At the time when he was brought for treatment, the little girl was twenty months old. The boy had become hot-tempered, liable to fits of rage in which he went pale with jealousy, and said of his sister: "They only love her, they only kiss her, nothing's the same since she came." He wanted to have a cord so that he could hang himself. The child confided to the analyst all his conclusions in respect of birth, and was not afraid to ask questions. He said: "I didn't believe it when they told me Mother was in bed because she had fallen down stairs. . . . A chum said that babies grow inside the mother's leg. . . ." The analyst was of opinion that a simple explanation of all these puzzles would have cured the lad, but the father forbade any mention of such "dirty subjects" in his son's presence. One can only deplore these unreasonable prejudices.[1]

When such a situation arises, we need to be on the alert, for very serious consequences may ensue: regressions in character formation, and intellectual regressions. I have already furnished examples showing that intellectual backwardness may be due to a hankering for the

[1] Sophie Morgenstern, La psychanalyse infantile et son rôle dans l'hygiène mentale, p. 74.

TWO TYPICAL MOTIFS 223

return of the early days of childhood, or else to curiosity concerning forbidden topics. Now, in the convergence we are studying, the two situations become welded together.

But there is a more direct expression of this sense of exclusion than any of the foregoing—perhaps the most direct of all—namely, a demand for love, attended by manifestations of obstinacy and other undesirable character traits.

Aubrey, a child of five, was under observation by one of my pupils. She had a younger brother, and her parents sent her to a boarding-school. This served to enhance her feeling of exclusion. She talked unceasingly of her parents and her little brother. But when her father and mother came to visit her, she barely so much as looked at them—which may have been her way of expressing the grudge she bore them. If the parents of her schoolmates came on visiting days, Audrey was greatly excited. Her conduct at school was dominated by the endeavour to attract attention to herself, to be cared for by the grown-ups, while at the same time she behaved in a most obstinate manner. She talked in a loud and screechy voice; she upset things and was constantly responsible for breakages; she was systematically disobedient; she wetted her clothes, and was pleased at the trouble she caused those who had to wash them; when she found that some one was particularly busy, she would clamour to be kissed; she deliberately stirred up quarrels so that a teacher was forced to intervene (e.g. she would snatch a pencil out of a schoolfellow's hand, and would start screaming and demanding the mistress' protection before ever the real owner of the object in question had had time to protest); at the slightest reprimand she cried aloud, "Don't you love me? Don't you love me?" She

224 THE MIND OF THE CHILD

was constantly asking questions (another device for attracting attention to herself), and this brings us back to the theme of curiosity concerning forbidden topics. Ida Löwy, one of Adler's pupils, records a similar case of a boy fourteen years old. After his sister's confirmation he became noisy and disobedient. Quite early in life the lad had been sent away from home (= excluded), and his parents more or less ignored his existence. He lived for three years in a sanatorium where he considered he had been underfed. His sister, on the contrary, had had all her heart could desire at home, and when she was sent to school at Prague had been fed on a very generous scale (here we cannot but feel that another component, issuing from the weaning complex, may have joined the rest). But the day when he saw his sister all decked out in her confirmation dress proved too much for him. In order to attract notice to himself, to become a centre of interest, he had recourses to infantile methods of revolt: noisy behaviour, disobedience. Once the boy had been led to realise what was amiss, in three weeks he calmed down and was able to live on the best of terms with his sister.[1]

The feeling of exclusion is fed from other and very important sources, namely those which flow from the ego complexes. The mere comparison of oneself with others, of differentiating oneself from others, of looking upon oneself as a being distinct from one's neighbours or distinct from members of the opposite sex, tends to awaken the sentiment of exclusion. Rank has often insisted on this fact, though he uses a different ter-

[1] Ida Löwy, Kränkung und Verwahrlosung, a section in Adler and Furtmüller's book Heilen und Bilden, p. 124.

TWO TYPICAL MOTIFS

225

minology; and it seems to me that it now plays a leading role in this expert's analyses.[1]

All the feelings of inferiority which are in any way related to the mutilation complex may serve to strengthen the sentiment of exclusion. Especially is this so when the feeling of inferiority is connected with an organic defect, with an infirmity which brings about a real exclusion. Here, again, objective data are reinforced by the complexes.

Such conditions of inferiority and their psychological results are of especial interest to Adler and his school. Consider, for instance, the case of a little girl who suffered from infantile paralysis when she was a year old. The upshot was that she had one leg shorter than the other with a stiff knee and an incurable limp. At school she was the butt of her schoolfellows. The organic defect was the centre of feelings of inferiority which developed in ways determined by various complexes. She fancied that the mistress did not like her (exclusion), and she had to be removed to another school; she declared that she would never be able to marry; thanks to a mutilation complex she became affected with a sense of guilt for which there was no reasonable warrant, but which made her regard herself as responsible for her condition. Thus she lapsed into neurosis.[2]

Here is another case recorded by one of Adler's pupils. It is that of a boy of eight who was blind of one eye. Until he was five, he lived in the country; then he was brought to stay with an aunt in Vienna, and it was there that he lost one of his eyes through an accident; wishing

---

[1] Otto Rank, Technik der Psychoanalyse, vol. ii, the chapter entitled Gleichheit und Verschiedenheit.

[2] Case reported by Else Sumpf in Adler and Furtmüller's Heilen und Bilden, p. 163.

P

226 THE MIND OF THE CHILD

to regress to the days before this disaster, he showed his longing by a strong desire to live in the country. He was of a harsh disposition and turbulent in his behaviour, cuffing boys bigger than himself, and always wanting to play the leading role. Sometimes he stayed out all night. These various characteristics were the outcome of the regression, of his yearning for the days of early childhood (fugues), and of a vigorous protest against the feeling of exclusion. It seems to me, moreover, that there must have been a close connexion between the longing for a country life and for early childhood (the mother's breast), on the one hand, and the sentiment of exclusion on the other. Removal from country to town and the loss of an eye would appear to have been felt as parts of one and the same shock.[1]

It will be readily understood that the feeling of exclusion may derive from the familiar motif "I am not really my parents' child," from the various fantasies of heroic birth, and from the allied tales of children stolen by gypsies. This notion may arise at a very early age. Wulff records the case of a girl eighteen months old who suffered from anxiety and from phobias after having been told a story about a child sold to a pedlar. She nestled down in a corner of the sofa saying again and again: "Mother, don't give me away to any one; Mother, keep me."[2] But it is obvious that the idea "I am not really my parents' child" will tend to become exceptionally vivid when this creation of the collective unconscious is reinforced by real facts (just as in Else Sumpf's case the mutilation complex was reinforced by an actual infirmity).

---

[1] Case reported by Ida Löwy in Adler and Furtmüller's Heilen und Bilden, p. 124.

[2] Phobies chez un enfant d'un an et demi.

TWO TYPICAL MOTIFS 227

This happens in adopted children or in a child whose father or mother has remarried.

In little girls, the Diana complex may greatly intensify the feeling of exclusion.

The reader will remember my patient Cecilia, the girl who knew her own mind very well, but as regards the choice of a profession vacillated between physical culture, medicine, and aviation. Here a strong Diana complex was accompanied by a no less strong feeling of exclusion. The latter underlay the obstinacy and rebelliousness, with occasional thoughts of suicide, on account of which Cecilia was placed under my care. The Diana complex was linked with the motif of forbidden curiosity. Cecilia resented the fact that her parents had never told her the truth about the important problems of sex. As so often happens, their reticence had made her withdraw herself thenceforward from their influence, and this had a good deal to do with her general attitude of revolt and independence. As the analysis proceeded, the sexual problem became urgent once more, until at last the young woman ventured to ask me in plain terms for a full scientific account of the topic. I referred her to Forel's book. We were to have had several more sittings, but Cecilia, having now got what she wanted, did not visit me again. Furthermore, I had lent her several books on psychoanalysis, which she omitted to restore to me— her neglect being probably the outcome of vestiges of a vengeful attitude which had not been completely dispelled by the analysis.

In Linette, whose case is partly recorded in my *Studies in Psychoanalysis,* and to whom I have alluded several times in the course of the present work, there were various factors combining to bring about a strong sense of exclusion. Linette manifested fraternal rivalry and

228 THE MIND OF THE CHILD

also suffered from the Diana complex. Curiosity, too, played its part. The convergence of the three motifs was vividly displayed in her enmity towards the brother who had been born when she was five years old, and whom she would have been delighted to see carried off for good and all in the wheelbarrow—provided that the wheelbarrow was brought back! She considered that she had been excluded for her brother's benefit. The position was made worse by the fact that she was the daughter by her mother's first husband. Besides this, when her brother was born a mischievous and stupid servant was continually saying to her: "Now that you have a little brother, no one will care for you any more."

For a long time Linette made a peculiar mistake in spelling. In the case of words ending in a mute "e" or a mute "e" followed by an "s," she would write the "s" when it had no business to be there and would leave it out in the other cases. Now, whereas her own name ended in a mute "e," her brother's name ended in "es." Her misspelling was a way of keeping her end up. But there was over-determination, for the Diana complex played a part. Linette called "s" a serpent, and she said that a final "s" which was not sounded was "a serpent who does nothing." In a word, for her this letter had become a phallic symbol, the final "s" representing all her brother's privileges. Then, the expression "who does nothing" is emblematic of the girl's curiosity. The "serpent who does nothing" in spelling was as annoying to her as the apparently superfluous organ she had noticed in her brother, an organ which had no discoverable function. At this stage she became disagreeable and exacting, the motif "I am shut out" being at work. As she made herself a nuisance at home, she was sent to a boarding-school; but, since her brother stayed with

TWO TYPICAL MOTIFS 229

the parents, this served only to intensify her sense of unsatisfied claims. One day when she came back for a holiday (she was then about twelve), she sat down beside her brother's bed, in earlier days her own bed, to cut the pages of a book, and "carelessly" left the open penknife in the middle of the bed—this representing the same desire to mutilate her brother that was manifested in the suppression of the final "s." A little later, sublimation began, and when she came home for the holidays the first thing she did was to cut her brother's hair. There had arrived upon the scene a second brother of whom she was very fond, and towards whom her attitude was quasi-maternal; but he, likewise, had to submit to the hair-cutting ritual. On one occasion when she came home, her mother had just cut the little brother's hair, and when Linette arrived she exclaimed: "How horrid of you, Mummy! There is nothing left to cut." When she was seventeen, the same system of affects was still going strong. By now the elder of the two brothers had been sent to a boarding-school, whilst Linette was again living at home. She felt herself avenged at last! But the boy had left a litter on the table in his room, and Linette declared it was an eyesore to see a clutter like that "doing nothing." For us who have followed her life story, it is obvious that the expression "doing nothing" is no more than a later edition of "the serpent who does nothing" and which vexed her so greatly when she was six years old. Now she swept all the stuff cumbering her brother's table into a dark corner, and installed herself and her work at this same table although she had the choice of other and far more commodious tables at her disposal in the house. About this time she talked aloud in her sleep; this habit of hers was of fairly frequent occurrence, and denoted the existence of somnambulism

230 THE MIND OF THE CHILD

in the larval state. In this particular dream she said to the younger of her two brothers, assuming the tone of annoyance proper to a person who has a bone to pick with another, "What on earth are you doing with that poker?" Again we get a reference to old-time "serpent who does nothing." Linette's vengeful attitude of mind peeped out in a hundred and one little actions and words. The infantile motifs persisted but were kept within reasonable bounds behind ingeniously constructed dissimulations; sometimes they even assumed an aspect which was the very obverse of what they really were. Thus at this period Linette went through a phase wherein she declared that for nothing in the whole world would she consent to be a boy, but would have liked to be a stag. She assumed at times the pose of an innocent victim, and became very fond of Racine's *Iphigénie* wherein the heroine is condemned to be sacrificed on Diana's altar.

When the situations we have just been studying attain a greater degree of intensity, paranoia and ideas of persecution are apt to arise. In Chapter Four of this book I alluded to a case reported by Odier. Here, after the birth of another child, the boy in question felt himself cold-shouldered by his mother because she would not disclose how babies came into the world. Thereupon mythomania set in, which, when the lad attained his nineteenth year, was pressed into the service of a syndrome of persecution. He invented all kinds of pretexts and excuses for his actions, even for the most innocent of his doings, in order to defend himself against the punishments and ill usage which, in his own imagination, his parents, the foreman, and his workmates, inflicted upon him.

TWO TYPICAL MOTIFS 231

Else Sumpf tells of a girl who was perfectly normal up to the age of ten. Then she became somewhat clumsy in her acts. It was found on examination that she was short-sighted. She had hitherto been a good pupil, but now she failed to point out places on the map, and her teachers considered her absent-minded and lacking in intelligence. Her clumsiness increased; she took to stammering. Her spectacles made her feel that she was ugly; at home she was forbidden to read, at school she was shunned by her classmates, who fancied she had a contagious disease of the eyes. When she grew up she expressed a desire to continue her studies, but her grandmother laughed at the idea of the young woman becoming a blue-stocking. Little by little the sense of inferiority gained ground and she felt she was shut out, avoided by every one; she fancied that people spoke ill of her; she was on the verge of suffering from a veritable mania of persecution.[1]

I want the reader to understand quite clearly that we are not accounting for the existence of a psychosis by saying it is due to certain complexes. Nevertheless, each psychosis is characterised by an undue activation of a definite area within the network of the complexes—this being a matter of much interest whose details have still to be worked out. What is called dementia praecox is an example of retreat and narcissism carried to an extreme; in melancholia there are abundant elements of masochism and of a sense of punishment; and the paranoiac affected with ideas of persecution is one who has multiplied to the nth power the feeling of exclusion. I do not mean to imply that such intensifications of this, that, or the other complex are to be solely or chiefly explained as the out-

[1] Else Sumpf's contribution to Adler and Furtmüller's Heilen und Bilden, p. 161.

232 THE MIND OF THE CHILD

come of psychological traumatism. Perhaps there are some cases in which the influence of such shocks preponderates, and others in which an anatomico-physiological explanation would be more appropriate. The attempt has, in fact, been made to distinguish on these lines between two types of dementia praecox. As regards the interrelationship between psychological and physiological outlooks, we have to recognise that to the complexes, "psychological areas," there must certainly correspond cerebral areas—which must be thought of dynamically, rather than as very strictly localised—which can be activated both by psychical and by physico-chemical agencies. Such a way of regarding the matter has become essential where insanity is concerned, but it is no less valid as regards the neuroses and even as regards mere "faults of character." When we explain a neurosis or a defect in character as the outcome of a complex, now one and now another, this does not mean that we suppose the psychological explanation to be all-sufficing.

Another very typical symptom of the motif of exclusion is theft. Nor need we be surprised, for we have already seen that thieving is an expression for the desire to be avenged. From this point of view and in the light of our present knowledge it is instructive to read once again Alfhild Tamm's book dealing with three cases of children suffering from thievish inclinations. Especially interesting is the one concerning the Jewish boy of nine who stole because he wanted enough money to buy goods and to set himself up as a pedlar like his grandfather. There are also, in his case, fantasies of a return to the mother's womb, to his native land (Russia), to a far-off country; there is likewise an identification with the grandfather, an identification which we have earlier found to contain

TWO TYPICAL MOTIFS 233

elements of revenge; further, the boy suffers greatly from an uneasy feeling, a sense of exclusion, so natural to a child who is forced to pass his life in a foreign environment (the lad is a Russian Jew).

Another instance of a child prone to theft is furnished by Ida Löwy. A girl of eleven, pale-faced, weak, vain, and jealous; being an illegitimate child, she has a well-developed and obvious sense of being shut out; her parents separated, and each of them chose another mate when the girl was still very young; her mother was of Jewish extraction, and, since the child has been placed in a Catholic school, she feels that she is despised on account of her Jewish blood; she longs for affection, and everywhere sees her advances repulsed; thus she is led to believe that she must buy the love which does not flow towards her of its own accord, and she steals from her grandmother in order to propitiate her schoolmates. This is a fine example of "rationalisation," and, in its way, admirably expresses the connexion between theft and love claims. Such rationalisations are composed of elements A and B which are linked together in the unconscious and are perceived by the conscious; but their relationship to M is not perceived with any precision, and is replaced by the relationship P which is a more or less imaginary one. Elsewhere I have given an example of this system of rationalisation in the case of a little girl in whom feelings of rivalry in regard to a younger sister and the consequent sense of being cold-shouldered led to her stealing in order to have the wherewithal to take care of her little sister. The child studied by Ida Löwy suffers, in addition to the symptoms enumerated above, from restless nights, when, like Linette, she talks in her sleep. Somnambulism is usually interpreted as an expression of nostalgia, etc., and it will,

234 THE MIND OF THE CHILD

therefore, not surprise the reader to learn how closely it is associated with feelings of exclusion and with the making of claims.

In Bertrand's case, too, the youthful kleptomaniac in whom fraternal rivalry was allied with curiosity (the reader will recall the boy's dreams of detectives, underground passages, explorations, and so on), the motif of exclusion was no less obvious.

Thus we see that children are peculiarly sensitive to all those situations which provoke in them, rightly or wrongly, a feeling of exclusion. Temporary disgrace and withdrawal of affection, even the simple threat "If you do that, no one will love you any more," touch the child on the raw. Psychoanalysts are inclined to think that a menace of the sort is highly logical and most efficacious, and should, indeed, be substituted for all other forms of punishment (whether of the violent or of the bickering kind) too much in vogue even in our day. Of course, there is no question here of corporal punishment, which cannot possibly form part of any education worthy the name. Physical violence towards children, though it may appear to bring about good results, only does so at the cost of developing masochistic trends—in which case the remedy is worse than the disease. Even the milder punishment of a threat to withdraw affection from the child must be used with discretion lest we engender a feeling of exclusion; especially, we need to be careful in this respect when the child is already under the harrow of the exclusion complex. In certain acute cases it may happen that the mere pretence at depriving the child of affection is enough to make it feel that it is being most violently and cruelly chastised. Barbara Low reports the case of "a boy of six, who had been tiresome and

TWO TYPICAL MOTIFS 235

obstreperous when much younger, then docile and quiet in disposition." But, at the end of his first term in the kindergarten, he showed himself "morose and aloof, unwilling to respond to the teacher's very sympathetic advances or to the other children's companionship; he moped, was aggressive at home, and ceased to take his former interest in physical and mental activities. During the first weeks of school life it happened that the kindergarten mistress pursued her usual policy of leaving the new child somewhat alone with the idea of giving him time to settle down and develop on his own lines. . . ." In this particular case the policy was ill-advised, for subsequent analysis showed that the child had suffered from a sense of being excluded ever since his younger brother's birth. But the hostile emotions aroused in him by the advent of a baby which had deprived him of his close companionship with his mother were repressed and compensated by his re-establishment as "the important elder brother." They were revivified and able to manifest themselves in the sequel, "under disguise," with his entry into the school "and the repetition, as it seemed to him, of the 'punishing' (i.e. ignoring) attitude of the mother-figure (the teacher)."[1]

When discussing curiosity in regard to forbidden topics, I showed that there were two questions uppermost in the child mind, namely, the difference between little boys and little girls, and the origins of life, especially where human babies were concerned. Upon these two problems two complexes are grafted: the complex of mutilation, and the complex of birth. But it is not difficult to see that a third problem naturally arises out of these initial ones: What is the relation of the father to the mother, of the man to the woman? No child is

[1] Barbara Low, The Unconscious in Action, pp. 73 et seq.

236 THE MIND OF THE CHILD

capable of formulating this third problem with so much clarity as the two fundamental ones; nevertheless, the fact is that when a child sees or hears something of the intimate sexual relations between its parents (or other adults), it is always profoundly moved and sometimes completely distraught. Grown-ups have every reason to beware of dealing such a shock. Even when the history of one of our subjects leads us to suppose that this shock was not dealt in a very sudden or brutal fashion, it may all the same have led to the results which we know to have occurred in more marked cases. One cannot but think that we are here in the presence of a primitive and hereditary system which needs a mere touch to set it in motion.

Children have their own theories respecting this problem, as they have in respect of the two fundamental ones. Having perceived what goes on between their parents and between animals, and inspired, no doubt, by the primitive schemata residing in their own minds, they piece their observations together, and out of this material they construct their theories. Such theories are invariably the same: sexual relations are interpreted as being an act of violence and brutality, as an attack on the woman by the man; the woman is suffocated, crushed, sacrificed. Sophie Morgenstern writes: "The idea that coitus is an act of cruelty and violence prevails among all the children who can be led to talk of the matter."[1] This has been termed the "sadistic interpretation of coitus." It is natural to suppose that when children actually witness sexual relations, the shock gives rise to more vehement imaginings and may shake the youthful psyche to an even greater extent. All the more

[1] La psychanalyse infantile et son rôle dans l'hygiène mentale, p. 83.

TWO TYPICAL MOTIFS

reason for parents to avoid having even the youngest of children to sleep in their bedroom. Freud, recording cases of this sort, shows how they are responsible for many a nightmare. Indeed, for the most part, child nightmares are built upon such foundations. A boy of nine, pretending to be asleep, witnessed the whole scene, and was terrified at what he saw and heard. Soon afterwards he had a nightmare wherein an analogy was set up between what he had heard and his own relation to a younger brother whom he habitually ill-treated.[1]

Sophie Morgenstern had a boy of fourteen under observation. He, too, suffered from nightmares. This was the lad who declared that children see far more than grown-ups are wont to suppose, and, indeed, as a little child he had witnessed things which were the starting-point of his sexual obsessions in later life: he imagined that his father was torturing his mother; that only married women menstruate; he was haunted by the fancy that his father had drunk water from a glass wherein a blood-stained clout belonging to his mother was soaking; and so on.[2]

2. *The Victimised Woman*

Memories of this kind do not immediately come up in the analysis; they are usually dissimulated behind a screen, just as are infantile theories of mutilation and of birth. A perfectly natural screen is furnished by the remembrance of quarrels and other scenes of violence between the parents in daily life. It must never be for-

---

[1] Freud, La science des rêves, p. 573.
[2] La psychanalyse infantile et son rôle dans l'hygiène mentale, p. 69.

238 THE MIND OF THE CHILD

gotten that such scenes are frequent causes of psychological trauma, and where the memory has been scarred by them they will often collaborate with the earlier shock to produce the type of the victimised woman.

Here is an instructive instance culled from Pfister's *Love in Children* (pp. 163 et seq.). "A girl of fifteen detests her stepfather, who is a drunkard and ill-uses his family. He often beats his wife, whereupon the child passionately espouses her mother's cause. . . . Every night in her sleep, the girl finds her way to the umbrella-stand in the dark passage, and awakens there with screams of anxiety. . . ." Analysis brought out that she associated "umbrella" with her stepfather, who always placed his in the stand at the door; she was "afraid a man would jump out on me there," and proceeded to describe this man as like her stepfather. There was obviously a hate-love conflict going on in her unconscious, which owed its origin to "critical experiences and undesirable stimuli in the parental bedroom during early childhood," so that her desires were directed towards the person of the father. Since such desires cannot be openly manifested, they appear under a mask. We have here the effects of a combination between the early shock of witnessing the sexual act and paternal violence.

In the case of young Klara, reported on by Zulliger, the motif of the victimised woman is underlain by the customary sexual allusions, but it is reinforced by the fact that the girl's uncle is a butcher who treats his wife with the utmost brutality.[1]

The foregoing examples suffice to prove that the situation is by no means a simple one. But it is further complicated by the fact that, despite the child's theories in the matter, sooner or later the youngster acquires an

[1] Hans Zulliger, Gelöste Fesseln, p. 43.

TWO TYPICAL MOTIFS 239

intuitive feeling that the sexual act is a demonstration of love and is pleasurable. Cases of masturbation have been observed wherein the habit was acquired as the outcome of what the child had heard and seen concerning its parents' sexual relations. In fantasy it will, under such circumstances, take its father's or its mother's place while it masturbates.[1]

Taking all these things into consideration, we have to admit that the shock which awakens the child's curiosity and sadistic trends, is equally capable of arousing its Oedipus complex and the motif of exclusion. Although the love act is looked upon as brutal and terrible, it is nevertheless felt to be a desirable activity. The fact of being excluded from participation in this activity, and, further, of being excluded from all knowledge concerning it, is a genuine sorrow to the child; this exclusion joins company with another form of exclusion which consists in being sent to bed when grown-ups continue to stay awake, so that certain forms of insomnia appear in very early childhood, and seem to be determined by a lively protest against these manifold exclusions. In the memories of later life, the last-named form of exclusion serves as a screen to the first-named.

We have constantly to bear in mind this conjuncture of diverse and contradictory sentiments: the terrible, the desirable, the mysterious, the shutting out. Only by so doing shall we obtain a fairly adequate idea of the child's fears, and especially its night-terrors. The anguish felt at separation might well be called "the dread of being shut out." But fear of the sort is only too readily overdetermined, so that the motif of the victimised woman

[1] René Allendy, Les rêves et leur interprétation psychanalytique, p. 126.

THE MIND OF THE CHILD

and of a love that inspires dread play a great part in it—just as they do in nightmares. Dread of the dark, of ogres, of "the black man," of the wolf or the serpent, etc., is fed from the same spring. Some interesting observations have been made upon children who are frightened and set up a howl immediately they perceive that something is taking place between the parents. Such children will insist upon a pledge that each parent shall be in a separate bed, and tranquillity is sometimes not wholly restored until father or mother comes and sits by the cot.[1]

If the origins of masturbation are sometimes to be found in the same shock which gave rise to fear, we shall be more easily able to grasp why there is so close an association between masturbation and anxiety. This anxiety or dread would not in such a case be a simple fear of mutilation, for it would at the same time draw upon the other great well-springs of anxiety. Naturally enough, the motif of the victimised woman is related to the mutilation complex, and readily joins forces with the Diana theme. This is what happened in Klara's case to which I recently referred. She had received a shock on the day when her uncle, the butcher, had pretended to stab her with a knife. A friend had put an end to this ill-conceived pleasantry by crying: "She's already got a cleft in her belly, and doesn't need a second!" Klara was deeply wounded by such a rude joke and wept. In giving a description of the scene to Zulliger she showed great indignation, and said: "Yet it isn't my fault if I'm a girl."

[1] The observations are signed "eine Mutter," and have been published under the title Die Entstehung von Pavor nocturnus bei einem Kinde. Another study of night-terrors has been made by Heinrich Meng in his Neurasthenie, Neuropathie, Psychopathie des Kindes.

TWO TYPICAL MOTIFS 241

Very various symptoms may be traced back to the shock caused by witnessing the act of sexual intercourse. In addition to the states of anxiety I have been discussing, this initial shock may give rise to asthma (catch in the breath, panting). Dr. Allendy told me of such a case observed by himself in a boy of six. Two or three visits to the analyst sufficed to bring about a great improvement in the child's condition. The attacks of asthma came on when the boy had got into trouble at school (inferiority), or when he had been playing with a little girl who wanted him to join her in games wherein exhibitionism and palpation were the main elements. But the auditive perception of the parents' sexual intercourse and the tabu placed upon the subject played the central part in his symptoms. The analyst's frank explanation of the questions troubling the lad's mind very soon brought relief.

When a child has been the victim of this typical shock whence the motif of the victimised woman arises, it tends in imagination to play the role of one or other of the parents whose sexual intercourse it has heard or actually witnessed. But it does not follow that a boy will invariably put himself in the father's place, and a girl in that of the mother. The roles may be reversed, and in this case the situation is a very significant one, and is related to a specific form of character, i.e. masculinity and aggressiveness in the girl, and femininity and masochism in the boy. Such situations have their roots deep down in the primitive, and ancient mythologies are a proof of this fact. Let me recall the legend of Tiresias who had witnessed the coupling of two serpents. Thereafter he wounded the female, and then he found that he himself had been changed into a woman. You could not find a story more effectively illustrative of psychoanalytical

242 THE MIND OF THE CHILD

outlooks, and all the other episodes of this myth are equally significant.[1] But in this assumption of another's role there is a strong ego complex at work; the child is endeavouring to find its own feet, and is not always successful. Nothing is more characteristic than the hesitancy exhibited by some persons in respect of the love scenes they have witnessed in early childhood. My patient Jacques did not "know in which bed" he was, and his whole character is built upon a hesitant attitude, for he cannot decide whether to accept the virile or the feminine role in life. The shock is further shown in another symptom, for whenever this complex was being analysed he had a slight attack of asthma and kept on panting. Ida E. is another case in point. She keeps in touch with the forgotten scene which has produced a trauma in her psyche by dreaming that she does not know whether she is in her own bed, in that of her uncle, or in her aunt's. Shortly after, she has another dream in which she is giving advice relative to marriage. The person she is advising is obviously herself, though in the dream this figure remains vague and unsubstantial. In her endeavour to furnish a description of this vague personality she makes use of the same expressions which served her turn in the former dream to describe her hesitation as to the bed in which she found herself; which, being interpreted, means that her hesitation is near akin to that other hesitation she feels in deciding as to the situation of her own ego.

In the investigations made in various schools as to whether the pupils would rather be "a boy or a girl," the Diana complex was much in evidence, and among the boys there were a few who preferred the idea of being a girl, thereby proving themselves exceptions to

[1] Cf. A. H. Krappe, Mythologie universelle, p. 302.

TWO TYPICAL MOTIFS

the general rule. Quite possibly, if these boys were submitted to a careful analysis we should find in them the motif of the victimised woman, with the superadded refusal (because of continued attachment to the mother) to accept the executioner's role. This actually comes out in the simplest and most direct way in some of the answers. One boy of eight who was in a boarding-school, the son of divorced parents, would have preferred to be a girl, making his avowal with tears in his eyes.

"Why?"

"Because men are so unkind."

"But all men are not unkind."

"Oh yes, they are because they are so strong."

Naturally this motif becomes much more precise if we go further with the analysis. My patient Gustave was completely under the dominion of the motif of the victimised woman: as a dim memory of childhood he has the vision of a cow that was slaughtered and all covered with blood; in one of his dreams, the man is required to drink the woman's blood. But Gustave himself is downright in his refusal to accept the executioner's role. This primary refusal determines his rejection of manly behaviour, for men's ways are deemed brutal; he assumes a feminine attitude to which are subjoined the complexes of mutilation, refuge, and retreat. In addition, he suffers from persistent insomnia, and "mystery" in any form has always occupied his mind.

Sophie Morgenstern, too, reports the case of a boy who dreamed that a man had to drink a woman's blood. She notes in passing that the fantasies of her little patient recall the symbolism of the rites and beliefs of primitive peoples. In Gustave's case the associations called up by his dream touched upon many a theme of the collective unconscious: the chalice filled with blood, dragon's blood

244 THE MIND OF THE CHILD

(two of the motifs in the legends of Parsifal and of Siegfried). Jung gives us some arresting suggestions in relation to the chalice and the dragon, and their association.[1] It was this motif of the victimised woman I had in mind when I wrote (apropos of the mutilation complex) that certain boys deliberately renounce a privilege which they feel has been unjustly conferred upon them; in some way or other they find a means to mutilate themselves, symbolically at least, and they identify themselves with womankind. This mechanism is at work on every plane of the intellectual life. Erwin, Zulliger's little patient, began to work badly at arithmetic because a small girl friend of his had been humiliated and laughed at when she was unable to find a correct answer to a very simple problem; the boy put himself in her shoes, blushed when she blushed, and from that day onwards refused to accept a part in life which was nominally superior to hers.[2]

The adoption by a child of a paternal or a maternal attitude, of a masculine or feminine role, or of a superior or inferior position, brings us face to face with the important problem of identification.

---

[1] C. G. Jung, Wandlungen und Symbole der Libido, p. 351.
[2] Hans Zulliger, Psychoanalytische Erfahrungen aus der Volksschulpraxis, p. 104.

CHAPTER TWELVE

THE SUPER-EGO

1. *Identification*

THE term "identification" in psychoanalysis is used to denote a more complete and a wider form of imitation wherein the whole being, including the unconscious, collaborates. A child which identifies itself with another, does not merely imitate this person's mannerisms, but even moulds its whole character upon that of its exemplar, going so far as to imitate illnesses under the form of neurotic symptoms. As regards neurotic troubles, physicians have frequently attributed to heredity what in reality is due to identification. In the course of the present study I have referred to a girl who, seized with the desire to occupy her mother's place, began by imitating the elder woman's headaches. This procedure is encountered again and again in innumerable subjects. Freud considers that character is built-up by laying down a succession of strata in which it is not difficult to detect the sequence of the identifications adopted as the personality developed. The most fundamental of these identifications is that relating to the imitation of the parents, and this primary identification gives the key-note to all the consequent ones.[1]

Identification may take place by means of various mechanisms. For the sake of simplification, I shall confine myself to the description of two forms of identification, that which is due to emulation and that which is due to love. Where the former is active, the subject endeavours

---

[1] Freud, Psychologie collective et analyse du moi.

246 THE MIND OF THE CHILD

to become as like the rival as possible so as to attain to equality; in the latter, the subject tries to reconstitute, by means of introversion, an equivalent for the beloved object which has had to be renounced (introjection of the object). One models the behaviour upon this object in the hope of finding it within oneself). Among boys (following the Oedipean law) identification with the father generally occupies the first place, that with the mother, the second. The act of renunciation which colours the latter is due to the necessity of sharing the mother with the father and with the other members of the family group. Among girls, the opposite sequence is the rule: in the beginning they imitate the mother in order to take her place; whereas they renounce the father and "introject" him.

This "introjection of the beloved object" is the subtler of the two mechanisms. Nevertheless we can obtain a good idea of its working by the study of simple examples furnished by the observation of children. Freud, quoting a case from Markuszewicz's article in the "International Journal for Psychoanalysis" (vol. vi, 1920), tells us of a boy who had had the misfortune to lose a kitten. All of a sudden the youngster began to declare that he himself was this kitten, and he took to walking about on all fours. He further refused to eat anything at the table, etc. In a case of my own, a young girl furnished me with a parallel instance, and an even completer form of identification. When Myrrha was a child, her favourite dog Bichon died. The animal had been used to follow her wherever she went. In order to console herself for this loss, little Myrrha began "to be Bichon," she would gambol like the dog and snuff around like him. First of all the imitation was purely physical, but as she grew up she identified herself with the dog mentally. A large

THE SUPER-EGO 247

portion of her character was based upon this early identification. Although she had an inclination to dissociation of consciousness, in respect of the dog-identification she never went so far; but a second personality resided within her, and both she and her friends were well aware of this isolated individual, and, with a common accord, they all called it "Bichon." The presence of Bichon announced itself by Myrrha's suddenly assuming the voice and the ways of a baby, by yapping as of a puppy, and by the expression of ideas to match.

Identification with an admired model explains the formation of the "imago," of the "ego-ideal," which, more or less unconsciously, attracts the ego to itself and moulds this ego to resemble itself.[1]

2. *The Father-Ideal*

But at this point matters become more complicated. The father—and I shall confine myself to him for simplicity's sake—plays the principal part only during the early years of a child's life; soon thereafter (as we have learned when studying the Oedipus complex), father-substitutes appear in the shape of other elders, masters, managers, chiefs, etc. In the case of a boy, the process of identification usually travels along the following lines: simple and direct identification with the father is not possible over any length of time; the child more often chooses a "father-ideal" who, in certain character traits, is the opposite of the real father; an uncle, a god-father, a grandfather will play the substitute role in the first instance, to be replaced in the sequel by the teacher, the professor, and, then, by another man who

[1] Freud, Essais de psychanalyse, Chapter Three, Le moi et le soi.

248 THE MIND OF THE CHILD

has made a name for himself in the past or in the present

In Victor Hugo's case, for instance, the child early rejected identification with his father who was a general under the empire, and chose as model his godfather, Lahorie, a conspirator against Napoleon and, consequently, an exile; when the lad was fifteen, he chose for exemplar Chateaubriand, who was an avatar of the same imago for he, too, was an opponent of the emperor (the symbol of the father), and it was at this moment that our future poet wrote: "I shall be another Chateaubriand or nothing." Much later in life, at the age of fifty, when on December 2, 1851, a new Napoleon established himself by a coup d'état, Victor Hugo felt that he, too, had been "proscribed" like Lahorie, and during his exile he recapitulated Chateaubriand's itinerary during the latter's life as refugee.

Various influences are at work to lead a boy to choose his father as ideal. First of all there are two opposing Oedipean causes which, in Victor Hugo's case, converge so that we have on the one hand hostility to the father, whilst on the other hand there exists a prohibition (tabu) against taking the father's place. The same mechanism may be suspected to be active in my patient Karl, who at first wanted to be a doctor of medicine like his father, and who later would not have practised this profession at any price. If the parents do not live on amicable terms, and if, then, the boy takes up the cudgels in his mother's defence (as was the case with Victor Hugo), we can readily understand how the imagined (and often real) contrast between the actual father and the ideal father becomes accentuated in the subject's mind. Furthermore, it behoves us to remember the disillusionment suffered by a boy in respect of his father, when one day

THE SUPER-EGO 249

the latter's foibles are shown up, when the father is discovered to be neither all-powerful, nor omniscient, nor perfect, nor superior to other men, as the child had fondly supposed. The disappointment, which may be sudden and so harmful as to leave a trauma in the psyche, is liable to be consequent upon the boy's detection of the father in deliberate falsehood, or upon the revelation of his parents' sexual intercourse, or what not. It is usual to look for its appearance towards the fifth year of life, just at the time when the Oedipean trends are making themselves more particularly manifest.[1]

The choice of a father-ideal converges towards the fantasy "I am not the child of my parents," and by this means it rejoins the myth concerning reincarnation and heroic (miraculous) birth. There is thus a compensatory element in the choice. In Victor Hugo, simultaneously with the growth of the father-ideal system of mechanisms, there was a considerable development of those connected with reincarnation or second birth (notably in the form of a "family novel" wherein he traced his origins, in all good faith, from ancestors who had belonged to the aristocracy). Certain young kleptomaniacs to whom I have referred above, identified themselves with the grandfather, and this identification harboured an element of revenge running parallel to the theft itself. I have had a boy of sixteen under my care who, in addition to being a thief, was likewise a liar and wished people to think that his parents were well-to-do—whereas in reality they were very poor and modest folk. At our first interview he offered "to take me out in the car." We see that his mendacity was a method of compensation, so that he told fairy-tales about his noble lineage. Indeed, I fancy that "compensation" lies at the root of many a falsehood!

[1] Cf. Ferenczi, Die Anpassung der Familie an das Kind.

250 THE MIND OF THE CHILD

This boy's mother had married again after her divorce; his so-called father was, therefore, not his real father, and we know from cases already adduced that such a situation is liable to set in motion the well-known motif "I am not my parents' child," a motif that belongs to the primitive and mythical age of mankind, and which in the case under consideration is given objective justification.

3. Conscience

And yet it is undeniable that a child is in very fact "the child of its parents." It is the parents who, by way of the first identifications, set up in the child's mind the tribunal which Freud began by terming the "ego ideal" and now inclines to speak of as the "super-ego." The term denotes the supreme authority whose business it is to hold many of the instinctive impulses in leash. I prefer, here, to use Freud's terminology, and to speak of the super-ego; but there have been various other ways of incorporating what is substantially the same notion. Jung, for instance, speaks of a man's guiding and satisfying idea of himself, as his "persona." Pierre Bovet has, independently, developed another aspect of the question by deriving the religious sentiment from filial trends.[1] Again, de Saussure has proposed to introduce in this connexion the notion of "instinctive inhibitions" as an apter term. Certainly this suggestion does not lack interest; but we must always remember that the task of an analyst is to reduce facts, not to their instinctive elements, but to the complexes. Now, Freud's super-ego is precisely such a complex, and for that very reason—

[1] Pierre Bovet, Le sentiment religieux et la psychologie de l'enfant.

THE SUPER-EGO 251

at least until further notice—is a more opportune term than any notion of "instinctive inhibitions."[1]

The super-ego is not to be identified with "conscience," with the "moral consciousness." It is, as it were, the psychological organ of which the moral consciousness is one of the functions; it is a complex whose duty is to form an opposition to the other complexes and to regulate their activities. And yet it is from these other complexes that the super-ego absorbs the forces which will be turned back against them in the sequel.

By laying bare the part which identification with the parents plays in the formation of the super-ego, we come to realise how intimate are the ties between the super-ego and the Oedipus complex (which portrays the original state of the filial sentiments). Freud considers that the strength of the super-ego is proportional to the initial strength of the Oedipus complex and to the energy displayed in the struggle to overcome it.

The commands and prohibitions issued by the parents (or by those who act for the parents) are at first felt by the child to constitute external constraints. Then, on a certain day, they come to be more or less accepted —"introjected"—and are henceforward transformed into interior constraints: it is at this moment that the super-ego makes its appearance on the stage. Even before Freud's attention had turned towards these particular issues, Pierre Bovet had shown this mechanism to be at work: a respect for orders given presupposes a respect for the person who issues the orders.[2] At times we are able to watch the passage from one stage to the other at the very moment in which it is effected. When Peter had done something

---

[1] Cf. de Saussure, L'instinct d'inhibition.

[2] Pierre Bovet, Les conditions de l'obligation de conscience, p. 55.

252 THE MIND OF THE CHILD

naughty, he took hold of his own ear and led himself into the darkened room where he was usually made to stay for punishment. His mother asked what he was doing there. The boy replied: "I told him not to slide down the banisters, but he wouldn't obey me. So I took him by the ear and made him come into this room." —"But who on earth are you talking about?"—"Peter, of course!"[1]

Thus it is plain that, from a certain point of view, the super-ego represents the parents in the psyche of a child. We shall, therefore, do well to bear the following formula in mind: The super-ego tends to behave towards the ego as the parents behave towards the child. Such a formula will help to explain many a situation which might otherwise perplex us.

Some children can never undertake any activity without falling into disaster. Fate comes in for a share of the blame; or else God and the devil are made responsible for these mishaps. But "fate" (or what you will) is, in the child's unconscious, identical with the father in respect of whom the youngster has always felt himself to be inferior, and whose words weigh upon the youthful mind like a doom. "You must not do that; you'll never make a name for yourself"—and so on. Henceforward an interior voice is constantly admonishing the child in these identical words, which have the force of a law.

Again, parental quarrels, and especially a divorce, will create a cleavage in the very heart of the super-ego. It is essential that there should exist a perfect unity of command in the tribunal of the super-ego if it is to function adequately as a regulatory mechanism. Sophie Morgenstern tells of a boy whose troubles began when his mother left her husband. The child was then sent

[1] Ernst Schneider, Die Abwehr der Selbstbefriedigung.

THE SUPER-EGO 253

to a boarding-school, where he was very unhappy; later on, he was exceedingly pleased when he was once more allowed to come home; but his joy was marred by the presence of his father's second wife for whom he felt neither love nor hatred, but an undefined sentiment. Analysis made it clear that the boy was suffering "from the conflicts engendered by the differing identifications of the super-ego."[1] It would be interesting to study afresh, in the light of this idea, many of the young people who have passed through my hands and whose childhood was troubled on account of parental squabbles, of divorce, or of the remarriage of a father or a mother.

As might be expected, any upset in the delicate poise of the super-ego is liable to find expression in deficiencies of character and in a lack of moral standards. Thus theft, lying, uncleanliness, cruelty, and what not, which have so far been interpreted as regressions and, in especial, as regressions to the anal-sadistic stage, may be open to another interpretation which by no means excludes those already adduced. Such a point of view has proved of inestimable value to Aichhorn in his analyses of abnormal children and of juvenile offenders.[2] In addition to the conflict between several contradictory identifications, we have to take into account a perfectly normal though no less unfortunate identification which is made with parents who are themselves lacking in moral tone. "Like father, like son."

Side by side with the Oedipus complex, and related to it, we have, further, to recognise the existence of certain spectacular elements. Hence the motif of "God's eye" looking down on us and seeing everything everywhere (very naturally associated with paternal supervision).

[1] Sophie Morgenstern, Prophylaxie infantile des névroses, p. 80.
[2] August Aichhorn, Verwahrloste Jugend.

254   THE MIND OF THE CHILD

The thought of this all-seeing eye haunted young Heinz's mind, so that he came to detest religion and religious instruction.[1] Victor Hugo elaborates the same theme in his poem *La Conscience*; here we find a convergence which proves an abundant source of inspiration; there is also an Oedipus element in the work, associated with the spectacular complex. Further, we cannot ignore certain primitive components in the whole idea of this eye which is all-seeing, which is compared to the sun, is an attribute of that "God in his heaven" who stalks through various mythologies before becoming "the eye of a moral God" (Varuna, Zeus, Jahveh, etc.).[2]

An important element in the composition of the super-ego is modesty, which is a modification introduced into the spectacular complex (prohibition of the pleasure the subject experiences in "showing off"). Another addition to the make-up of the super-ego is disgust, which is a modification introduced by the anal complex and the whole series of "the ethics of the sphincters" (the child is forbidden to be dirty, etc.). Nor must we lose sight of the fact that under such conditions the child will react by asserting itself, and may develop a character which is stubborn, pigheaded, or the like. Further, we must never forget that modesty and disgust are moral factors which develop in close relation to the attitude the child adopts towards its parents (or other guardians and educators); behaviour of the sort is specially and primarily adopted in relation to them. Very interesting to observe is the period of a "double standard of morality." During this traditional period the child will behave quite properly so long as it is in the parents' presence, but will completely relapse when it finds itself alone or in the

[1] Hans Zulliger, Gelöste Fesseln, p. 34.
[2] A. H. Krappe, Mythologie universelle, p. 39.

THE SUPER-EGO   255

company of other children. Anna Freud tells us an
amusing story of a boy who showed her a cow-pat as
if it was a most sensational thing to see; then, suddenly,
he pulled himself up, became shamefaced, and got himself
out of the difficulty by a lie: "I didn't really know what
it was." He had certainly made a mistake—but not
concerning the object in question! He had forgotten that
he was talking to a grown-up, and had behaved as though
he was playing with persons of his own age. In their
company he felt no scruples, and did not think it necessary
to mask the fact that such things added a zest to his life.[1]

4. *Self-Chastisement*

It is in connexion with the super-ego that the ego-
complexes arise; and it is in relationship to this super-ego
(which the subject feels to be "superior") that the ego
proper has to find its place. This will inevitably give
rise to inferiority and mutilation sentiments; but since
the super-ego (like the parents) is set up as a kind of
tribunal or judge whose duty it is to inflict punishment,
feelings of guilt are an unavoidable result.

When I say that the super-ego deals out punishment, I
must not be interpreted as holding that an abstraction has
become a concrete fact. The phrase, however, epitomises
a fact which is not only concrete but is also extremely
important and sometimes tragical. When a child estab-
lishes its super-ego, when it introjects the admonitions,
the orders, and the prohibitions of its parents or teachers,
it simultaneously introjects the corresponding sanctions.
In other words, it accepts the punishment (mutilation)
which ought to be inflicted when it infringes the

[1] Anna Freud, Introduction to Psychoanalysis for Teachers.

256   THE MIND OF THE CHILD

tabus. Because of such acceptance, it acquires a sense of guilt when it has "done wrong." Nay more, it substitutes its own self for the executive authority which would inflict punishment—as did little Peter when he took himself by the ear and led himself to the place of punishment.

This mechanism of self-punishment is of great moment, and is more far-reaching in its consequences than might be supposed at a first glance.[1] It is not any less significant because, in great measure, it works in the unconscious. (The reader must never forget that the zone of the super-ego extends far deeper than the conscious, and I wish to point out in this connexion that, even supposing that what has hitherto been termed "conscience" were identical with the super-ego—which it is not—it would be desirable in psychoanalysis to have a special term for use in this connexion, since it would certainly be confusing and clumsy to speak of an "unconscious conscience." In English, French, and German alike, Freud's term "super-ego," "sur-moi," "Ueberich," is indispensable.) We know that the unconscious stands guard upon the nervous paths along which the physiological functions of the organism are guided, just as it determines the functions of consciousness. This explains how self-punishment may manifest itself either by psychological or by physiological symptoms. A child which, having practised masturbation, has introjected, has accepted, the customary punishment by mutilation, will, in the unconscious, actually achieve a "mutilation" of one sort or another. It will suffer from a reduction in bodily vigour or mental energy, from weakness of memory, from a defect of attention, or from some nervous symptom manifested in this organ or in that—although in many

[1] Cf. René Allendy, La justice intérieure, especially Chapter Five.

THE SUPER-EGO 257

instances we have no ground for regarding these troubles as a direct physiological outcome of masturbation.

Psychoanalysts are agreed to-day that nervous symptoms in general are explicable, not only as "wish-fulfilments," as expressions of a complex, but also as self-punishment which is the expression of a condemnation of the wish or the complex. There are cases in which this latter interpretation is peculiarly apposite. Here are four which have come within my own experience.

Fernand, a little boy with a strong spectacular trend, playing with two girls in the open country, insisted upon their stripping to the skin, while he did the same thing. He then sent them home, totally nude, whereas he was discreet enough to dress again before he went back. They were punished with a sound whipping, whilst he got off scot free. The upshot was that he had a lively sense of guilt, and punished himself in various ways: by feelings of inferiority; by a feminine identification (mutilation); and, above all, by an attack of eczema. This disorder, affecting the skin (nudity), often manifests itself as a punishment for indulgence in spectacular inclinations. As far as Fernand was concerned, I think it must also be regarded as an equivalent for the weals which he would have had if he had been whipped in accordance with (as he thought) his deserts.

In Bernard, indulgence in spectacular trends was punished by an attack of writer's cramp, and by timidity on various social occasions when, as he kept on saying, he "ought to have taken the front place." The action of "taking the front place," like that of holding a pen and signing his name, was regarded in the unconscious as the equivalent of indecent behaviour.

The third case is that of Gabrielle, in whom spectacular

258 THE MIND OF THE CHILD

inclinations were punished at puberty by the onset of agoraphobia. Here, the action of making herself conspicuous by crossing a public square had been unconsciously assimilated to a blameworthy display of the genital organs.

My fourth case is of a different nature. Nelly had an elder sister who had been afflicted with paralysis in consequence of a fall. Now this fall had taken place when the elder sister had been sent away for a few days to a boarding-school at the time of Nelly's birth. Poor Nelly came to regard herself as responsible, through having been born, for her sister's mishap. She applied the lex talionis, a simple and straightforward method of punishment much in vogue in the unconscious. She found it difficult to walk, and could only keep afoot for a very short time, although there was no organic disorder to explain the remarkable weakness of her legs. She was merely imitating her sister's paralysis.

The punishment which an inward and often wholly unconscious sense of guilt demands may sometimes be achieved by a side wind, by finesse as it were. The subject will behave in such a way as to incur a punishment objectively administered. Félix Boehm describes a girl who was a confirmed story-teller, and in whom this symptom was linked with a sense of guilt deriving from the Oedipus complex. Her whole life had been established upon an unconscious falsehood, upon the determination to show herself indifferent to the father whom she adored. Her feeling of guilt induced her to tell deliberate lies, very stupid ones, which brought punishment upon her.[1]

In such cases, which are common enough, objective punishment misses its mark, serving only to encourage what it is intended to prevent. The mechanism in question

[1] Félix Boehm, Une enfant menteuse.

THE SUPER-EGO 259

may reach tragical proportions. Aichhorn has shown this clearly in his study of juvenile criminals. The sense of guilt may bear on childish peccadilloes, which have sometimes been altogether imaginary, but of which the sufferer, under stress of complexes, takes a very serious view. Hence there arises so strong an unconscious need for punishment that the boy or girl thus affected may commit actual crimes in order to be satisfactorily punished.[1] Once more psychoanalysis teaches us to be on our guard against appearances. I may reiterate in this connexion how unjust it is to accuse us of seeing only the worst aspects of human nature. Though it be true that, in many instances, analysis has disclosed the suspect foundations of "good" actions, here we find it teaching us that a criminal may be a criminal through excess of morality!

The foregoing considerations will have led the reader to recognise that the super-ego does not always conduct itself with the wisdom of a judge, but often behaves like a blind tyrant. It is a psychological reality, not an ethical and philosophical imperative; or, at any rate, the ethical and the philosophical are no more than certain facets of the super-ego, and must not be confounded with its essence. The punishments which the subject, influenced by unconscious motivation, metes out to himself or succeeds in making others mete out to him, are as stupid as they are brutal. They consist, for the most part, either of mutilation or of an enforcement of the principle of an eye for an eye and a tooth for a tooth, so that we cannot fail to recognise once again the survival of primitive trends in the unconscious. The super-ego

[1] Verwahrloste Jugend, p. 283. Cf. also Freud, Essais de psychanalyse, Le moi et le soi, p. 222.

260 THE MIND OF THE CHILD

cannot be explained exclusively in terms of parental identifications which account only for the individual and highly evolved elements of the super-ego ("the ego-ideal"), There are other elements of the super-ego which are deeply rooted in the primitive, making it terrible and immoderate like the tabus of primitive societies.

In certain cases, these formidable aspects of the super-ego assume a dangerous preponderance, and when that happens we may speak of a regression of the super-ego towards its primitive elements. Such a regression is prone to occur in a masochist. Let me remind the reader of our discussion of the Prometheus complex. Georg, eight years old, often dreams that a black man seizes him and cuts off his legs. When he is asked, "What do you do if you miss the train?"—"I want to cut my throat."—"What if you have broken a thing which belongs to some one else?"—"I cut off my hand."[1]

Since the super-ego and the ego sometimes clash as if they were two distinct persons (like the father and the child) it is by no means absurd, even though it may sound strange to speak of "a masochistic attitude of the ego towards the super-ego." Here again we have to do with cases in which punishment misses its mark because it is too successful, because it is secretly felt to be pleasurable. Psychoanalytical writers have likewise referred to "a sadistic attitude of the super-ego towards the ego," this being the counterpart of the same situation. It arises especially when the super-ego has been modelled upon the image of a father who was brutal, or too strict, or unduly exacting.

We see, then, that although the super-ego rises into the most abstract realms of the categorical imperative,

[1] S. Spielrein, Einige kleine Mitteilungen aus dem Kinderleben: Traum eines Masochisten, p. 99.

THE SUPER-EGO

261

it is not free from instinctive and primitive elements which advantage it by endowing it with their energy, so as to make of it a "divine instinct" (as Rousseau termed conscience); but which are perpetually tending to encroach. Sadism (cruelty) is, as I have pointed out, capable of being sublimated into severity towards oneself into asceticism; but we cannot afford to blink the fact that such transformations run the risk of "regressing" to their primitive elements. These dramatic aspects of human nature, aspects wherein the good and the bad are as closely intertwined as two wrestlers in the heat of struggle, must never be lost sight of, and it is difficult to decide which of the two is victor and which is vanquished. A trifle may change the issue of the combat, and education is one of the elements of this "trifle." That is precisely what makes education so arduous an art, and it is the victory of a "trifle" which adds lustre and dignity to the educative process.

CONCLUSION

HINTS TO EDUCATORS

My readers must not expect from the present work anything which it has not tried to furnish. It makes no attempt to teach the technique of psychoanalysis as applied to children, and still less does it aim at formulating a methodology of education. The author's sole ambition has been to depict the child mind as revealed to us by psychoanalysis. Nothing more than this was foreshadowed in the title. I believe, however, that from the foregoing exposition parents and educators can deduce certain useful inferences—as follows.

1. First of all we have to realise that the earliest days of childhood play a role whose importance has so far been grossly underestimated, not to say completely ignored. It is usually assumed that the "serious" task of education must begin round and about the twelfth year of life; some persons hold that before a child is seven years old education "is of no moment." Now, according to the findings of psychoanalysts, a child of seven has already gone beyond the age when its affective life is plastic, for the decisive shocks come before the sixth and even before the fourth year. A child of tender age should never be handed over to the care of second-rate persons. Psychoanalysis emphasises the fact that a very young child's psychical development is already well advanced and extremely complex, so that education is of primary importance from the outset.

2. The recognition of this fact would be somewhat alarming were it not that psychoanalysts have further been able to throw light upon the chief shocks to which those passing through the first years of childhood are exposed. The foregoing pages have been mainly devoted

266 THE MIND OF THE CHILD

to an account of the shocks attendant upon weaning and upon separation from the mother; to the Oedipus conflict which disturbs a child's relationships with its parents; to rivalry among brothers and sisters; to the extreme sensitiveness of the child mind, a sensitiveness which often induces the feeling of exclusion; etc. Elders who have been enlightened regarding these weak spots will be to some extent forearmed, in some degree able to mitigate the shocks in question.

3. A separate and express mention must be made of what can be classed in the aggregate as the sexual shocks of childhood. Grown-ups are far too apt to ignore them; and their importance, though it be not exclusive (as the language of some psychoanalysts seems to imply), is certainly very great. The problems with which a child is faced when it discovers the difference between the sexes; the questions that torment it as concerns birth; the dangers that arise when it witnesses the intimate sexual relationships of adults; the quasi-universality of masturbation in infancy, the frequency of masturbation at puberty, and the profound sense of guilt which may arise in these connexions; the need for frank explanations and for the avoidance of threats as regards masturbation, and as regards the whole realm of the sexual life where children are concerned—these are various matters of which parents and educators must never lose sight.

4. One of the leading characteristics of the psycho-analytical outlook is that we must never trust appearances. All the facts of human life, and not our dreams alone, have a latent content which differs from their manifest content. This applies, for instance, to the whole of a child's behaviour. Behind what the child actually does we shall be well-advised to search for what may have been its hidden desires, whereof the action may often

HINTS TO EDUCATORS

be no more than a substitute or a symbol. The symbolism of a child's dreams, games, fantasies, and drawings is peculiarly instructive, and an intimate knowledge of psychoanalysis is not always requisite to enable the grown-up observer to draw useful inferences in these matters.

5. The difference between the manifest content which is conscious, and the latent content which is unconscious, must above all be taken into account when we wish to understand how a child is reacting to our rules and regulations, to our chidings and our chastisements. We fancy that we are addressing the child's conscious mind, but really it is the unconscious which replies! We have seen how futile punishment can be when it is secretly longed for by a masochist child or by a child that suffers from an exaggerated sense of guilt; and we have likewise seen that the most trifling manifestation of disapproval may sometimes be regarded by a child as a terribly severe punishment. We may do great harm by simply "leaving a child alone" in the hope that it will spontaneously react in the way we desire!

6. The mechanism of displacement or transference which underlies symbolism and the substitution of the manifest for the latent, and which thus confuses the issues, can also give us valuable help. The possibility that a tendency can be displaced or transferred from one object to another, in accordance with certain laws which it is becoming possible to formulate,[1] opens to us the possibilities of that sublimation which is pre-eminently the process through which education must work—so that, instead of repressing trends regarded as undesirable, it will effect derivations, will orient a tendency towards new goals.

[1] Cf. my Mobilisation de l'énergie.

268   THE MIND OF THE CHILD

7. The motive force of these sublimations and successful transformations of instinct is to be found in the super-ego, which, in its turn, is conditioned by the identifications of the child with its parents and with its earliest teachers. This fact should inspire in grown-ups who have to deal with young children a lofty ideal of their task. The "voice of conscience" is always in some measure the voice of parents. The study of identification throws a strong light upon the primary educational value of example. Of course it seems trite to say that example is better than precept, but the old saw acquires a new profundity when we consider it in the light of the theory of identification.

8. Thus psychoanalytical knowledge, even though theoretical and elementary, can open fresh horizons to parents and teachers, can supply them with unprecedentedly effective means of action. One who knows a child better will certainly know better how to behave towards it. All the same, he who would plumb the depths of child psychology, which analysis shows to be so different from our own, will need something more than superficial information. The same wall, the same repression, separates our conscious from our unconscious and forms the barrier between the grown-up mind and the child mind. The adult unconscious, as described by Freud, is mainly a survival of the childish conscious. We have "forgotten," that is to say we have repressed, the child we once were, and this is the doom that weighs upon education, for it prevents us grown-ups from understanding our children. The adult who would know, would understand, a child, must rediscover the child in himself. He must break down the hidden barriers in his own mind, and nothing but a far-reaching analysis of his own self will enable him to do so. That is why

HINTS TO EDUCATORS

professional teachers have been recommended to have themselves analysed at the outset of their career. Were we consistent, we should make the same recommendation to all prospective parents. The actual fact is that in most of the cases in which we discover psychological disorders in a child, it is the parents who need psychoanalysis more than the child. Still, in the extant state of our customs and at the present level of our knowledge (or of our ignorance), to demand the universalisation of psychoanalysis is a tall order!

9. In conclusion I wish to insist that the recommendations made in this book come within the realm of the ordinary work of the educationist. When a child is suffering from serious or stubborn psychological disorders, there is presumably need for methodical analysis by a specialist. The discussion of that necessity would lead me beyond the scope of the present work, although most of my instances have been drawn from methodical psychoanalyses. Where else, indeed, could so concrete and so abundant material be found?

BIBLIOGRAPHY

ADLER, ALFRED, Le tempérament nerveux, Payot, Paris, 1926. Original German: Ueber den nervösen Charakter, Bergmann, Wiesbaden, second edition, 1919.

ADLER AND FURTMÜLLER, Heilen und Bilden, Bergmann, Munich, 1922.

AICHHORN, AUGUST, Verwahrloste Jugend, Internat. psychoanalytischer Verlag, Vienna, Leipzig, and Zurich, 1925.

ALLENDY, RENÉ, L'orientation des idées médicales, "Sans Pareil," Paris, 1929.

Les rêves et leur interprétation psychanalytique, Alcan, Paris, 1926.

La justice intérieure.

BASHKIRTSEFF, MARIE, Journal de Marie Bashkirtseff (first edition, 1887), Nelson, Paris, abridged edition.

BAUDOUIN, CHARLES, Ein Fall von Kleptomanie, "Zeitschrift für psychoanalytische Pädagogik," vol. iv, Nos. 8 and 9, 1930, Verlag der Zeitschrift für psychoanalytische Pädagogik, Vienna.

Freud et la psychanalyse éducative, Editions du Loup, Paris.

Leidvoller Verlust und Regression im Kindesalter, "Zeitschrift für psychoanalytische Pädagogik," vol. iii, Nos. 5–6, 1929.

Mobilisation de l'énergie, Pelman, Paris, 1931.

Psychanalyse de l'art, Alcan, Paris, 1929.

Psychoanalysis and Aesthetics, Allen & Unwin, 1924.

La psychanalyse et l'éducation morale, Communication to the Fifth International Congress of moral education held in Paris, 1930. Reprinted in "Action et Pensée," vol. vi, No. 11, 1930, Institut de psychogogie, Geneva.

272 THE MIND OF THE CHILD

Studies in Psychoanalysis, Allen & Unwin, London, 1922.

La régression et les phénomènes de recul en psychologie, "Journal de Psychologie Normale et Pathologique," vol. xxv, November–December issue, 1928, Alcan, Paris.

BLANCHARD, PHYLLIS, The Care of the Adolescent Girl, Kegan Paul, Trench, Trübner, London, 1921.

BLEULER, E., Natürliche Symbolik und Kosmogonie, "Internat. Zeitschrift für ärztliche Psychoanalyse," vol. i, 1913, p. 556, Heller, Leipzig.

BOEHM, FÉLIX, Une enfant menteuse, "Revue Française de Psychanalyse," vol. ii, No. 1, 1928, p. 204, Doin, Paris. Also published in "Zeitschrift für psychoanalytische Pädagogik," vol. ii, No. 1, October, 1927.

BONAPARTE, MARIE, Prophylaxie infantile des névroses, Communication to the Fifth Congress of French-speaking psychoanalysts. Reprinted in "Revue Française de Psychanalyse," vol. iv, No. 1, Paris, 1930.

BOVET, PIERRE, Les conditions de l'obligation de conscience, "Année Psychologique," vol. xviii, 1912, p. 55.

The Fighting Instinct, Allen & Unwin, London, 1923.

La psychanalyse et l'éducation, Payot, Lausanne, 1920.

Le sentiment religieux et la psychologie de l'enfant, Delachaux & Niestlé, Neuchâtel, 1925.

CHADWICK, MARY, Le phantasme d'être Dieu chez les enfants, "Revue Française de Psychanalyse," vol. i, 1927; also published under the title Die Gott-Phantasie bei Kindern, "Imago," vol. xiii, 1927, p. 383, Internat. psychoanalytischer Verlag, Vienna.

COLETTE, Sido, Ferenczi, Paris, 1930.

CULLERRE, Les enfants nerveux, Payot, Paris, 1914.

BIBLIOGRAPHY 273

DREVER, Instinct in Man.

FERENCZI, S., Die Anpassung der Familie an das Kind, "Zeitschrift für psychoanalytische Pädagogik," vol. ii, 1928, p. 239.

FRIEDJUNG, JOSEPH K., Un cas de fétichisme concernant le linge chez un enfant d'un an, "Zeitschrift für psychoanalytische Pädagogik," vol. ii, No. 1, 1927; also published in the "Revue Française de Psychanalyse," vol. ii, No. 1, 1928, p. 204.

FREUD, ANNA, Considérations sur l'analyse des enfants, "Revue Française de Psychanalyse," vol. ii, 1928, p. 397; also published in "Internat. Zeitschrift für Psychoanalyse," vol. xiv, No. 2, 1928, p. 153.
Introduction to Psychoanalysis for Teachers, Allen & Unwin, London, 1931.

FREUD, SIGMUND, Eine Kinderheitserrinnerung aus Dichtung und Wahrheit, "Imago," vol. v, No. 2, 1917, p. 49.
Essais de psychanalyse: Au delà du principe de plaisir, Payot, Paris, 1924.
Essais de psychanalyse: La guerre et ses déceptions, Payot, Paris, 1924.
Essais de psychanalyse: Le moi et le soi, Payot, Paris, 1924.
Introduction à la psychanalyse, Payot, Paris, 1926.
Introductory lectures on Psychoanalysis, translated by Joan Rivière, Preface by Ernest Jones, George Allen & Unwin, London, 1922. Revised edition, 1929.
Preface to August Aichhorn's book mentioned above.
Psychanalyse et médecine: Ma vie et la psychanalyse; and, Psychanalyse et médecine, Gallimard, Paris, 1927.
Psychanalyse collective et analyse du moi, Payot, Paris, 1924.
Psychopathologie de la vie quotidienne, Payot, Paris, 1922.

8

274 THE MIND OF THE CHILD

The Interpretation of Dreams, translated by A. A. Brill, George Allen & Unwin, London, 1913. Completely revised edition, 1932.

La science des rêves, Alcan, Paris, 1926.

Totem et tabou, Payot, Paris, 1924.

Trois essais sur la théorie de la sexualité, Nouvelle Revue Française "Les Documents Bleus," Paris, 1923, No. 1.

Un souvenir d'enfance de Léonard de Vinci, Gallimard, Paris, 1927.

FURTMÜLLER, see ADLER AND FURTMÜLLER.

GERSON, ADOLF, Die Scham, "Abhandlungen aus dem Gebiete der Sexualforschung," vol. i, No. 5, 1918–1919, Marcus & Weber, Bonn.

GRABER, G. H., Aus der Analyse eines nachtwandelnden Knaben, "Zeitschrift für psychoanalytische Pädagogik," vol. iv, No. 1, 1930, p. 69.

Zeugung und Geburt in der Vorstellung des Kindes, "Zeitschrift für psychoanalytische Pädagogik," vol. i, Nos. 7, 8, and 9, 1927, p. 244.

Redehemmung und Analerotik, "Zeitschrift für psychoanalytische Pädagogik," vol. ii, Nos. 11 and 12, 1928.

Unterwürfigkeit, "Zeitschrift für psychoanalytische Pädagogik," vol. ii, No. 2, 1927, p. 53.

GREEN, GEORGE H., Psychoanalysis in the Class-room, University of London Press, London, 1921.

HEALY, WILLIAM, Mental Conflicts and Misconduct, Kegan Paul, Trench, Trübner, London, 1919.

HERMANN, IMRE, Un enfant veut savoir d'où viennent les enfants, "Revue Française de Psychanalyse," vol. ii, No. 2, 1928, p. 386.

JANET, PIERRE, Psychological Healing, 2 vols., George Allen & Unwin, London, 1925.

JONES, ERNEST, Papers on Psychoanalysis, third edition, Ballière, London, 1923.

BIBLIOGRAPHY 275

JUNG, C. G., Psychologische Typen, Rascher, Zurich, 1921. Wandlungen und Symbole der Libido, "Jahrbuch für psychoanalytische und psychopathologische Forschungen," vol. iii, 1911, and vol. iv, 1912, Deuticke, Vienna and Leipzig.

KRAPPE, ALEXANDER HAGGERTY, Mythologie universelle, Payot, Paris, 1930.

LA BRUYÈRE, Caractères.

LAY, WILFRID, The Child's Unconscious Mind, Kegan Paul, London, 1919. Man's Unconscious Conflict, Kegan Paul, London, 1919; Dodd, Mead, New York, 1920.

LEY, MADELEINE, Petites voix, Stock, Paris, 1930.

LOW, BARBARA, The Unconscious in Action, University of London Press, London, 1928.

LÖWY, IDA, Kränkung und Verwahrlosung, see above, ADLER AND FURTMÜLLER.

MARKUSZEWICH, R., Beitrag zum autistischen Denken bei Kindern, "Internationale Zeitschrift für Psychoanalyse," vol. vi, 1920, p. 248, Internat. psychoanalytischer Verlag, Vienna and Leipzig.

MARRO, ANTOINE, La puberté, Schleicher, Paris, 1901.

MAURRAS, CHARLES, La musique intérieure, Grasset, Paris, 1925.

MENG, HEINRICH, Neurasthenie, Neuropathie, Psychopathie des Kindes, in Das psychoanalytische Volksbuch, Hippokrates Verlag, Stuttgart, 1927.

MILLER, H. CRICHTON, The New Psychology and the Teacher, Jarrold, London, 1924.

MORGENSTERN, SOPHIE, La psychanalyse infantile et son rôle dans l'hygiène mentale, Communication to the Fifth Congress of French-speaking psychoanalysts, held in Paris, 1930. Published in the' 'Revue Française de Psychanalyse," vol. iv, No. 1, 193—1931.

276 THE MIND OF THE CHILD

ODIER, CHARLES, Curiosité morbide, "Archives de Psychologie," vol. xxi, 1929, p. 83.

PFEIFER, S., Aeusserungen infantil-erotischer Triebe im Spiele, "Imago," vol. v, No. 4, 1919, p. 243.

PFISTER, OSKAR, Die Behandlung schwererziehbarer und abnormer Kinder, "Schriften zur Seelenkunde und Erziehungskunst," vol. i, Bircher, Berne and Leipzig, 1921.

Love in Children, Allen & Unwin, London, 1924.

La psychanalyse au service des éducateurs, Bircher, Berne and Leipzig, 1921 : published in German under the title, Was bietet die Psychanalyse dem Erzieher, Klinkhardt, Leipzig and Berlin, 1917.

PICHON, E., Sur les traitements psychothérapiques courts d'inspiration freudienne chez les enfants, "Revue Française de Psychanalyse," vol. ii, No. 4, 1928.

PIPAL, KARL, Er möchte ein Mädchen sein, "Zeitschrift für psychoanalytische Pädagogik," vol. iii, July, 1929, p. 324.

Gewohnheiten beim Denken und Lernen, "Zeitschrift für psych. Pädagogik," vol. ii, Nos. 11–12, 1928, p. 386.

RANK, OTTO, Der Mythus von der Geburt des Helden, "Schriften zur angewandten Seelenkunde," vol. v, Deuticke, Vienna and Leipzig, 1909.

Technik der Psychoanalyse, vol. ii, Deuticke, Vienna and Leipzig, 1929.

Le traumatisme de la naissance, Payot, Paris, 1928; German original, Das Trauma der Geburt und seine Bedeutung für die Psychoanalyse, Internat. psychoan. Verlag, Vienna, Leipzig, Zurich, 1924.

RIVERS, W. H. R., Instinct and the Unconscious, second edition, Cambridge University Press, 1922.

SARASIN, PHILIPP, Goethes Mignon, eine psychoanalytische Studie : Goethes Jugendgeschichte, "Imago," vol. xv, 1929, p. 349.

BIBLIOGRAPHY 277

SAUSSURE, R., L'instinct d'inhibition, "Revue Française de Psychanalyse," vol. iii, No. 3, p. 429.

SCHNEIDER, ERNST, Die Abwehr der Selbstbefriedigung, "Zeitschrift für psychoanalytische Pädogogik," vol. ii, Nos. 4, 5, and 6, 1928.

Kinderfehler, Entstehung und Behandlung, a contribution to Das psychoanalytische Volksbuch, Hippokrates Verlag, Stuttgart, 1927.

Zur Psychologie des Lausbuben, "Zeitschrift für psychoanalytische Pädagogik," vol. ii, October, 1927, p. 12.

Zur Sexualforschung des Kindes, "Zeitschrift für psychoanalytische Pädagogik," vol. i, Nos. 7, 8, and 9, 1927.

SEARL, Un cas de bégaiement chez un enfant, "Revue Française de Psychanalyse," 1927, p. 758; also published in "Internat. Zeitschrift für Psychoanalyse," vol. xiii, No. 3, 1927.

SPIELEREIN, S., Einige kleine Mitteilungen aus dem Kinderleben: Traum eines Masochisten, "Zeitschrift für psychoanalytische Pädagogik," vol. ii, No. 3, 1929, p. 99.

STAÜB, HUGO, Psychoanalyse und Strafrecht, a contribution to Das psychoanalytische Volksbuch, Hyppokrates Verlag, Stuttgart, 1927.

STEGMAN, MARGARETE, Identifizierung mit dem Vater, "Internat. Zeitschrift für ärztliche Psychoanalyse," vol. i, 1913, p. 531, Heller, Vienna and Leipzig.

STENDHAL, Vie de Henri Brulard.

STERBA, EDITHA, Nacktheit und Scham, "Zeitschrift für psychoanalytische Pädagogik," vol. iii, November–December, 1928, p. 58.

STERBA, RICHARD, Eine Zwangshandlung aus der Latentzeit, "Zeitschrift für psychoanalytische Pädagogik," vol. ii, No. 10, 1928.

278 THE MIND OF THE CHILD

SUMPF, ELSE, Die Störung des Persönlichkeitsgefühls in der Neurose, see above under ADLER AND FURTMÜLLER.

TAMM, A., Drei Fälle von Stehlen bei Kindern, "Zeitschrift für psychoanalytische Pädagogik," vol. ii, No. 1, 1927, p. 6.

WESTERMANN, HOLSTIJN-VISSERUNG, Ein Traum eines dreijährigen Mädchens, "Zeitschrift für psychoanalytische Pädagogik," November–December, 1929, p. 476.

WITTELS, FRITZ, Verdrängung und Zwangsideen in der Kindheit, "Zeitschrift für psychoanalytische Pädagogik," vol. ii, Nos. 8 and 9, 1928.
Set the Children Free! Allen & Unwin, London, 1932.

WULFF, Phobies d'un enfant d'un an et demi, "Revue Française de Psychanalyse," 1927, p. 757; also published in "Internat. Zeitschrift für Psychanalyse," vol. xiii, No. 3, 1927.

ZULLIGER, HANS, Eltern, Schule und sexuelle Aufklärung, "Zeitschrift für psychoanalytische Pädagogik," vol. i, Nos. 7, 8, and 9, 1927.
La psychanalyse et les écoles nouvelles, "Revue Française de Psychanalyse," vol. ii, No. 4, 1928.

Psychoanalytische Erfahrung aus der Volksschulpraxis, Bircher, Berne and Leipzig, 1921; French version, La psychanalyse à l'école, Flammarion, Paris, 1930.

INDEX

Abwehr der Selbstbefriedigung, 189, 252
"Action Française," 48
"Action et Pensée," 194
ADLER, 23, 43, 48, 51, 54, 75, 87, 108, 118, 119, 122, 123, 127, 138, 139, 142, 143, 144, 155, 156, 163, 196, 197, 209, 224, 225, 226, 231
ADLER and FURTMÜLLER, 43, 75, 123, 139, 143, 144, 209, 224, 225, 226, 231
Aeusserungen infantil-erotischer Triebe im Spiele, 212
AICHHORN, 20, 165, 195, 253, 259
ALLENDY, 184, 239, 241, 256
Anpassung der Familie an das Kind, 103, 172, 249
AUGUSTINE, 37
Aus der Analyse eines nachtwandelnden Knaben, 193

BASHKIRTSEFF, 181–186, 201
BAUDOUIN, 159, 184, 192, 201, 216, 219
Behandlung schwererziehbarer und abnormer Kinder, 57, 72, 192
BERGSON, 122
BLANCHARD, 119, 120
BLEULER, 151, 152
BOEHM, 65, 258
BONAPARTE, Marie, 18, 47, 65, 79, 116, 117, 118, 128
BONAPARTE, Napoleon, *see* Napoleon
BOVET, 23, 161, 162, 164, 165, 250, 251
BRUYÈRE, *see* LA BRUYÈRE

Caractères, 86

Care of the Adolescent Girl, 120
Cas de begaiement chez un enfant, 76
Cas de fétichisme concernant le linge chez un enfant d'un an, 178
CHADWICK, 167, 201
Chanson de Juillet, 146
CHATEAUBRIAND, 185, 248
CHAVANNES, *see* PUVIS DE CHAVANNES
Child's Unconscious Mind, 62
Civilisation and its Discontents, 26
CODET, 172
COLETTE, 145
Conditions de l'obligation de conscience, 251
Conscience, 35, 254
CORIAT, 44
CULLERRE, 37
Curiosité morbide, 91

DARWIN, 60
DEMOSTHENES, 119
Dichtung und Wahrheit, 41
Drei Fälle von Stehlen bei Kindern, 164
Drever, 23

Ego and the Id, 50
Einige kleine Mitteilungen aus dem Kinderleben, 260
EINSTEIN, 18
Eltern, Schule und sexuelle Aufklarung, 151
Enfant menteuse, 65, 258
Enfants nerveux, 37
Entstehung von Pavor nocturnus bei einem Kinde, 240
Er möchte ein Mädchen sein, 128

280 THE MIND OF THE CHILD

Essais de psychanalyse,
  Au delà du principe de plaisir, 175
  Guerre et ses déceptions, 83
  Moi et soi, 247, 259

Fall von Kleptomanie, 157
FERENCZI, 79, 103, 172, 249
Fighting Instinct, 23
Flight into Reality, 99
FOREL, 227
FREUD, Anna, 54, 159, 160, 163, 214, 254
FREUD, Sigmund, 17, 18, 20, 21, 23, 24, 25, 26, 28, 30, 31, 35, 41, 49, 50, 51, 53, 60, 70, 82, 83, 96, 97, 98, 108, 109, 115, 122, 123, 128, 149, 153, 157, 158, 173, 175, 178, 179, 201, 203, 237, 245, 246, 247, 250, 251, 256, 259, 268
Freud et la psychanalyse éducative, 17
FRIEDJUNG, 177, 178
FURTMÜLLER, *see* ADLER and FURTMÜLLER

Geburtproblem, 157
Gelöste Fesseln, 113, 114, 160, 212, 238, 254
Generations-Umkehrungs-Phantasie, 164
GERSON, 74
GOETHE, 41
Goethes Jugendgeschichte, 41
Goethes Mignon, eine psychoanalytische Studie, 41
GRABER, 157, 188, 189, 192, 193, 196, 211, 212, 214, 215, 216
Grands initiés, 89
GREEN, 46, 47, 118, 167, 196, 199

Heilen und Bilden, 43, 75, 123, 139, 143, 144, 209, 224, 225, 226, 231
HERMANN, 39

Holstijn-Vissering, 40
Homme qui rit, 165
HUGO, 35, 41, 48, 58, 165, 185, 248, 249, 254

Identifizierung mit dem Vater, 63
Instinct and the Unconscious, 184
Instinct in Man, 23
Instinct d'inhibition, 251
"International Journal of Psychoanalysis," 246
"Internationale Zeitschrift für Psychoanalyse," 76
Interpretation of Dreams, 35
Introduction à la psychanalyse, 98, 173
Introduction to Psychoanalysis, 153
Introduction to Psychoanalysis for Teachers, 54, 160, 254
Iphigénie, 230

James, 24
JANET, 102, 155, 171
JONES, 20, 79, 82, 88, 93, 97, 98, 99, 100, 163, 164, 211
JUNG, 198, 219, 244, 250
Justice intérieure, 256

Kindheitserinnerung aus Dichtung und Wahrheit, 41
Kinderfehler, Entstehung und Behandlung, 76, 90
Kränkung und Verwahrlosung, 224
KRAPPE, 242, 254

LA BRUYÈRE, 86
LAFORGUE, 172
LAHORIE, 248
LAY, 44, 62, 151
Leidvoller Verlust und Regression im Kindesalter, 192
LEONARDO DA VINCI, 96
Leonardo da Vinci, 97

INDEX

LEY, 146
Love in Children, 65, 87, 93, 209, 238
LOW, 41, 50, 61, 62, 71, 73, 77, 78, 79, 94, 95, 158, 234, 235
LÖWY, 224, 226, 233
LUCRETIUS, 153

Man's Unconscious Conflict, 44, 151
MARKUSZEWICZ, 246
MARRO, 141
MAURRAS, 48
Meaning of Dreams, 44
MENG, 240
MILLER, 137, 139, 140, 141, 142, 158, 167
Mobilisation de l'énergie, 26, 78, 197, 198, 203, 207, 216, 267
MORGENSTERN, 93, 99, 153, 222, 236, 237, 243, 252, 253
Musique intérieure, 48
Mythologie universelle, 242, 254
Mythus von der Geburt des Helden, 159, 219

Nacktheit und Scham, 86
NAPOLEON, 59, 248
Natürliche Symbolik und Kosmogonie, 152
Neurasthenie, Neuropathie, Psychopathie des Kindes, 240
New Psychology and the Teacher, 137, 139, 140, 141, 158, 167

ODIER, 90, 91, 102, 230
Orientation des idées médicales, 184

Papers on Psychoanalysis, 20, 79, 82, 88, 93, 99, 100, 164, 211
PASCAL, 52
PERRET, 133
Petites Voix, 146
PFEIFER, 154, 212

PFISTER, 57, 58, 60, 65, 72, 73, 82, 86, 87, 92, 93, 100, 151, 179, 192, 209, 210, 238
Phantasme d'être Dieu chez les enfants, 167, 201
Phobies chez un enfant d'un an et demi, 226
PICHON, 64
PIPAL, 128, 129, 173
Prophylaxie infantile des névroses, 18, 67, 79, 117, 118, 128, 253
Psychanalyse de l'art, 25, 56, 78, 159, 201, 207, 219
Psychanalyse et l'éducation, 162, 165
Psychanalyse et l'éducation morale, 194
Psychanalyse et les écoles nouvelles, 55
Psychanalyse et médecine, 20
Psychanalyse infantile et son rôle dans l'hygiène mentale, 93, 99, 153, 222, 236, 237
Psychanalysis in the Class-Room, 47, 118
Psychoanalyse und Strafrecht, 138
Psychoanalytische Erfahrungen aus der Volksschulpraxis, 112, 218, 244
Psychological Healing, 171
Psychologie collective et analyse du moi, 245
Psychologie et l'action, 184
Puberté, 141
PUVIS DE CHAVANNES, 198

RACINE, 230
RANK, 100, 153, 159, 161, 171, 172, 219, 224, 225
Redehemmung und Analerotik, 212
Régression et les phénomènes de recul en psychologie, 187, 197, 216
Rêves et leur interprétation psychanalytique, 239
"Revue Française de Psychanalyse," 39, 55, 76, 126

282 THE MIND OF THE CHILD

RICHARD, 133
RIVERS, 184
ROUSSEAU, 261

SACHS, 100
Sainte Geneviève veillant sur Paris,
198, 200
Salambô, 89
SARASIN, 41
SAUSSURE, 250, 251
Scham, 74
SCHNEIDER, 56, 76, 90, 149, 189,
252
SCHURÉ, 89
Science des rêves, 35, 237
SEARL, 76, 99
*Sentiment religieuse et la psychologie
de l'enfant,* 250
SHAW, 208
Sido, 145
SPIELREIN, 70, 260
STAUB, 138
STEGMAN, 62, 63
STENDHAL, 52, 53
STERBA, Editha, 84, 86
STERBA, Richard, 81
Studies in Psychoanalysis, 23, 227
SUMPF, 225, 231
*Sur les traitements psychothérapiques
courts d'inspiration freudienne chez
les enfants,* 64

TAMM, 164, 232
Technik der Psychoanalyse, 225
Tempérament nerveux, 118, 163
Totem and Tabu, 60

Traum eines dreijährigen Mädchens,
40
Traum eines Masochisten, 260
Traumatisme de la naissance, 171
*Trois essais sur la théorie de la
sexualité,* 149, 173, 179

Unbehagen in der Kultur, 26
Unconscious in Action, 41, 59, 62,
71, 73, 78, 79, 94, 95, 158, 235
Unterwürfigkeit, 189

*Verdrängung und Zwangsideen in der
Kindheit,* 81
Verwahrloste Jugend, 20, 165, 253,
259
Vie de Henri Brulard, 52
VINCI, *see* LEONARDO
VISSERING, *see* HOLSTIJN-VISSER-
ING

Wandlungen und Symbole der Libido,
219, 244
*Was bietet die Psychanalyse dem
Erzieher,* 73, 82
WITTELS, 81
WULFF, 226

ZULLIGER, 55, 73, 111, 112, 113,
114, 125, 126, 150, 151, 158,
160, 200, 201, 212, 217, 218,
219, 238, 240, 244, 254
Zur Psychologie des Lausbuben, 56
Zur Sexualforschung des Kindes, 149
Zwangshandlung aus der Latenzzeit,
81